Jean Maine

J Feingold

No died Nov. 23, 1996
in hijacked jetliner crash.

MO

BRIAN TETLEY

MO

THE STORY OF

MOHAMED AMIN

FRONT-LINE CAMERAMAN

FOREWORD BY
BOB GELDOF

MOONSTONE BOOKS · LONDON

Acknowledgements

I'm indebted to Al Ventner, John Platter and Ronald Robson for a large part of this book.

And to Michael Wooldridge, Brendan Farrow, Peter Marshall, David Martin, Peter Seidlitz, Tim Arlott, Tom Hudson, Al Wells, Abdul Rahman Ramadhan, Michael Roe, Bob Cheek, Peter Searle, Roy Lipscombe, Brian Quinn, Sean Hawkins, Henry Reuter, Mohamed Shaffi, Saidi Suleiman Salim, Jerry Shah, Harriet Bisley, and Patrick Orr for their anecdotes, recollections and impressions.

Also to John McHaffie, John Edlin, and Brendan Farrow for editing; Barbara Lawrence and Helen van Houten for copy editing, Juliet Antao for preparing the original manuscript and to Nazma Rawji for her long and uncomplaining hours in preparing and typesetting one revised manuscript after another.

And, of course, to Mo.

First published 1988 by Moonstone Books Ltd
PO Box 736 London NW1 6TX

British Library Cataloguing in Publication Data

Tetley, Brian
    Mo: The Story of Mohamed Amin
    I. Biography
    I. Title   II. Photography

ISBN 1 869828 03 8

© 1988 Camerapix

Editor: John Edlin
Design: Craig Dodd
Typeset: Juliet Antao and Nazma Rawji

Printed by Mandarin Offset

Contents

Your May issue, with the 'Moving Pictures' essay was very good. However, it should be noted that the Visnews crew that shot the film for the British Broadcasting Corporation was led by a veteran still photographer and cinematographer named Mohamed Amin. Amin has not received the attention he deserves.
Burnham Wore, Owenton, Kentucky

A letter in the June 1985 issue of the *American Photographer*

'For so fearlessly forcing the world to face the truth about African Famine that governments had to take action and . . . for currently continuing courageous camera coverage of the homeless and hungry all over the world.'
Citation for the Valiant for Truth Award, 1986, awarded to Mohamed Amin by the Order of Christian Unity.

Any danger spot is tenable if men — brave men — will make it so.
John F. Kennedy 1961

Author's Note

In this book all the organizations are referred to by their professional acronyms: in America the major ones are NBC — National Broadcasting Company; ABC — American Broadcasting Company; and CBS — Columbia Broadcasting System. In Canada, CBC — Canadian Broadcasting Corporation. In Britain, BBC — British Broadcasting Corporation; and ITN — Independent Television News, owned by the network of Britain's commercial television companies. Australia has many independent stations as well as ABC — Australian Broadcasting Corporation. In Europe and elsewhere there are both state broadcasting and independent broadcasting networks. All are members of the European Broadcasting Union — EBU.

Communications technology has an elaborate lexicon of phrases such as 'sat feeds' — satellite television transmissions; ENG — electronic news gathering; and, by comparison, old-fashioned terminology like 'dope sheets' which refer to the factual information provided by a cameraman when he ships his film or tapes. Other language derives directly from the cinema — take, expose, cut, shoot, and so on. And some, like 'hacks' for reporters, are journalese.

The same applies to the printing industry: 'proofs' are the finished pages of yet-to-be-printed books; 'separations' are the colour pictures divided into four or more colours before printing; 'dummies' are mock-ups of projected books without the final text or pictures, designed to show publishers what the finished publication will look and feel like.

In all cases I have tried to ensure that context clarifies meaning.

Live Aid's Bob Geldof, the Boomtown Rats pop group leader, who inspired millions to respond to the tragic images filmed by Mohamed Amin.

Foreword by Bob Geldof

Sometime in the last days of October 1984 I turned on the television and saw something that was to change my life.

I was confronted by something so horrendous I was wrenched violently from the complacency of another rather dispiriting day and pinioned — unable to turn away from the misery of another world inhabited by people only recognizable as humans by their magnificent dignity.

I do not know why Mo Amin's pictures did this to me. God knows, if you watch an average night's news you are confronted with enough scenes of horror to seriously question man's sanity. But the tube also has the ability to reduce, to shrink events and make them bearable in the context of your living-room. Ultimately, one becomes immune, if not anaesthetized.

But the pitiless, unrelenting gaze of this camera was different. Somehow this was not objective journalism but confrontation. There was a dare here: 'I dare you to turn away, I dare you to do nothing'. Mo Amin had succeeded above all else in showing you his own disgust and shame and anger and making it yours also.

It is certainly true that were it not for that now historic broadcast, millions would be dead. There would have been no Band, Live or Sport Aid, no mass outpouring of humanity's compassion. No questioning of statutes, laws and values both inside and outside Africa. No reappraisal of development, of the nature of international aid, no debate on the mire that Africa had become.

In that brief, shocking but glorious moment Amin had transcended the role of journalist-cameraman and perhaps unwittingly become the visual interpreter of man's stinking conscience.

He had always been amongst that breed considered extraordinary. He continues to upset us with his unrelenting and passionate lens. He is without question an extraordinary man.

I thank God that I was home that autumn evening. I thank God I was watching that channel, and I thank God that Mo Amin sickened and shamed me. Long may he do so.

One year after the devastating famine of 1984 Mohamed Amin returned to Mekele in Ethiopia to film the survivors of the holocaust — restored to health by the greatest act of giving the world has known.

Introduction: We Are the World

'There comes a time when we heed a certain call
When the world must come together as one
There are people dying
And it's time to lend a hand to life
The greatest gift of all . . . '

— We Are the World

It's 19 October 1984. The place is Korem in northern Ethiopia. People lie dying, not from war or disease but simply of hunger. They lie in their thousands in the open: in freezing rain, in searing sun. If they had the strength to look for shelter they would find none. If they had the strength to look for food they would find none.

It's like the Holocaust, but these are not the victims of hatred — only of indifference. In Europe, millions of tons of grain lie rotting in stores — too much for people already glutted with the realization of plenty. Here in Korem they shrivel before your eyes: wasted with the pain of starving and yet in their bearing there is dignity to match the hopelessness in their eyes.

It's like something out of the Bible. Gently, caringly, a television cameraman moves among the dying and the dead with his cameras. He limps as he walks. What passes between him and the victims and thus through his lens is so elemental, and so profound, that four days from today it will change the world.

It's 28 January 1985. Early morning in Los Angeles, California, USA, and forty-five pop stars are belting out a revivalist-style hymn of hope that's destined to become one of the hit singles of the decade — the world's own anthem of love.

There's Kenny Rogers, undisputed king of country and western, Bruce Springsteen, Lionel Richie, Bob Dylan, the balladeer of protest, Diana Ross, Michael Jackson, Harry Belafonte, Dionne Warwick, and Ray Charles. So many, in fact, that nobody's quite able to put a value on this unique gathering.

They've been here since ten o'clock last night and they won't be leaving

The USA for Africa session in Los Angeles on 27-28 January 1985 when the superstars of American pop music, who formed the United Support of Artists for Africa under the leadership of Harry Belafonte, recorded the mega-hit, *We Are The World*, composed by Michael Jackson and Lionel Richie. It sold millions and raised more than US$50 million for victims of the Ethiopian famine and other stricken countries in Africa. (*Picture by Henry Diltz*)

Mohamed Amin at work. The inspiration for USA for Africa arose out of the work of the Kenya-born frontline cameraman, whose historic reports filmed in the highlands of Ethiopia shook the conscience of the entire world. It took months of persuasion by Amin to obtain permission from the Ethiopian authorities to visit the worst-hit areas. Long plagued by rebel wars, they feared his filmwork would focus on guerilla activity and not the plight of the starving.

until eight o'clock this morning. They're here because of Ken Kragen, and Harry Belafonte, and an Irishman called Bob Geldof who's flown over from Britain for this moment. And, of course, because of Mohamed Amin, the television cameraman who filmed the horror of Ethiopia '84.

This day is one they'll all remember. One the world will remember, too. On radio stations everywhere, in practically every language on earth, people will send in requests for *We Are the World*.

This is their requiem for the hungry and the homeless. Producer Quincy Jones is making it memorable: a heart cry from the famous for starving millions.

'Hopefully,' says Lionel Richie, 'what we're trying to do here is something that's going to be everlasting, or at least a link in making people aware of the true value of life. . . . It's a party for life.'

Kim Carnes says: 'If we can bottle the spirit we have in this room and send it round the world we will have no problems.'

Ray Charles says: 'For me it's a great opportunity to contribute to a beautiful cause, a wonderful cause. I'm honoured to be a part of it.'

Kenny Rogers says: 'I see that these people really do care . . . they're just like everybody else.'

Stevie Wonder says: 'It's out of a dream, all this energy together, energy that can really change the world. . . . We've all got to use modern technology properly to bring people closer together. That helps them see how everyone is alike. . . .'

As early as 1980 UN agencies and relief organizations began to warn of famine in Africa, and in Ethiopia in particular. Appeals for aid and food fell on deaf ears as the hungry continued to die. By the spring of 1984 the famine had reached a magnitude difficult to comprehend.

In the penultimate decade of the twentieth century it was not really possible for a human mind to envisage half the population of London wasting away for want of food. Jobless people in Europe and America didn't really understand, any more than those in safe and secure jobs with comfortable homes, that five million people could die of hunger. Not in societies where surplus food made mountains.

In October 1984 Mohamed Amin could not believe what he saw. Nothing, he was to say later, nothing that he had experienced in twenty-five years of covering wars, disasters, riots, and other famines could have prepared him for this.

This son of a railway worker is one of a courageous few who daily put their lives on the line: an elite that included such friends as the late cameramen Ernie Pyle, *Time's* Priya Ramrakha and *Time-Life's* Bob Capa — all killed in action taking news pictures. They are legends.

In 1985 Mohamed Amin would mourn the death of another friend and colleague, Neil Davis, killed in action for America's NBC television network covering an abortive coup in Thailand.

The last half century has seen a revolution in global communications. Today it is literally possible to sit by a warm fire and witness, as Mohamed Amin demonstrated, the truth of C. P. Snow's 1969 prediction that 'many millions of people in the poor countries are going to starve to death before our eyes . . . we will see them doing so on our television sets.'

Television images shape our lives with powerful force: none more so than the news films made by cameramen in the front line of dramatic events. These images are broadcast by the world's television networks.

In Europe, the European Broadcast Union operates the Eurovision News Exchange. EBU subscribers take a choice of newsfilm from a range of material offered by members and by the television news agencies.

The largest of these agencies, Visnews, based in London, syndicates its services daily to more than 420 television stations in nearly 100 countries around the world.

Mohamed Amin is the African bureau chief for Visnews, based in Nairobi.

1 Kid with a Box Brownie

In August 1943 prejudice and bigotry wore many faces. One was colonialism, which was nearing its end, though few if any could have predicted how soon. The British, fighting to preserve the Empire, had enlisted those subjects regarded as second-and-third-class citizens, sometimes not even as citizens at all, to fight on their side. Many Africans fought against the Italians in Ethiopia and Somalia. Others went across the Indian Ocean to do battle in the jungles of India, Burma and Malaya.

Nairobi, the Kenya capital, an offspring of the Grand Empire, was itself born at the zenith of Imperial might and splendour as a shantytown railhead on 30 May 1899.

Forty-four years later, this improbable town, a mile above sea level, had begun to blossom with spaciousness and dignity — but not equality. By some unstated rule the races were as severely segregated as if by royal ordinance — though no laws to this effect had passed through the statute books of the Crown Colony. Through self-sustaining levels of economic and class privilege, the races themselves fell into their respective ghettos.

Those Africans in the British forces abroad, some of whom would never return, had been recruited from such locations as Eastlands and Shauri Moyo, low-class, overcrowded, residential estates. The Europeans lived in tree-clad, pleasantly gardened suburbs called Parklands and Muthaiga.

In between, in such places as Eastleigh, lived the buffer community: the Asians, many of whom had arrived with the railway and stayed on to develop this wild and wonderful land astride the Equator.

It was in Eastleigh on 29 August 1943 that Mohamed Amin was born. At that time Nairobi was still a small and unpretentious town, a settlement of 250,000 people. By 1988, swollen to more than one million citizens, its suburban periphery extended on every side, over rolling plain and up forested escarpment. Eastleigh itself had become a forlorn part of the inner city core. But it has changed little in physical appearance. It has that depressing atmosphere of raw utility found in British council housing estates, some rather dilapidated maisonettes and flats and bleak shopping centres.

Mohamed's father, Sardar Mohamed, born on 30 April 1910 in Jullundur, Punjab, migrated from India when he was seventeen after he heard of the opportunities in East Africa. He paid three-and-a-half rupees for a passport and travelled to Bombay where he boarded the British India

Navigation Company's steamship *Kampala* for the seven-day voyage to Mombasa. There he took the train to Nairobi and spent his first three nights in the capital in a cheap lodging house on River Road, a busy downtown concourse.

His first job was as a mason in the Public Works Department in Eldoret, on the high plateau of Uasin Gishu, north-west of Nairobi. Six months later he moved to Kakamega, in western Kenya, with the same department. After eighteen months, in 1929, he travelled to Nakuru in the Rift Valley to join the Kenya-Uganda Railways corporation as a mason. It was the Uganda Railway, the 'Lunatic Line', which, in 1899, had made railhead at the swamp known in the Maa language of the Maasai as Nairobi, meaning the 'place of cold waters' or 'the beginning of all beauty'.

For two years Sardar Mohamed was based in different towns such as Nakuru, Kisumu — the Lake Victoria port — and Eldoret, in charge of the buildings and bridges in those areas. Finally he was sent to Nairobi, where he was when war broke out in 1939 and he went home to marry Azmat Bibi.

The wedding took place in Jullundur in May 1940. In June, the couple travelled to Bombay to board the SS *Katlina*. At the last moment, Sardar Mohamed changed his mind and cancelled his double berth. It was an augury perhaps of the uncanny intuition which his son would inherit. SS *Katlina* was torpedoed and sank with the loss of all passengers and crew, but for a sole survivor.

Returning to Kenya soon after, Sardar was posted to Namasagali, a remote paddle steamer base on the shores of Lake Kioga in Uganda, and then began a period of transfers from Kisumu to Jinja and then Kampala in Uganda, where he settled for eighteen months before returning — for three months in 1941 — to Jinja, where his first son, Iqbal, was born. Two years later, during a posting to Nairobi, Mohamed Amin was born. Very early in his career, friends and colleagues shortened his first name to 'Mo'.

In charge of station construction and maintenance along an extensive network of track, his father was at home in most of East Africa. He travelled great distances in his own camping coach, often taking Iqbal and Mo with him. They thus acquired a taste for travel and adventure very early.

Deeply devout, pious and outwardly austere, Sardar was also a warm and loving father. Early on he implanted in his sons those virtues of independence, initiative and straight-talking which he cherished. He was far removed from his contemporaries in the supervisory section who fawned on their European superiors, presenting them with gifts in anticipation of patronage and privilege to come. Sardar Mohamed sought no man's favour. He trod his own forthright, independent path, placing value on hard work, integrity, pride and honesty.

His disdain for subservience and preference for straight-talking brought a rebuke — a 'hardship' posting in 1952 to far-off Dar es Salaam, seven hundred miles south of Nairobi, at the far corner of what, by then, had become the East African Railways and Harbours Corporation. Dar es Salaam, sultry and humid, was in more ways than one the end of the line. But for Mohamed Amin the transfer could not have happened at a better time. The carefree, sunny childhood days which he had enjoyed in Eastleigh were at an end for everyone.

In 1952, Kenya was on the brink of civil war and revolution. The Mau Mau movement had become a fully-fledged freedom army and had taken the battle against colonialism to the armed forces of Kenya's colonial government in forests and countryside. In October, after declaring a State of Emergency, the British seized Kenyan African leader Jomo Kenyatta and others at night and hustled them away to spend almost a decade incarcerated in Kenya's remote north. Parts of Eastleigh became barbed-wire, open-air concentration camps for thousands of Africans rounded up on suspicion of supporting, harbouring and sympathizing with members of the Mau Mau freedom fighters and their cause.

In Dar es Salaam the battle for freedom waged by the young teacher Mwalimu Julius Nyerere was more persuasion than force. A League of Nations mandated territory, Tanganyika at first was administered on the League's behalf by the British. In 1946, after the Second World War, it became a United Nations trusteeship, again administered by the British. Throughout the 1950s, by comparison with Nairobi, Dar es Salaam was indeed what its Swahili name means, a 'haven of peace' — not at all a bad place for Mo to spend the most formative years of his life.

Sardar Mohamed and his family were the first to move into a new railways estate, on the fringes of bush country still plentifully populated with wildlife. It opened up new worlds for Iqbal, Mo and their younger brothers and sisters, introducing them to Africa's wildlife which would become one of Mo's consuming passions.

Each morning, he recalls, they would scout through the house, peering out of all the windows to see if a lion or a leopard was in the garden. The youngsters quickly adapted to this new environment, delighting in the thought of waking up to find a giraffe in the garden, or an elephant demolishing the vegetable plot. For their young hearts and imaginations this was no hardship posting at all. Once they woke up in time to see a lion kill a zebra. Few ten-year-olds recall such drama outside their bedroom windows.

He went to the Indian Secondary School for Asian children, another mark of the segregation which existed in Britain's colonial territories in Africa. But the teaching staff were both Asian and European and there was none of the prejudice Mo might be expected to remember. He was brash — to the point of bullying — and his instinct for taking command was quickly spotted. Almost at once he became a form prefect with power and authority. His determination to let nothing — and nobody — stand in his way was evident. His lifelong friend, BBC producer Roy Lipscombe, describes the young Amin as 'demanding'. Undoubtedly, he was. He hectored, bullied, and dominated, instinctively knowing how much he could demand and how far he might push.

Indecision played no part in his character or his relationships. Those who knew him were often aggravated by his attitude, but he would bustle along, a twinkle in his eye, to straighten out hurt feelings — never by apology, and always maintaining he was right — displaying early an almost irresistible charm, and an adroit ability to persuade which won over those he needed.

He neither sought popularity nor courted favour, unless for professional or business advantage. Indeed, his independence and self-reliance have remained monumental. Unlike his eye for a picture or nose for news, he sees life altogether in black and white, without room for half measures, ambiguity or qualification.

From the moment he acquired a second-hand Box Brownie camera for forty shillings when he was eleven, he was never in doubt about the career he would follow — though those first pictures, keepsake snaps of family and friends, scarcely serve as indication of what was to come.

Yet he had found his vocation, and the art and the chemistry of photography became his passion. Even as a youngster he was tireless to the point of hyperactivity, both in his enthusiasms and in his attention to detail. But his plea to join the school photographic society was turned down. He was told he was too young and a Box Brownie, after all, was only a toy. Few men in pursuit of a goal are as determined and persistent (sometimes ruthless) as Mohamed Amin. Then, as now, he let nothing deflect him from his single-minded purpose. In hindsight he regards his subsequent battle to join the society as a major element of his career today.

'When I tried to join the society I was in Form One and I was told that I would not be allowed to join until I was in Form Four. The teacher who ran the society was adamant. He said that there was no way I could join.

'Since my Box Brownie did not impress anybody, I asked a friend whose father had a Rolleicord camera — in those days one of the best — to lend me his dad's camera. He lived across the road from my house.

'But the father said it was far too precious to be taken to school. So I persuaded my friend to borrow it for the day without his father's knowledge — which he did — and I would make sure he got it back.

'So I took it to the teacher and said: "I have access to a Rolleicord camera. Won't you reconsider my request to rejoin the Society?"'

The teacher was so impressed with the Rolleicord that he relented and let Amin join. The camera was returned, unused and undamaged, the same day. But the father found out what had happened and lambasted his son with a hockey stick and locked up the camera.

'I never had access to that camera again,' says Mo. 'So whenever the teacher asked where it was I had to say that it had been damaged and sent for repairs. In fact I never, ever saw it again. But it got me into the society and that gave me access to the equipment there including a camera.

'I spent as much time as possible covering school events like drama, sports and festivals. One of the arrangements in the school was that 19 outside photographers were not allowed to cover school functions. We were allowed to sell the pictures to the students. Half the revenue went to the society and the other half to the photographer. By doing this I was able to raise enough money to buy my own equipment, although it took three years or so.'

Membership of the society was important in two senses. It provided Mohamed Amin with the facility to learn the art and the science of photography and so consummate what would be a lifelong passion. At the same time it taught him the commercial value of photography. He worked hard, learning how to process film and produce prints, and he joined the Scout movement. It was through these two associations that the first pictures with the by-line *by Mohamed Amin* were published.

As a member of the party that went to Government House, Dar es Salaam, during the Scouts' 1958 Bob-a-Job week to meet the Governor, Sir Richard Turnbull, he used the school's Rolleiflex to take 'official pictures' of the occasion. Back in the society's darkroom — a broom cupboard beneath the staircase — he carefully processed his film. Selecting the best negatives, he printed three or four pictures. When they had dried, he put them in an envelope and went to the office of the *Tanganyika Standard*, the country's leading newspaper. Editor Brendon Grimshaw, now living in retirement in the Seychelles, chose two of the unknown schoolboy's prints, scaled them for reduction and sent them off to the process department to be made into half-tone blocks — the images etched with acid as dots on a zinc or copper plate. The pictures appeared on Page One of next day's paper.

Mo was elated. 'I felt on top of the world. My first published pictures were on the front page of the leading newspaper in the country. This was a tremendous boost. In fact, I carried the newspaper around for days and showed it to all my friends and sent copies to my friends overseas. I must have bought about fifty papers on that day.' Significantly, he adds: 'I got one guinea [£1.05] for each picture.'

He became a regular visitor to the newspaper offices. 'As I recall, he used to turn up at the newspaper, still in his school shorts, offering pictures of various events,' remembers David Martin, a journalist on that paper who now runs a publishing company in Harare, Zimbabwe. 'As I also recall, they were not particularly great pictures in those days.'

Still, it's unlikely that anything since, including awards, honours, and commendations, have equalled Mo's feelings at that first acknowledgement of his competence with a camera. It added considerably to the prestige he already enjoyed at school.

Two years before this he had obtained his first official accreditation, to cover the fledgling East African Safari Rally. Few thirteen-year-old schoolboys have the assurance, or the determination, to pass themselves off as professional Press photographers, especially when nothing of their work has been printed. But though gauche, and with his frame still to fill out, young Mo did. And at that early age he already met challenges with a look-'em-straight-in-the-eye response that brooked no opposition.

Another reason for prestige at school was his ownership of a motor scooter. It had become essential to carry him from one assignment to another, and his enthusiasm and output grew with every new picture in print.

The vehicle, which cost his father 100 shillings a month in hire purchase repayments, was as important to Amin as his camera and typewriter. Ironically, he had acquired the typewriter before the camera, as he realized that without a typewriter on which to present his captions, letters of introduction and invoices for work rendered, submitted or published, all would be wasted.

Before his sixteenth birthday he broke into the pages of *Drum*, the magazine of black consciousness in Africa throughout the late 1950s, the 1960s, and 70s. It was under the control of ex-*Picture Post* editor, Sir Tom Hopkinson, who for the *Post* in Britain had recruited some of the greatest photographers and writers in western journalism. They included Bert Hardy and Slim Hewitt whose own careers — from still photographers to BBC-TV cameramen — in many ways anticipated Mo's own.

When the *Post* shut down, Hopkinson was invited to Johannesburg by South African dilettante Jim Bailey, a rich and aristocratic farmer, to work on *Drum*. It was an immediate success and within a very short time Bailey had established separate regional editions in East and West Africa.

That Hopkinson should unequivocally accept and publish Mohamed Amin's work says everything. Few people, if any, knew more about Press pictures or the function of the news and feature photographer. Hopkinson's was the kind of pictorial journalism only equalled by the *Post's* contemporaries in America, *Life* and *Look*.

'The Twenties were not to be merely the decade which followed the two previous ones,' he recalls in *Picture Post: 1938-50*, published in 1985. 'They were to mark the beginning of a new era, an era of experiment and self-expression, through which a new attitude to life, surely indeed a new kind of men and women, would emerge from the shadows of the past into a sunlit future. Clearly the new spirit of the age demanded a new form of journalism through which to spread its message.

'But before this could come into existence there had to be the journalists, and there had to be the instrument. That instrument proved to be a new kind of camera. . . . Only in the mid-1920s, with development of small format cameras, did the photo-journalist begin to acquire the equipment needed for his job — that of telling a story in pictures in much the same way that the reporter tells it with his pen. . . . The Leica, with its small format, thirty-six pictures on a film, ease of operation and quiet mechanism — to which before long was added a wide range of interchangeable lenses — brought photography out of the studio and into the stream of everyday life. . . . '

Hopkinson then describes the new breed of news cameraman which took advantage of the new cameras. His words describe exactly the spirit

Mohamed Amin and the scooter with which he launched his photographic career when he was a thirteen-year-old schoolboy and won accreditation as a Press photographer covering the gruelling East African Safari Rally.

which was to characterize the work of Mohamed Amin. 'The first and most renowned of these was Dr Erich Salomon, a doctor of law and a skilled linguist. Salomon started taking news pictures only in 1928, but within two years his pictures of political conferences and his stolen pictures of murder trials had won him a European reputation.

'Until 1932 Salomon operated with an Ermanox before switching to the Leica. For trial scenes he used such devices as secreting his camera inside a bowler hat or small attache case, and he would at times gain entry to a discussion among high-ranking diplomats disguised as a waiter or house-painter.

'But his finest disguise was his own cool assurance, enabling him to attach himself to the train of some eminent personage entering the buildings — he was always immaculately dressed — or to occupy the seat of a missing delegate. Once inside he would operate his cameras with such confidence and tact that everyone assumed he had full official authority in his pocket.'

This last paragraph, except for the 'always' immaculately dressed, might easily have been about Mohamed Amin.

Drum was not alone in recognizing the Dar es Salaam teenager. His work was soon on the pages of the most competitive newspaper community in the world — London's Fleet Street — in papers like *The Times*, *Daily Express*, *Daily Mail*, *Daily Telegraph* and *Daily Mirror*.

His schoolboy successes did nothing to endear him to full-time photographers in Tanganyika. He threatened their livelihood. It was no surprise, therefore, when he turned up at events to find gatemen and security guards barring his way, on instructions from his seniors. Little did they realize they were providing him with an invaluable apprenticeship in perseverance, initiative and ingenuity. The lessons he learned at this stage have made the difference between success and failure ever since.

He quickly learned the value of persistence and the need never to take 'No' for an answer. The fact that he learned to overcome obstacles to gain his objective was supremely significant. It also confirmed his own belief in his professional competence.

Far from nipping his career in the bud, Dar es Salaam's community of photographic elders put an edge to the youngster's determination. He talked, cajoled, persuaded and sometimes blustered. But, as he recalls, 'at the end of the day I seemed to get where I wanted to get'. As he still does.

But he didn't get quite far enough when, at the age of sixteen, he set out on his Grand Adventure — an overland journey to Europe with just 400 shillings, his scooter and a Goan friend, Thambi, riding pillion. 'I had extra carrying space on the pillion,' remembers Mo, 'and I thought, why go alone?'

By the shortest land route Tanganyika was around 5,000 miles from Britain. The first leg alone involved a journey of something like a thousand miles just to cross the Equator, most of it over dirt roads. In East Africa, tarmac was virtually unheard of outside the main cities. The dirt road from 23

Mohamed Amin, as a schoolboy, waits outside Aga Khan Girls High School in Dar es Salaam. Some of his earliest pictures were used in the school's magazine 'by his kind permission'.

Dar es Salaam north to Nairobi wound through rough bush country and climbed gradually upwards to more than a mile above sea level.

Mo, who has subsequently planned all his travels down to the last detail, paid scant attention to roads or weather. With one suitcase he and Thambi set off, blissfully ignorant of the countryside they had to cross or the difficulties they would face. 'We felt', he says, 'we could work at various places on the way to raise enough money to finish the journey.'

When they arrived at Morogoro the youngsters found the hotel too expensive. Son of a railwayman, Mo mounted up and the scooter bucked over the potholes of the little town to the railway station on the old German-built Central line from Dar es Salaam to Kigoma on the shores of Lake Tanganyika. It was typically teutonic — cold and austere — but the stationmaster was sympathetic. Thambi slept on the floor, Mo on the stationmaster's desk.

Early in the morning it began to rain and the downpour beat a tattoo on the corrugated iron roof. The noise woke them up. At first light, the two teenagers emerged to find the landscape sodden: the baked dirt road leading out of Morogoro to Korogwe at the foot of the Usumbara Mountains had become a sea of mud. Outside the town they asked an African what the road ahead was like. He told them it was rough for a few miles and then 'like a piece of concrete'.

In the event, the 100-mile journey took them the best part of four days. Almost every yard of the way lorries and vehicles and cars lay abandoned, axle-deep in the mud. Every few hundred yards the scooter broadsided and flipped, throwing the two youngsters off. They slept where they stopped — one night under a tree, soaked to the skin, another in a well-covered glade in a wayside thicket. This was wild country, roamed by elephant, lion, leopard, rhino and myriad plains game.

He recalls that he was woken by something tickling his face. He thought it was Thambi's hair and he gave his friend's sleeping bag a good thump. The response startled him. There was an aggrieved snort, warm rancid breath on his face and the hasty departure of a heavy body. In the morning the two found the pug marks of a lion at the spot.

Battered almost beyond recognition, the scooter eventually chugged into Korogwe, its two riders smeared with mud, their baggage soiled and dirty; but after a wash and a rest they quickly recovered and rode on through Moshi, where Mo's friends lived, and Arusha to Namanga, the border crossing into Kenya. From there, they rode into Nairobi. Altogether this first leg took about a week.

Many of his relatives lived in the Kenya capital, including his uncle, Niaz Mohamed, who had a house in Pangani. It was to there they headed. Mo was half-expected. His parents, frantic with worry, had already circulated the news of his 'absconscion'. Mohamed Shaffi, his cousin, who now works for him as a cameraman, was about eight when the two teenagers arrived. 'It was raining very hard. And they were very scruffy and very tired,' he recollects.

Young Mohamed Amin and his Goan friend, Thambi, reach the Kenya border at
Namanga on the first leg of their planned 5,000-mile overland journey to Britain.
In the event, after covering 1,500 miles they were turned back at the Sudan-
Uganda border because they had no passports or travel documents.

Shaffi's father was understanding; he admired their spirit. 'He was very good,' Mo recalls. 'He gave us somewhere to rest and when we wanted to get on our way he gave us some money.'

The two made it north-west from Nairobi, through Kampala and up to the Sudan border, where their way was barred. Neither had even a rudimentary travel document let alone a passport. Their money was running out, too.

In three or four weeks on an underpowered scooter they had covered around 1,500 miles on the kind of killer roads which earned the East African Safari Rally, which ran through all three East African countries in those years, its reputation as the ultimate test of man and machine.

'So we turned round and rode all the way back to my uncle's house in Nairobi and on down to Dar es Salaam where I was given a thoroughly good thrashing by my father,' Mohamed Amin remembers. 'He didn't think very much of the adventure at all.'

It had lasted two months and he had learned a great deal. The scooter was a write-off, but he sold it for 100 shillings and began casting his eye over an assortment of second-hand VWs. To his mind, these vehicles had all the virtues of the people he liked. They were reliable and hard-working, able to rough it, and they were economically priced.

To earn the money to pay for the VW, he redoubled his photographic work. The annual magazine of the Aga Khan Girls High School in Dar es Salaam carried the following: 'The Editors acknowledge most gratefully permission to use the photographs taken by Mohamed Amin.' He had begun to understand the importance of copyright and the value of repeat usage of pictures. It must have pleased his vanity to grant 'permission' for the use of his pictures.

In 1962, the Indian Secondary School changed its name to Azania Secondary School. Henceforth all Dar es Salaam's children would begin life with equal education, for 1961 had closed with Nyerere's cherished dreams of Independence fulfilled. Colonialism was abolished at midnight on 8 December 1961.

His cameras were among the hundreds that exploded in thousands of flashes when the flag of the new nation was hauled up the flagpole to replace the Union Jack. The pictures appeared in *Drum* and newspapers throughout East and Central Africa. For the first time, too, his work and name went around the world. He had covered the celebrations for The Associated Press, beginning a relationship that continues unbroken.

He was now eighteen and a senior schoolboy, and the annual report of the school Photographic Society noted:

> Photography proved a paying hobby for many, and only a few members depended on their parents for recurrent expenses.
> Some earned a guinea or two, now and then, by sending a photograph to some local newspaper or foreign magazine.

He had no doubt about his choice of career, just as he was sure he would never be anyone else's employee. He had taken his first and only 27

An early news picture from the camera of Mohamed Amin: Mwalimu Julius Nyerere, leader of Tanganyika, tours the streets of the capital Dar es Salaam with a visiting freedom fighter.

Recording Tanganyika's Independence celebrations in 1961 for the Associated Press and other world media, Mohamed Amin captured the happiness of President-elect Julius Nyerere with Britain's Prince Philip, who handed over the instruments of independence.

photographic job when he was just sixteen after an advertisement in a Dar es Salaam newspaper had caught his eye: 'Photographer wanted'. He applied with a portfolio of his published work.

The man who answered his letter was Tony Dunn of the Aga Khan's *Nation* group who, twenty-five years later, as London correspondent of the *Nation*, would profile Mo's year of success, 1985. Working hours were from nine to twelve and two to five but he did not disclose the fact that he was still a schoolboy. He was offered the job.

'I worked out that I could report in for roll call and the first school period which was at eight and then leave for work at nine and return to take the last period. Being a prefect helped, since I was hardly going to report myself. I was missing but it wasn't that blatant — although the teachers must have wondered why I was out of class so much.'

The interruption in his academic career was not long. The *Nation* office in Dar es Salaam was minuscule and the darkroom even smaller — the office toilet. His system was to carry the chemical trays and a red light into the toilet when it was vacant. 'We stood the enlarger on the seat,' he remembers. 'The only really bad thing was the lack of fresh air.' Anybody in desperate need had to dash out of the office to find another toilet.

Saturday morning work was mandatory but developing was usually done on the Monday. One Saturday, however, Dunn was insistent that Mo go along to photograph some workmen digging holes in the capital's main road, close to the famous Askari monument to the dead and fallen of two world wars.

'They were installing cables and I thought to myself, "There's not much of a story — or picture — in this",' he recalls. Dunn told him to process the film and make some prints. The accountant, who doled out the printing paper against a stock sheet wherever it was requested, was not on duty. 'I asked him if it was important. Dunn said yes it was and I said I could borrow three or four pieces of printing paper from a friend, Sheny, and return it on Monday.' His friend ran a photographic shop and studio.

Next day he went through the *Nation*. None of his pictures had been used. His anger mounted. He was convinced the whole exercise had been deliberate. On the Monday, he asked Dunn if there had been any intention of using the material. Dunn told him no.

'I still don't know what he was trying to prove, but I had no doubts about what to do.'

He went to his desk, cleared away his papers, returned to Dunn's office, threw the office keys on the desk and told him: 'Stuff your job.' He never collected the only pay packet for which he ever worked.

In December 1962, in the middle of his school exams he quit. 'I remember', he says, 'that I decided in the middle of the exams that there was no point going through the exams because, however well or not so well I did, I'd just get a piece of paper from the school which I didn't need. Because this was when Tanganyika was going through the transition — it was all happening at that time.

'A good photographer doesn't need to go to a college to learn photography. I believe that if you are interested in photography you teach yourself. It's a question of trial and error. The more you practise in the field, the better you will be. Some of the best photographers around have had no formal photographic training. In fact, I think that to some extent those who go to colleges to learn photography are never really as good as those who have taught themselves. Because they have learned at school they go very much by the theories: it's all chemistry and physics and that's just very complicated; it doesn't work practically in the field.

'For example, if I told a college-trained photographer how we sometimes process our film, he would be horrified because occasionally we process film in paper developer to gain time. That's because very often you are racing against time, and speed is essential.

'I wanted to make my mark covering what was a major story. So I left school. And I still feel it was the right decision. I would have wasted four or five years of my life going to college, and I may not have had the same opportunities.'

And, recalling his one and only job, he vowed that he would always be his own master. Indeed, he had already decided the name of the company he would form.

2 Isle of Blood

Never in history has one continent experienced such a decade of turmoil, turbulence and transition as Africa in the 1960s. Almost everywhere the old order was swept away — in some cases to be replaced by new and unaccustomed freedoms, elsewhere by systems more authoritarian than those they displaced.

In time, many of the new leaders would come to know the young man who spent the evening of 24 March 1963 in Dar es Salaam filling in business registration Form 5 (Section 14), issued by the office of the Registrar-General of Tanganyika. The name he put down for the fledgling company was Minipix of Post Office Box 20345, Dar es Salaam, telephone 20953.

He already had a studio. One of his friends, Aziz Khaki, had offered to rent him half of his shop. It was a simple one-storey affair of block and mortar with a corrugated iron roof. Steel shutters were drawn across it at night for security. There was a reception area for customers, a darkroom and a small studio for portrait work.

Aziz's sister, Dolly, was a radiant and striking raven-haired model. The young photographer and she knew each other. He had met her in 1962 when he covered a fashion show in which she was taking part. The dresses she wore were her own designs.

Dolly ran a fashion shop just behind the Ismaili Mosque off the capital's Independence Avenue and she and Mohamed Amin became friends. Their affair began, he says, in the darkroom. 'I kissed her while I was printing her pictures. She used to visit me because she wanted to know how you developed pictures.'

What really developed was a lifelong love affair. Though he was from an orthodox Muslim family, he had already made up his mind to marry Dolly, who was an Ismaili, one of the Aga Khan's followers. For herself, she had thoughts of no one else but the wavy-haired teenager with the steely resolve and almost hypnotic personality.

There was another reason for his anxiety to get to work at once. Besides his older brother Iqbal, he had three younger brothers — Manir, born eight years after him, Alim ten years after him, and Hanif, fifteen years younger. He also had three sisters, Sugra, Sagira and Nazira. Home life was good. His mother, Azmat, made sure they were well fed, clothed and happy. But money was limited and, in 1963, in the wake of Independence,

In a Dar es Salaam coffee shop, Mohamed Amin and the girl he later married, fashion designer and model Dolly Khaki, discuss their future during 1963. The young photographer rented his first studio and darkroom from Dolly's brother, Aziz.

his father was anticipating retirement. At 53, his thoughts were turning more and more towards his homeland, which had been partitioned during his time in East Africa. His birthplace, Jullundur, now lay well inside India's share of the Punjab following the 1947 partition, and Sardar Mohamed was thinking of moving to that part which now lay within Islamic Pakistan. He intended that his family should return with him. Amin did not intend to go and needed to be assured of his independence.

Iqbal, who had been training with the East African Posts and Telecommunications Corporation in Kenya, was one of a handful of Asians and Europeans hastily recruited before Independence to provide the newly free nation with skilled personnel. He wanted to continue his studies in Britain and flew there on 24 December 1963.

His brother, too, had made up his mind. He was sure his future lay in Africa and this thought was uppermost in his mind as he completed the registration form.

Next morning, however, as he walked to the Registrar-General's office, he was still not satisfied with the name he had chosen. 'Mini' suggested something small, which did not suit this ambitious youngster.

Obviously his business must start small but it need not remain so. Pausing, he withdrew the form from the envelope and with his pen crossed out the 'Mini'. Above, in neat block letters, he wrote 'Camera'. Minutes later he bounced up the steps of the Registrar-General's office and pushed the form across the counter with the twenty shillings registration fee. Thus Camerapix was born.

The sign the teenager hung above his studio when the company opened for its first day of business read:

CAMERAPIX

STUDIO, PRESS AND COMMERCIAL PHOTOGRAPHERS

One service offered was the processing of black and white film at a shilling a roll. He had calculated this would cover the cost of chemicals, equipment and his time in the darkroom.

Indeed, his very first customer, a young African, handed him a roll of black and white film. But when Mo developed it the negatives were blank, although the frame numbers confirmed there was nothing wrong with the processing. With a shrug of his shoulders he realized that whatever explanation he gave would be met with disbelief. He was right. The customer gazed at him with the look of one convinced he was dealing with a charlatan. 'He didn't believe a word I said. It was obvious he thought that I had developed his roll wrongly.' The customer refused to pay and although the shop had only been open for two hours young Amin locked it up and took the board back to the sign writer.

Back in position an hour later, it read simply:

Press Photographers Only

As a matter of routine, right from the beginning Mohamed Amin worked a fourteen-to-fifteen-hour-day, and a seven-day week, developing relationships with clients, and every day learning something new about the fascinating, unpredictable world of news.

'I just worked. I used to come to the office in the morning and clean it all. I used to beat the carpets without any shame at all. I didn't give a damn who saw me do it. Then I spent the day taking pictures and writing captions and sending them to various newspapers.'

He is almost pathological about work. Even in the 1980s, waking early and unable to get back to sleep, he gets dressed and goes to his office sometimes as early as four a.m.

'I think, subconsciously to a degree, that God has given me life and it's not a life that I want to spend lying on the beach. You must achieve something with your life. It's not to waste. And I just feel that I don't need to rest any more than I have to rest in this life. I can rest later when I'm dead. Then nobody's going to bother me.'

In the meantime, from those very early years, driven by a relentless sense of destiny, he has bothered many who labour in his shadows, caught up in his work compulsion to the point of exhaustion. 'There were a number of times that I actually slept in the office. I didn't have to sleep in the office. I could have gone home. But I just wanted to work. In my early years, half the time in any month I think I actually spent the night in the office. I just slept on the table. I would work for as long as I could and then clear the table and sleep on it for three or four hours, wake up at two or three in the morning and go on again. I just enjoyed working.'

His energy soon paid off. The established freelancers in Dar es Salaam were not at all pleased by the success of this brash young upstart. But just how intensely they resented him he had no idea until the day he sought advice from one of the capital's veteran photojournalists.

Amin had bought a flash and wanted to know in which position he should set the switch on his camera body for electronic use. His poker-faced rival pointed out the wrong position. The result was a disaster, every picture an unusable half frame.

'At that moment,' he recalls, 'I figured — never trust anybody. And always check and double-check.' It is a rule he stands by almost religiously — sometimes to the irritation of all involved — but it undoubtedly accounts for his achievements where others, less exacting, fail to deliver.

'I felt really let down and very bitter at being deliberately misled. In fact, when I confronted the photographer later he agreed that he had done it because I was competing with him and he had been working at the job for years.

'It was a very nasty thing to do and I promised myself that if ever any   35

Opening day for a new business, 25 March 1963. Twenty-year-old Mohamed Amin waits with a friend to welcome the first customer to Camerapix — with disastrous consequences. When Amin developed the customer's roll of film in his darkroom it was blank and the customer refused to pay. So, hours after this picture was taken, Mo changed his sign — and his business — to that of Press Photographers Only.

1958: Mohamed Amin in the Photographic Society's darkroom at the Dar es Salaam Indian Secondary School.

photographers came to me for any advice I would never mislead them but go out of my way to try to help them and point them in the right direction. This is something I have conscientiously done ever since — even with my direct competitors. I've always tried to help in whatever way I can, always bearing in mind what happened to me. I must never let that happen to anyone looking for advice from me.'

Former CBS cameraman Abdul Qayum Isaq, who now runs a television production outfit, was a callow photographer with one of Mohamed Amin's rivals for some time. 'I really wanted to be a cameraman but nobody was interested in giving me the experience or teaching me.'

Then he went to Amin who spent long hours passing on his experience to the enthusiastic youngster. Soon Qayum's film work began to earn plaudits from the Visnews editors and other organizations.

But, like so many, Qayum found Amin's pace too hot. 'He's impossible to work for,' he says. 'He never stops — and he expects everybody else to continue at the same incredible pace. I wanted to stay alive so I quit. But he taught me everything I know.'

If the young Amin had rivals, he also had friends. He soon acquired official accreditation from the Tanganyika Government. His Press card, approved by one of President Nyerere's top aides, Colonel Hesham Mbita, who had taken a liking to the tireless youngster, gave him the right to move to the front of the crowd at State functions and other events without being hassled by security — or rival photographers — and put him shoulder to shoulder with the old guard.

He learned quickly that any official-looking piece of paper could be a passport to closed places and an asset in dealing with stubborn or bullying officialdom. Years later, he lent his Diners Club credit card to a *Newsweek* correspondent who showed it to the security guards at Mombasa's Kilindini Port and was admitted without question.

At this stage, however, Amin knew nothing of cinefilm or television and it's unlikely he ever would have taken much interest but for talk he overheard about the money to be earned from the television networks. He gave it little thought, however, until he received a 'tip-off' on a strong story.

Two liberal white South Africans, imprisoned for their opposition to the apartheid regime, had broken jail in Pretoria and stolen a Cessna as their getaway plane to fly to Dar es Salaam. Nyerere's Tanganyika had become a well-known haven for those opposed to colonialism, racism and apartheid.

He hurried to his friend Sheny, who had a sixteen-millimetre, hand-cranked, clockwork Bolex which shot silent film. Each take of the 100-foot reel was limited to little over half-a-minute (around twenty feet) after which the motor had to be wound up again. Compared with later cameras it was a serious limitation — though it forced a generation of news cameramen, including young Mohamed Amin, to shoot really tight stories, and to make every 'take' count.

Sheny opened the Bolex and wound the reel in place before handing the camera to Amin who, with hasty thanks, hurried out to the second-hand Volkswagen he had acquired.

At the airport, he prepared his still cameras, hung the Bolex over one shoulder and, waving his Press pass, sauntered casually through the security to the parking apron waiting for the Cessna to taxi in.

He had never used a cine camera before, so he spent the first few minutes shooting stills before asking the two tired runaways if they would co-operate a little longer while he shot a news film for British television. On the way back to his studio he called in at Sheny's to return the Bolex — and to ask him to unload the film. Then, as he processed and printed his stills and filed his story for the local East African press, and *Drum* and AP, who, he knew, would certainly want the pictures, he pushed it out of his mind. When he did remember, he realized he had no idea who would use it, or even where to send it.

A contact in the British High Commission in Dar es Salaam gave him the London headquarters addresses of the British Broadcasting Corporation (BBC), the British Commonwealth International Newsfilm Agency (BCI-NA) — the original name for Visnews — and Independent Television News (ITN) together with the advice: 'I hear ITN pays best.'

It was all he needed to know. Compiling a 'dope' sheet listing each take on the reel, together with background notes and a cutting from the *Tanganyika Standard* which had used his story, he air-freighted the package with charges collect.

Speculative offerings from unknowns, addressed simply to 'The Editor,' rarely get used. His first news film however was shown on ITN's peak-time bulletin. Fast asleep at the time, he only learned of his success two days later when he opened a cable from ITN Editor Geoffrey Cox. It was a milestone in his career; though more significant to him was ITN's cheque for £25 — substantially more than he got from sales of the same story to the press.

With the right equipment and contacts, he calculated, he could more than double his money on any story he covered by combining news film coverage with stills. After this first success he was rarely without Sheny's Bolex on his stills assignments. It became so much a part of him that he came to be known as 'Six Camera Mo', the man with a necklace of still and cine cameras draped across his shoulders. Soon, for the way he managed to meet the requirements of rival newspapers and television stations with just one pair of eyes, he became something of a legend.

Besides news stories he produced features, many of them concerned with Tanganyika's incomparable wilderness areas. His interest and enthusiasm for Africa's wildlife grew all the time. So did his fascination with Africa's tribal cultures. He was particularly impressed by the proud independence of the nomadic Maasai, as prominent in Tanganyika as they were across the border in Kenya. To reach Tanganyika's Maasailand,

Known as Six Camera Mo, Amin
learned early in life the logistics —
and the burden — of filming the
same assignment for several rival
clients.

When Bobby Kennedy visited Tanzania with his wife Ethel and children, Mohamed Amin covered the visit flying throughout the country in the Kennedy's chartered plane.

Mohamed Amin at a welcoming cocktail party at Arusha, northern Tanzania, for Prince Bernhard of the Netherlands in 1963 when, as President of the World Wildlife Fund, he paid a visit to the country's famed national parks — Serengeti, Manyara and Ngorongoro. When he saw young Amin covering his visit with a sixteen-millimetre, hand-cranked Bolex, the Prince — a keen wildlife photographer — sought the cameraman's help in loading his own Bolex and asked him how to operate it.

however, was not easy.

In such a vast country, roads were few, rough and often impassable during the rains. Although costly, flying made a lot of sense and as he counted the cost of his trips upcountry, he resolved that one day he would learn to fly — to the horror of those he'd driven in his Beetle.

He'd already had some near-fatal crashes. One occurred when he was driving home to change to cover an evening function. By good fortune, Dolly was not with him. 'Normally she would come home with me and wait while I changed,' he remembers. 'This time, thank God, she did not. I was blinded by an oncoming Peugeot 504 with full lights blazing. All I know is that I hit something.'

The something turned out to be a big lorry without lights parked in the middle of the road. He was thrown out of the car as the Beetle went straight under the truck and had its top sliced off. Anybody with him would have been killed instantly.

The driver of the Peugeot stopped. He was Eduardo Chivambo Mondlane, head of the Mozambique freedom fighting organization *Frente de Libertaçao de Mozambique* — Frelimo — based in Dar es Salaam. He picked up the unconscious body and drove straight to the city's government hospital.

'By this time I had come around and had a lot of pain in my chest but did not know if I was badly injured or not. I was put in a wheelchair and wheeled into a cubicle waiting for my turn to be examined.

'A friend of mine, Mohinder Singh Matharoo, chief photographer for the Ministry of Information who lived close to my house, was driving to the city when he saw the wreckage and was told on the spot: "The driver is dead".

'There were a lot of people around the truck. Because I had been thrown out and taken away almost instantly nobody knew what had happened and just assumed I was inside the mangled wreck.'

'It was his first "fatal" crash,' recalls Roy Lipscombe, in those days a reporter on the *Tanganyika Standard*. 'Everyone in the office who saw his car said no man could have lived.'

'Mohinder finally found me in the hospital while I was still waiting to be examined,' Mo remembers, 'and he took me straight away to the private Aga Khan Hospital, where they X-rayed me. There were two broken ribs which were quite painful.'

Next day, bruised and battered, he flew to Pemba and Zanzibar, the island that was to give him his first news triumph, to cover the State visit of President Nyerere.

In the two centuries since the Sultans of Oman first extended their domain to absorb the islands offshore from Dar es Salaam virtually nothing on Zanzibar had changed. The wealth of the ruling Barghash dynasty was founded on 200 years of slave trading. At its height, in the late nineteenth century, as many as 30,000 slaves a year were trekked down from the interior in cruel, inhuman caravans and embarked, at Bagamoyo

During Kenya's Independence celebrations in December 1963, Mzee Jomo Kenyatta, the Kenya Prime Minister and President-elect, listens to a point from the outgoing Governor-General and first British High Commissioner to Kenya, Sir Malcolm MacDonald.

One of the first of hundreds of Mohamed Amin action pictures that were to hit the world's front pages — a looter flees the wrath of rebel soldiers during the January 1964 Tanganyika Army mutiny in Dar es Salaam. The mutiny came in the wake of the Zanzibar coup.

Right: The future Sultan of Zanzibar, Prince Seyyid Jamshid bin Abdullah, quenching his thirst from a bucket of well water on a hunting expedition in the island's Josani Forest. After he became Sultan he was overthrown in 1964 by peasant rebels led by John Okello, a semi-literate Acholi tribesman from northern Uganda.

Below: Self-styled Field Marshal John Okello, poses with some of his 600-strong peasant army while the island runs red with the blood of between 12,000 and 13,000 victims. Okello was soon disowned by the first President, Sheikh Abeid Karume.

on the mainland north of the capital, for the slave market in Zanzibar town presided over by notorious slave traders like Tipu Tip.

In 1866, Scottish missionary and explorer David Livingstone rested in a house overlooking the market, before setting out for the interior on his crusade to end the evil trade. Yet, a century later the Sultan was still indulging himself in the manner of his ancestors. He claimed a royal rent from the island's British tenants, which, together with the earnings from clove plantations, placed his family among the wealthiest of all Arab royalty.

In 1955, for example, a 1,500-ton ocean-going luxury yacht was built in England for the Sultan, Seyyid Sir Abdullah Khalifa, at a cost of £350,000. Named the mv *Seyyid Khalifa*, it joined its predecessor, a no-less luxurious royal yacht, the *Salaama*, cruising the warm Indian Ocean waters.

The photographer often accompanied the Sultan's son, Prince Seyyid Jamshid bin Abdullah, on hunting expeditions — mainly pig-sticking in the dank jungles of the island. The future Sultan's extravagant lifestyle, in decadent contrast to the abject poverty of his subjects, many of whom were descended from slaves, made perfect material for picture features.

On 9 December 1963 Prince Philip renounced Britain's guardianship of the Sultanate. Mo Amin was there, for press and television. Then, on the morning of 11 December, he took an East African Airways flight from Zanzibar to Nairobi, trailing Prince Philip, who at midnight that same day stood at attention with Mzee Jomo Kenyatta, the Kenya Prime Minister, as the British flag was lowered for the last time and the new Kenya flag raised.

Photographers and cameramen were assigned places in foxhole-style dugouts close by the flagpoles which lined the site of the ceremonies at Uhuru Gardens near Nairobi's Wilson Airport. As the British flag was lowered, the lights went out. The plan was for the floodlamps to burst into light as the Kenya flag unfurled at the top of the staff. But the rope snagged and there was a slight delay.

Prince Philip leaned over and whispered something to the African statesman which brought a wide grin in response. It was learnt later that the Prince had told Kenyatta: 'You've still got time to change your mind if you wish.' Seconds later thunderous cheers greeted Kenya's entry into the ranks of the world's free and sovereign states.

Exactly one month later, on Saturday 11 January 1964, the young photographer received a telephone call from an old contact, forty-year-old Marxist revolutionary Abdulrahman Mohamed Babu, organizer of Zanzibar's extreme left-wing Umma — 'Masses' — Party.

After spending six years behind a Post Office Savings Bank counter in Acton, West London, and dabbling in journalism, Babu, of mixed Arab-Comorian descent, had returned from England in the 1950s. He had fled Zanzibar in a dugout canoe the day before, after laying the groundwork for an uprising planned for Sunday 12 January.

46   'If you want a big story you should be in Zanzibar tomorrow.'

'Why?'

'There's a big story. Take your cameras. You'll get an exclusive.'

'What kind of story?'

Babu would say no more. When Amin learned from his own sources that the Sultan had given the opposition Afro-Shirazi Party permission to hold a fete, he dismissed the story as non-newsworthy and thought no more about it. Until 0430 on Sunday 12 January, when he was woken by the telephone and a voice saying: 'There's shooting all over Zanzibar.' He was at Dar es Salaam airport in time to board the 0700 flight to Zanzibar. But when it reached the island the pilot was refused landing permission.

Back at Dar es Salaam airport he rang Associated Press correspondent Dennis Neeld, and five minutes later Neeld and a newly arrived colleague, Bob Ryder, jumped into Amin's car and raced out of town along the coast road to Bagamoyo, forty-five miles away. The old slaving centre was a thriving dhow port — and boat was now the only way to reach Zanzibar.

As he and Neeld bargained with dhow captains who had no wish to go there at any price, the streets of the island, thirty miles across the sea, ran crimson with blood. In those first hours of what was to be a week of terror thousands died.

At three that morning 600 revolutionaries, under the command of John Okello, a semi-literate Acholi tribesman from Uganda's Lango District, had struck the island's Mtoni police barracks. Within days Okello himself was disowned; but not before he had indulged in blood-letting on a horrifying scale. At week's end, the death toll was officially estimated at between 12,000 and 13,000.

Still bargaining at Bagamoyo, Amin finally persuaded a bearded dhow veteran to carry his party across. Outside Zanzibar harbour they were challenged by one of Okello's motor patrol boats. A man on board recognized Mo and gave the dhow a tow into the harbour.

By the following morning resistance to the coup had virtually ended. With no military on the island, the British troops having left after Independence, the only armed force on Zanzibar consisted of a European police commissioner, James Sullivan, a European assistant, six European 'special reservists' and eighty Zanzibaris. Between them, they had five rifles, one revolver and a handful of ammunition.

When Mo's party landed in Zanzibar, Sullivan and the others had already left with the Sultan aboard the potentate's yacht, the *Salaama*. Later the royal party transferred to the bigger yacht and — turned away from Mombasa — berthed back at Dar es Salaam where this prince out of a live 'Arabian Nights' fantasy boarded a BOAC jet, chartered by the British Government, which took him and his forty-two-man entourage to that limbo of many forgotten exiles — England. It landed at Ringway Airport, Manchester.

Amin arranged with the captain that the dhow should ferry his film back to the mainland each day. To his astonishment telephone links with the mainland were fully operational, so he was able to ring Dolly in Dar es

Salaam and tell her when to drive out to Bagamoyo to meet the dhow.

For four days, through CBS, Visnews and ITN, his film from the bloody island of spice led world television bulletins. He also hit the front pages of the world's Press. Interest was all the greater because Zanzibar was a strategic area, and one of the bases for the United States satellite tracking stations for 'Project Mercury'.

Soon after landing on the island he was pressed into service to take the first official pictures of the revolution's leaders. One of them — Babu, his confidante — had become the new regime's Minister for External Affairs. Meeting Babu in a crowd of excited revolutionaries in Zanzibar's seething streets he told him he needed permission to charter a plane to ship his film. Time was critical, and the airport was still closed.

'Give me a piece of paper,' said Babu.

'I don't have any.'

Looking around him, Babu saw a discarded detergent carton, picked it up, tore off the flap and scribbled a crude but official note clearing a plane to land at Zanzibar.

One of his first newsfilm reports that week was the evacuation of sixty-one Americans, twelve Britons and five West Germans — together with nine Arabs the American consulate described as 'Lithuanians' — from the island by the American ship USS *Manley*.

Then, just after he completed a grisly film about mass graves and dhow 'funeral' ships used to dispose of corpses at sea, always followed by a sinister wake of dorsal fins, the British ship, HMS *Owen*, arrived to evacuate about 150 British citizens.

They included seven newsmen deported as 'prohibited immigrants' including Clyde Sangar of *The Guardian* in Britain, Priya Ramrakha of Kenya working for *Life* magazine, William Smith of *Time*, Jack Nugent *Newsweek*, Robert Conley *New York Times*, Peter Rand *New York Herald Tribune*, and Robert Miller of Toronto's *Globe and Mail*.

American Consul Fred Picard, who tried to intervene on their behalf, and his assistant were arrested at gunpoint at the Zanzibar Hotel where the newsmen had been detained.

Before boarding the ship the newsmen had been lined up against a wall. At first they thought they were going to be shot – but the Zanzibaris just wanted to take their pictures to make sure they never came back.

The story left Amin in no doubt about the merciless attitude the revolutionaries had to Arabs and Asians. As he stood on the wharf, filming the last of the British boarding the launch which was to carry them out to the anchored warship, he felt a hand on his shoulder. Two revolutionaries in tattered clothes and armed with machine guns took hold of his arms and tried to snatch his cameras. He resisted and held on to his precious equipment. As the launch was pushed off, he jumped on board. The startled Zanzibaris raised their weapons, trigger fingers tightening. British marines on the boat challenged Mo, but as the gap between vessel and steps widened, he reached into his camera bag and

pulled out the black passport with the gold crest of the British coat of arms
— No. 336186 — issued by the British High Commission in Dar es Salaam.
The marines nodded. The Zanzibaris watched the boat drift away.

Through it all he never stopped taking pictures.

When he arrived in Mombasa he shipped his film to London via Nairobi,
then took a charter flight back to Dar es Salaam.

Not yet twenty-one, his performance earned the admiration of the
hardened professionals in the CBS, UPIN and Visnews newsrooms. He
had been in a frontline situation all week and shown not only the courage
to film it, but the initiative and resource to get his film out for the world to
see. A great reputation was in the making. Within the week he had added
to it substantially.

The revolution created unease throughout East Africa, and there were
immediate repercussions. Two hours after midnight on Monday 20
January the First Battalion of the Tanganyika Rifles — two-thirds of the
country's army — stationed at Colito Barracks on the outskirts of Dar es
Salaam mutinied.

Before dawn they swooped on the homes of British officers seconded to
the Tanganyika Armed Forces, bundled them into lorries and took them to
the city's airport. There, they put them aboard an East African Airways
plane and ordered the pilot to fly them to Nairobi.

Later in the day, after sweeping through the capital at daybreak in an
orgy of looting that left at least six people dead and many wounded, they
collected their wives and children and put them on another plane to
Nairobi.

The whereabouts of President Julius Nyerere was a mystery. After
promising a delegation of mutineers to consider their demands he
vanished. It later transpired that he was smuggled out of State House by
the Army's British commanding officer, Brigadier Patrick Douglas, and
went into hiding for two days.

As police moved in to take control, arresting looters, the photographer
was at the heart of the action. Then a senior police officer arrested him and
marched him off to Dar es Salaam Central Police station. The cells were
already full so he was put inside one of the small offices behind the
counter.

'Basically, the whole scene was chaos and pandemonium,' he recalls.
'The police took my cameras and just shoved me in an office. I looked
through the keyhole and it was like a rugby scrum outside. Nobody
seemed to be in charge. I could see my cameras on a desk, unguarded, and
there was a lot of confusion and shouting.'

To his surprise, when he tried the handle of the door it swung open. He
sauntered out through the arguing police, public and soldiers, picked up
his cameras and, without quickening his pace, walked out to freedom. At
home, for the first and only time in his life he shaved off his beard, then
changed his clothes and went straight back to film the action.

On Tuesday evening Nyerere made a speech to the nation over Radio   49

Tanganyika calling the previous day 'a day of shame'. When Nyerere visited the barracks to address the mutineers he told the soldiers that they would have to lay down their arms before he would consider their grievances, but the troops refused. Nyerere, accompanied by expatriate Press officer George Rockey and aides, left to inspect the damage in the city centre.

By now, Dar es Salaam teemed with television cameramen from Europe and America come to cover the Zanzibar Revolution. They had grip boys to carry their baggage, and the latest cameras and sound equipment — not to mention sound recordists, producers and, of course, the ace, front-of-camera reporters who put words to the pictures.

Among them was the man known as 'the CBS marine' — tough, trouble-shooting Joe Masraf, a cameraman who had filmed virtually every major war of the last twenty-five years, from Spain to Vietnam.

Pitted against all these resources twenty-year-old Amin had one ancient borrowed Bolex camera. He remembers thinking it was a bit like trying to compete in an air race in a glider. But in the end it was not the camera but the man behind it who won the day.

'Touring the town late in the evening, I saw British officers coming ashore at the Presidential jetty off a British ship anchored offshore. I decided I must be ready for action early next day. Around sun-up I heard the thump of heavy gunfire and small-arms fire from the direction of the Colito Barracks, eight miles out of town. I headed that way. A mile short I was stopped at a road block manned by British marines.'

His ITN card established an immediate rapport with the marines. They told him it was 'bloody dangerous up there'. He just grinned — and asked if he could film them. He was allowed through.

'A British helicopter was circling the barracks with a loud-hailer. The man on the hailer was Captain M. S. H. Sarakikya, a Tanganyikan hero who had climbed Kilimanjaro's ice-capped 19,340-foot-high peak on Independence Day to hoist the new republic's flag on Africa's highest mountain. Sarakikya was calling on the mutineers to lay down their arms. Between his appeals the helicopter, armed with a light gun, was loosing off blank shells.

'They made a lot of noise but they were doing no damage. Some of the mutineers, but not many, were moving towards the football field, where they had been told to surrender. And some men in the guard room were firing back at the helicopter.' In response the gunship put a live shell through the guard house. The rebels began to capitulate.

Up to this time, filming from outside the gates, he had had the story all to himself but now NBC, BBC, CBS and other crews began to arrive. They got dramatic coverage of rebels fleeing the barracks and being flushed out of the bush by the low-flying helicopters. Heart sinking, he realized he could not compete.

'They had everything. All the technology you need to make a good story. And they had the action, too. Anyway, I filmed what I could with what I had.'

Then the barrack gates were opened and the film crews were allowed inside to record the arrests and the mopping up. At midday he saw the first television crew leave. They were stopped outside the gates by members of the Tanganyika Special Branch who confiscated their films. 'That was one crew which had nothing to show for their efforts,' he recalls. Then the same thing happened to another crew. Masraf and his CBS team also saw what was happening.

He watched as big Joe slit open the back seat of the crew's rented car — and stuffed his cans of film inside. Then, slowly, he and his team drove clear of the barracks till they too were pulled up and ordered out of the car. Smiling innocently, they denied possession of any exposed film and showed the guards rolls of unused stock, gesturing and chatting in a friendly, persuasive manner. But one of the Special Branch guards found the rip in the seat cover and pulled out the used films.

Amin was now the only one left inside the barracks. 'As I kept filming I was trying to work out ways of evading the security check outside the gates.'

Filming yet another helicopter coming into the barracks with more officers he realised this could be the way out. 'They were British helicopters and pilots,' he remembers. 'And because the barracks were under the control of the British, the Special Branch were not allowed inside.' As it came to rest, rotors still whirling, he ran across and shouted at the pilot.

'What the hell?' asked the man at the controls. 'Who are you?'

He flashed his ITN card and grimaced at the chaos around him.

Shouting to make himself heard above the roar of the engine, he said, 'I've got to get this film on a flight to London — and there's one leaving very soon. Can you give me a lift to the airport?'

'For ITN?' the pilot smiled. 'Any time, jump in.'

Seconds later the helicopter swirled over the gates. Angry and frustrated Joe Masraf and his crew gazed up at it, and when Amin hung his head out of the window the CBS ace shook his fist at him.

He replied with a V-salute. His car was still inside the barracks but he had his film; and ten minutes later he was checking it through the freight office of East African Airways for the flight to London.

Two days later, CBS news executive J. Segal, after viewing the only film showing the Tanganyika Army mutiny, was talking to his London office on a bad telephone connection:

'Who do you say this kid is?'

'Mohamed Amin.'

'Well make sure he stays on our payroll. I'd hate him to work for the opposition.'

3 Massacre on the Horn

Change in Africa during the 1960s was momentous and traumatic. After the euphoria of independence, many countries found themselves ill prepared for their responsibilities and unable to cope with the political conflicts and disillusion which followed. Those colonies that remained became the targets of freedom movements: many of them based in newly independent countries sympathetic to their goals.

Under Nyerere, Tanganyika became a major frontline country. The symbolic African idealist wanted no truck with the illegal white minority regime under Ian Smith which, in 1965, seized power in Rhodesia. He was also opposed to the Portuguese occupation of Mozambique and Angola, and a leading campaigner against apartheid in South Africa. This put him at loggerheads with Dr Hastings Kamuzu Banda of Malawi, who settled for pragmatic peaceful co-existence with the powerful white neighbours on whom his country's economic well-being depended. By contrast, Nyerere paid court to Mao Tse-tung's China, while the Russians and East Germans consolidated their presence in Zanzibar.

Across the waters of Lake Tanganyika, the Congo, that vast territory once ruled over by Belgium, still seethed with genocidal strife in a savage struggle for power among rival factions.

Cuba, Russia, East Germany, China and others were only too ready to stir this witches' brew. Never slow to recognize the potential of a situation, Amin began to extend his television news coverage, often on a speculative basis. Most of his work was used, and he won an increasing number of assignments.

Throughout 1964 he worked regularly for CBS. By now America had an obsessional interest in Russia's growing influence in Africa; the French, under de Gaulle, kept a covetous eye on their little possession on the Horn of Africa, French Somalia; and, of course, any good story from the former British colonies was grist to the television mills of Britain's BBC, and the broadcasters served by UPIN and Visnews.

Mohamed Amin became a thorn in the flesh to the Dar es Salaam-based stringers — all less energetic. UPIN's stringer in Tanganyika, Ahmed Sharif, was well into middle age. He ran a successful shop, Minicine, in the centre of Dar es Salaam. The occasional UPIN assignment gave him useful pin money. His great friend was the opposition Visnews stringer, Farouk Reporter, a man his own age. Neither depended on the television news agencies for their livelihood. Their philosophy was simple: 'Don't put your life on the line for fifty dollars.'

But nothing seemed risky about the March 1964 visit of British Commonwealth Secretary Duncan Sandys to Tanganyika and Zanzibar which they were assigned to cover. For all three the attraction was the money they could earn.

On the flight to Zanzibar, Sharif and Reporter admired Amin's brand-new Bolex camera which he had bought with the money he had made covering the revolution and the Dar es Salaam mutiny. On both occasions Sharif and Reporter had been noticeably absent.

'I was paid by the story, not by the day, and I thought I may as well get another story and earn another pound. No point wasting time in Zanzibar for half a day. So I decided I was going to cover one of the prisons — which was an obvious story to do — and I persuaded these other guys to come along with me and do it.'

They saw no harm in his suggestion. The detainee camps still held thousands of Arab prisoners. Even when they were refused permission at the first camp they still went along with his suggestion that they should try the Aga Khan's house which, Mo had heard, was being used for a similar purpose.

At the gates, he used his favourite ploy of chatting up the young guards and suggesting he should film them. The trick rarely failed. The guards were in an amiable mood and the three were given the run of the grounds and the mansion. Just as they were about to leave, however, the telephone rang.

The guard who replaced the receiver was a changed man. 'Suddenly,' Amin recalls, 'we had guns in our backs. We were made to stand out in the sun for hours and we were all near to collapse. The temperature was around 34°C (93°F) with eighty-five per cent humidity. These were not two young people like myself and even I was close to exhaustion.

'A cabinet minister arrived. He accused us of being imperialist spies, spat on us, kicked and slapped us. We were then locked up in a room, our cameras, bags and films confiscated.'

By morning Farouk had run out of the medication he carried for the pernicious haemorrhoids from which he suffered, while Ahmed, deprived of pan — a mild narcotic to which he was partial — became neurotic. 'Their plight was dreadful,' Mo remembers. 'They really hated me.'

It was forty-eight hours before the Zanzibari authorities relented and let them go, endorsing Mo's passport with a 'Prohibited Immigrant' stamp — the first of three he would collect within a span of thirty months from the hyper-sensitive governments of East Africa.

He never used his new Bolex again. Together with Farouk's and Ahmed's equipment the new Zanzibar Government requisitioned it to form the island's first film unit. Not that the two elder stringers ever needed their cine cameras again. Safely back in Dar es Salaam, they quit television news. 'They said they would never do a story again. But I was back scrounging for cameras from my friends again because I'd just lost my new camera.'

If Amin had wanted a strategy which would make Tanganyika, and much of East Africa, his exclusive beat he could have thought of none better. He now had a virtual monopoly in the area and it was only a matter of time before he was able to replace the confiscated Bolex.

Despite the Prohibited Immigrant stamp in his passport, he was allowed to enter Zanzibar on 25 April to cover the story of the Union — between Tanganyika and Zanzibar — which gave birth to today's Tanzania.

Like a cat — no matter which way fate tossed him — he always managed to land on his feet. The gauche young man, now approaching his twenty-first birthday, had filled out and become burly. The goatee beard he had cultivated and which he still has today gave him a maturity which belied his years. Cameras over his shoulders, he was at the seat of great events. He was already becoming something of a legend. He worked with exceptional energy. Rumour said he had designed a crossbar, which he strapped over his shoulders, on which he could mount three sixteen-millimetre cameras and focus and operate them simultaneously with a single sighting sensor and trigger. He denies it. He could fit only two cameras to his crossbar.

These events, including the often painful births of nations, proximity to new men in power, meetings in his stills studio with a rapidly widening range of acquaintances, were giving his life a very clear outline.

By now his father and mother were ready to leave East Africa for good. It never seriously occurred to them that he would not travel back 'home' with them, like the rest of their children. But he was never in any doubt for one moment.

With frequent assignments from the Press — even the wildlife pictures he took 'for fun' during the weekends had begun to make half-page spreads on the back pages of papers like *The Times* of London — and now television, he had no wish to leave Africa.

Early in 1965 his parents, sisters and brothers boarded a P & O liner, the SS *Karanja* in Dar es Salaam harbour, bound for Karachi. At the age of fifty-five, Sardar Mohamed was returning to his ancestral land on a pension of 500 shillings a month. As part of his terminal benefits, all his dependants were given one-way tickets on the Indian Ocean steamer. As Amin took his, he told his father: 'I'll come across later.' But, waving farewell as the steamer moved away from the quay, he knew it would never be used.

Jaunty, self-confident, he moved into bachelor quarters in the house of Salim, a neighbour on the Railways estate. He had total confidence in his abilities, could talk anyone into anything, never minded taking a risk, and seemed to have a charmed existence whatever he did. All he needed were more hands and equipment to meet the demands of his clients. He chose some novel ways of fulfilling them.

David Martin remembers him at work during the 1965 visit to Tanzania of Chinese Premier Chou En-lai. 'He had assignments from five television organizations and eight stills organizations. Obviously, he couldn't do everything himself so he hired a group of young Asians and taught them the most rudimentary photography.

'Throughout the Chou En-lai visit there was this crocodile procession of photographers led by Mohamed. He would move up to take a given shot and shoot for X seconds, then he would move on and the next in line would move into his place and do the same. He must have made a fortune out of that visit.'

Then, as now, he could summon up hypnotic charm when he wanted something. 'No, I don't want to talk to Mohamed,' Nairobi marketing executive Jerry Shah once told me with some vehemence, 'Every time I do it costs me money.'

Roy Lipscombe remembers their first meeting — the start of a lifelong friendship — hundreds of miles upcountry in Tanzania where they were covering a Presidential visit. Lipscombe had flown by charter plane for the *Tanganyika Standard*. Amin, working for Lipscombe's opposition, drove all the way in his Beetle.

'When the ceremony was over,' remembers Roy, 'Mo strode up and asked, almost demanded, that I should take his film, which was for a rival newspaper, back to Dar es Salaam with me in time for publication. I can't imagine now why I agreed. But I did.'

Persistence and perseverance are a newsman's greatest assets. Amin sees his job as taking pictures — and is obsessive about it. Nothing stands in his way.

'Once you agree to do a story it's important that you're first with it. You can't always win but generally speaking you should never lose. I can't actually remember a time when I've been on a story and been beaten into the ground, so to speak.'

For the 1965 state visit of Britain's Queen Elizabeth II and Prince Philip to Ethiopia and Sudan, Amin, assigned to cover the tour by Pathe News, whose newsreels ran in cinemas around the world, was one of a hundred or more cameramen and photographers.

It was during this visit that Emperor Haile Selassie presented the Queen with a thoroughbred from his royal stables. These were behind the Ghion Hotel which was once a part of the palace and connected by a private path.

'All the Press — and there were about 200 of us counting the reporters — were staying at the Ghion,' recalls Amin. 'Obviously, with the Queen's interest in horses, it was going to make a great picture. But although the stables were at the back of the hotel, the Emperor's officials insisted that we had to report at the palace and board the official buses. Since we couldn't use the private path this involved a long drive around half of the city to the official entrance.

'And when we got there it was the usual snafu and there was a delay. While we were waiting, the royal couple and the Emperor walked down 55 the path and into the stables and by the time we got there the presentation was over. So we weren't allowed to enter.

'We wrote a note and sent it in asking them if they would please make the presentation again. It was given to one of the Royal family's aides and the answer came back — no.

'That was when we decided we were going to boycott the rest of the visit. The Queen was still being shown around the Emperor's stud and we were standing outside the entrance where the royals would leave.

'So lining up our cameras on the ground, like a guard of honour without the cameramen, we all stood a yard or two behind. It was very clear that we were protesting and it was very obvious from their reaction when they came out that neither the Queen nor the Emperor knew what had happened. He asked his aide what the problem was.

'When he heard he talked to the Queen and then, just like two real professionals, they invited us in while the Emperor re-presented the horse to Her Majesty.'

During this tour, his determination always to be first earned him the dubious distinction of receiving two royal rebukes within the space of a week: something even that not many of the British palace staff can boast about. He has a great gift, even in the middle of the mob, of standing out from the others.

The first rebuke came during a garden party in Addis Ababa. 'I was filming Prince Philip talking to some schoolgirls, but eventually I became more interested in what he was talking about than actually filming.

'So I got closer and closer pretending that I was filming. Unfortunately, you can hear the drive on a thirty-five-millimetre cine camera and mine was not switched on. I was just interested in listening to one of the royals talking. I got very close. But Philip of course twigged what has happening. He turned around and in a very quiet voice said:

'"Why don't you fuck off".'

A few days later Mo found himself in the Sudan driving through the desert near Khartoum line abreast in two ten-ton trucks, ahead of the Queen's car. All was well until the road narrowed to a single lane when the lorry in which he was standing took the lead place. All he could see in his viewfinder were professional rivals happily clicking away in the other truck.

Outraged, he shouted at the driver of his lorry to stop so that he could climb down and go back to photograph the Queen's car as it approached. 'The convoy was going slow enough for me not to get left behind and anyway Khartoum was not that far away.'

But he had not reckoned with the courtesy of the Sudanese. The driver who had stopped to let him off would not go on without him. The royal motorcade ground to a halt.

Taking what he felt would almost certainly be exclusive royal portraits, he ignored the furore he had created until the Queen herself leaned over the side of her open-top vehicle, extended her arm, and shouted at him in the manner of one used to being obeyed:

'Get yourself out of the way — and take that truck with you!'

Soon after this he had learned that Frelimo was running a guerilla training camp at Bagamoyo, the dhow harbour he'd used for entering Zanzibar.

They had taken over a building put up more than half a century earlier by the Germans when the Kaiser claimed Tanganyika for himself and had converted it into barracks. He made his first visit directly to the door but he was met by a gun. Despite his pitch that he was working for news agencies sympathetic to Black Africa and freedom from colonialism, three more similar attempts failed.

Foiled in this conventional approach, he chartered a light plane at Dar es Salaam airport, removed the door, strapped himself in next to the pilot and zoomed above the palms, almost clipping the topmost branches. But Frelimo held its secrets close beneath the rustling branches. He returned empty-handed.

Next, he hired a small dhow and drifted in on the night breeze to the beach which led up to the camp. Arranging to be picked up just before sun-up, he dropped into the shallows and waded ashore with his cameras. But this commando-style operation resulted in failure too.

Finally, he forged a letter from the Frelimo chief himself, Eduardo Mondlane, the man who only months earlier had taken his unconscious body to the hospital. Somehow he had obtained a copy of his signature.

Now he typed a letter giving himself authority to enter the camp for filming, and carefully forged Mondlane's signature at the bottom. As a result, he was given the run of the camp for one whole day — shooting news footage and taking colour and black and white still pictures. They showed more than 300 freedom fighters being trained by Africans who had been instructed in ideology and hand-to-hand fighting in camps in the Soviet Union, Cairo, Peking, Cuba, and Algiers.

Subsequently the pictures appeared in North America, Europe, Africa and the Pacific zone including Australia, New Zealand and the Far East together with a page spread in the London *Observer* and *The Times*. They aroused shock and anger in equal proportions. His television film was widely used and the issue was debated in the Tanzania Parliament.

In November, no longer a Prohibited Immigrant after the island's union with Tanganyika, yet still needing a visa, he went to Zanzibar to cover Land Distribution Day — a heady occasion summing up what the revolution was all about. Sheikh Abeid Karume, President of the Island and Vice-President of Tanzania, was handing out plots to landless Zanzibaris.

The media were already tagging Karume's bastion island a Soviet submarine base and accusing him of destabilizing the Indian Ocean which was a peace zone. A massive military build-up was said to be taking place on the island with shipments of arms unloaded nightly from Russian, Polish, Bulgarian, East German and even Romanian ships. Washington

Opposite: When Amin stumbled on a secret camp in Zanzibar where Soviet personnel were training Zanzibari Armed Forces, his exclusive film and pictures led to debates in the British Parliament and the American Senate. It also led to his subsequent arrest and imprisonment in a notorious Zanzibar jail.

Opposite: One of a series of pictures taken in 1964 by Mohamed Amin of Mozambique freedom fighters undergoing training at a secret camp at Bagomoyo, Tanganyika, which sent a ripple around the world and sparked a debate in the Tanganyika Parliament.

Above: Mohamed Amin filming Tanganyikan President Mwalimu Julius Nyerere's first visit to Zanzibar after Sheikh Abeid Karume was installed in power. It was Nyerere who sent in his troops to help the new regime maintain its power base.

was especially worried. Its paranoia about Cuba resulted in an obsessive fear that Zanzibar might become Cuba's equivalent in Africa. He realised CBS would jump at evidence of such a military build-up on the island.

As he drove inland for the Land Distribution ceremony his sixth sense was working overtime. Not far from his destination he saw a new dirt road leading off into the jungle. It was unmarked and, judging by the debris and uprooted trees, recently built.

'I turned and drove along it for a few miles,' he recalls. 'Suddenly I found myself around a bend driving through an open and unguarded gateway as if it was the most natural thing in the world.'

Troops, wearing Cuban battle fatigues and East German helmets, were being drilled by European instructors. There were Soviet BRT-40 armed personnel carriers, and black crews undergoing training. On another site instructors were demonstrating the use of a flare pistol.

'It was like something out of a James Bond movie. And there I was in the middle of it. What could I do but get to work.'

He did so with typical care, returning to his car every few minutes to hide the film he had taken and to reload his cameras as a precaution against confiscation. The Soviet instructors were astonishingly co-operative. If he asked for a sequence to be restaged they complied. Moving through the camp he took pictures of heavy machine guns and anti-tank guns, personnel undergoing training in grenade handling and anti-personnel mines. All the instruction was given in heavily accented Swahili.

'I went unchallenged until I filmed close-ups of ammunition boxes with Russian markings on the side. Then I was stopped by a couple of Russians who asked if I was working for the Zanzibar Government.'

He paused, cleaning his lenses, before explaining carefully that he was on the island to photograph the Land Distribution ceremony as a guest of the government. Mr Karume, he explained to his incredulous listeners, was expected any moment and he was there to record his arrival for the East African press and television stations.

When he was told he was in the wrong location he feigned shock. 'But then', he lamented, 'I have wasted all my film.'

The Russians watched in disbelief as he produced the invitation and his official pass. 'This is a dreadful mistake,' he sighed, continuing his performance as a gullible and not very bright photographer. 'I am in serious trouble with my bosses.'

Beside themselves with anger, the Soviets told him they would detain him for interrogation. But he played the part of the harried, not too intelligent photographer convincingly:

'If you let me go I'll give you all the film I have taken. You can open it up and throw it away. But please, I beg you, leave me my unused film so that I can do my job and film the ceremony when it takes place.'

Even as he talked he was rooting in his camera bag, pulling out roll after roll of unused film, shredding the celluloid before their astonished eyes.

Then they asked him about the film in his two Bolex cine cameras.

'Not that,' he said. 'I've hardly used any, and what I have I need for the ceremony'.

But the Soviets were adamant, so he suggested he should remove the reel. He borrowed one of the guard's jackets and covered the camera. Before the Russians could answer he moved through them and, speaking in Swahili to one of the Zanzibari trainees, asked him to hold his camera. He then took out the spool with the unexposed film keeping the film that he had exposed on the take-up spool in the camera.

To his delight, the ruse worked. The Russians nodded and moved away. 'I never knew whether it was just my manner, or the name Karume and the official invitation which persuaded the Russians to leave me alone.'

The following day, *The Times* splashed his still pictures, as CBS and Visnews syndicated his dramatic film footage. The Visnews 'dope' sheet of 8 November 1965 which went out with Mo's film read:

TANZANIA: 1) Russians help train Zanzibar Army;
2) Zanzibar gives farms to peasants.

Two stories from Zanzibar: Soviet military advisers helping to train the island's army, and peasant families being given farms by the Tanzania Government.

Film shows: Zanzibar troops with Soviet military vehicles and advisers training in bush country near Zanzibar town; and first Vice-President Abeid Karume at the Land-Giving ceremony and helping to measure out the three acres allotted to each family.

As well as advisers, the Soviet Union has also provided vehicles, including armoured cars equipped with anti-aircraft guns and trucks.

The Chinese People's Republic has also given similar aid.

This clear evidence of Russia's presence in Zanzibar and the Indian Ocean was debated in both the British Parliament and the American Senate. Nothing about the prints made from the edit of his film identified the cameraman. But he forgot one thing. It was routine at Visnews to identify the camera operator on the 'dope' sheets which accompanied the film to their subscribers around the world. One of these was Soviet television in Moscow.

There, his name was passed on to Comrade V. A. Kiriev, head of the East African section in the Russian Foreign Ministry. Kiriev, in turn, reported Mohamed Amin's name in a confidential report to Ibrahim Makungu, Abeid Karume's head of security on the Clove Island. He had become a marked man.

By the end of 1965, he had already acquired an international reputation. In newsrooms throughout Europe and America, he was recognized as a man willing to go anywhere who could be relied upon to deliver the story and the pictures.

In August the following year, when President Charles de Gaulle visited the pocket colony of French Somalia, CBS assigned him to cover the story.   61

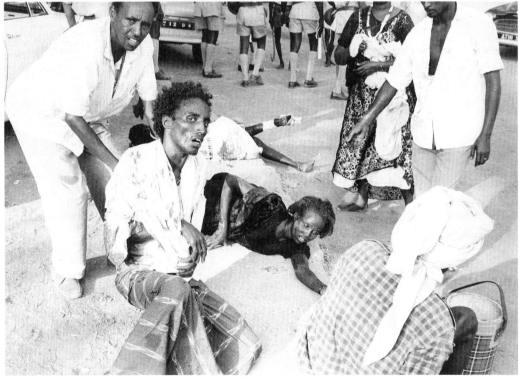

Opposite: In 1966, Mohamed Amin captured this portrait of President Charles de Gaulle during his visit to Djibouti (then French Somalia) when the French leader was determined by any means to retain his country's hold on this strategic country on the Horn of Africa.

Above: Conflict in Aden — in helmet and gas mask Mohamed Amin prepares to record the fighting in Aden's Crater area.

Opposite: In Djibouti's Lagarde Square, minutes before de Gaulle was to address a mass meeting, French Foreign Legionnaires opened fire on a crowd demonstrating against the French leader and France. It was a massacre that left several dead and many wounded. Amin's cameramen colleagues, who were taking lunch, missed the action when their drivers fled — taking their cameras, still in their cars, with them — leaving Amin with another exclusive.

63

It was a patch of arid desert patrolled by the French Foreign Legion and a handful of nomads, sandwiched between Somalia and Emperor Haile Selassie's Ethiopia. Djibouti — its one and only town — was a docks and Foreign Legion centre. It accounted for almost half of French Somalia's population. There was virtually nothing else but sand and sweltering heat, but de Gaulle was eager that France should hold on to this outpost, one of the most strategic points in the region. His visit was intended to make this clear.

On the morning of 26 August 1966 a large Press contingent followed the French leader on a tour of the port installations, breaking for lunch at the main hotel in the city's Lagarde Square where de Gaulle was scheduled to make a major address in the afternoon. All the bunting, chairs, and platforms were in position.

Leaving their camera equipment in the cars, his colleagues hurried into the dining room for lunch. 'I didn't bother with lunch. I went up to my room which had a balcony overlooking the square where de Gaulle was going to make his speech,' recalls Amin.

'After taking some shots of the large crowd that had already gathered, my Bolex camera was on its tripod and I was actually sitting there cleaning my cameras. Suddenly, around midday, somebody fired a shot. It seemed to come from the crowd.

'At this point the French Foreign Legion opened up with their machine guns, shooting randomly into the crowd.

'I did some quick takes from the balcony and then rushed down the stairs to film the massacre. People were lying dead at the side of the road. Others were dying, their legs and arms ripped off by machine gun bullets. Then a Legion ambulance, pretty large, drove up and the locals loaded the wounded, with blood pouring out of them and limbs missing, into the ambulance.

'A big Foreign Legionnaire came along shouting at me in French. I think he was telling me to get the hell out of there but since I don't understand a word of French I ignored him and in the confusion he didn't actually do anything.

'Then he ordered the Legionnaires to throw all the wounded out of the ambulance — about a dozen were critically injured, some dying — and they just threw them out like sacks of potatoes. Everybody was told that the ambulance was for the Legion and not for the locals.

'Despite the large contingent of photographers and cameramen who were in the restaurant, I had this story pretty much to myself. Their cameras were locked in their hired cars and their drivers had all fled for fear of being killed by the Foreign Legion.'

His film went to CBS with secondary footage to Visnews, whose script of 27 August reported:

General de Gaulle arrived on Thursday to an airport welcome which gave no indication of the trouble to come. The banners were predominantly welcoming, although a few demanded, and demonstrations, which started in a minor way, grew fiercer. Soon the main square, in which the President was scheduled to make a public address, was thronged with demonstrators — and there were clashes with police troops. Barricades of barbed wire and road blocks were quickly set up, and the African quarters of the capital were sealed by troops with sub-machine guns. The President cancelled his public address and instead spoke to the Djibouti Assembly. He told them the banners and agitation were not sufficient to express the democratic will of the nation.

After the demonstrations the wounded were left in the square as squads of troops and police moved in to clear the debris of clubs, bottles, clothing and stones.

Amin had the only pictures. Once again 'Mo's Luck' had put him where the action was and given him a major exclusive.

He followed in de Gaulle's wake when the French leader flew at once to Addis Ababa for a State visit to Ethiopia. At the capital's Bole Airport he was approached by a *Time-Life* correspondent.

Did he have pictures of the Djibouti massacre?

Yes, he'd shot some rolls of colour but he wasn't sure what was on them.

The *Time-Life* representative said they'd buy them. How much did Amin want?

'A thousand dollars.'

Without demur the American newsman agreed. The pictures made a gruesome spread in a subsequent issue of *Life*.

Then he flew to Pakistan to visit his parents at their new home in Faisalabad before flying back to Dar es Salaam on 8 September to find his post-box filled with congratulatory messages from CBS and Visnews lauding his coverage of the Djibouti rioting.

Fifteen days later, on 24 September 1966, with three other media men, he flew in a chartered four-seater Cessna from Dar es Salaam airport to Zanzibar to cover the State visit of Egyptian President Gamel Nasser.

Amin had just passed his twenty-third birthday, but his long mop of black wavy hair and goatee beard made him look a good deal older. It was about his twentieth visit to Zanzibar in as many months and the immigration officer looked down, checked his name against the Press list, and stamped the formal one-day visa into his passport.

Minutes later, as he waited to film the Egyptian President's arrival, he was approached by a burly African, sweating freely in a three-piece European suit. Asked to accompany the man, Mohamed Amin walked behind him, unworried. He thought he was going to be shown the Press vehicles arranged for cameramen to film the Egyptian leader's visit. Unknown to him he was followed by a colleague who saw four men bundle him into a car and drive away. The Soviets had marked him. Now the Zanzibaris had him.

4 'Solitary', Slings and Death Row

The nightmare grew from the moment the heavy doors leading to the sweltering, mouldering dungeons of Zanzibar's infamous Kilimamigu prison swung shut behind him. Before him, across a bare, concrete vestibule, stood a second door — a lattice-work of steel. When this too was locked behind him, he was pushed along a passageway lined with maximum security cells, four on each side.

As he was being locked in, he pleaded to write at least one letter. He addressed it to Mohamed Fazal, the Tanzanian Government Press Officer accompanying the official party with President Nasser.

> Dear Fazal,
>
> Please, you must help me urgently. I am being held for no reason in Kilimamigu prison. I was arrested this morning and I am being locked at the rear of the prison in the maximum security political section. If you have no luck with the Zanzibar authorities, please advise the British High Commission in Dar es Salaam and my clients, CBS, in New York, and Associated Press and Visnews in London. Also tell Dolly what has happened. Tell everyone to do what they can. I am desperate.
>
> Amin

'I also asked to be allowed to contact the Canadian High Commission in Dar es Salaam,' he recalls. 'It was looking after the interests of British citizens following Tanzania's break in diplomatic relations with Britain the December before over Rhodesia's Unilateral Declaration of Independence.

'The African guards refused, and I was hustled into a dark cell at revolver point. There I found an African who told me he had fled from the Portuguese colony of Mozambique seeking asylum in Zanzibar. He'd reported to the Zanzibar police on arrival and they'd immediately slapped him in jail.'

One guard gave him some cushions to rest on but before long a rough, bearded inquisitor — his name was Yusuf — hurried into the cell, ripped the cushions away and threw him a tattered and dirty sheet with the sneer: 'That's all you'll get in this place.' Later, he returned and hustled Amin out of the cell, with his camera equipment, into an interrogation room.

'I thought this was the end and that they were going to shoot me,' he remembers. Told to write down a list of all the things he had with him, he was then marched into another room and stripped naked. Eventually, his captors gave him back his trousers. When he returned to the cell the Mozambican had been moved. He was alone — locked up in a tiny cubicle no more than six feet square with one small hole for ventilation and a wooden door with a peep hole. He was to spend sixteen days in 'solitary'.

'There was no bed and I slept on a grimy concrete floor with that disgusting sheet, full of holes, as my only protection from hordes of mosquitoes. I can't ever remember crying before but I did in that terrible place and I beat my fists on the wall because my situation seemed so hopeless.'

Each morning, before sunup, he was given five minutes to use the primitive toilets but not allowed to bathe. Food was a plate of maize porridge in the morning and unwashed beans at night. For thirteen days he ate nothing. Drinking water came from the lavatory cistern.

When he refused to sweep his cell he was stripped, beaten with a broomstick and made to crawl naked along the floor of the compound in the midday heat.

On the sixteenth day of this nightmare, his cell door swung open and a body was pushed in. In the darkness, Amin squinted trying to make out who the man sprawled on the floor was.

Then he recognized his new companion. It was the Zanzibar Minister of Finance. But the man was too shocked to answer questions or even speak. 'If they can do this to their cabinet ministers,' he thought, 'what chance have I?'

The minister, Abdul Aziz Twala, was later killed on Abeid Karume's orders.

However, Amin was not given long to meditate. Later that day he was moved to a cell with two Arabs and two Africans. One Arab had been locked up almost a year. He had said he had no sympathy with the new government. The other was a former Radio Zanzibar disc jockey who had been inside for eight months — from the day security police had searched his home and found a toy gun. The two Africans had been there six months. They had no idea why they were being held. Talking to them, despite the heat, he felt a sudden chill.

Looking back, there has been nothing in Mohamed Amin's character or personality that evokes even a sentient feeling of self-pity. Resolute and determined, too often in his life he has been in potentially dangerous situations with only his own resourcefulness, quick wit, ready tongue and extempore ingenuity to rely on for escape.

More often even than most in his perilous profession, certainly much more often than any ordinary person, he has been eyeball to eyeball with death and outfaced it. He was ever an opportunist and a calculated taker of risks. There's no doubt, however, that it never entered his head he would be arrested for the film he had taken earlier in Zanzibar.

67

East German interrogators accused him of spying for Britain and America, and threatened to kill him unless he confessed. When he refused to take a tablet prescribed by an orderly in a tattered shabby white uniform he was beaten.

Yet, though he despaired, he did not give up. 'I think being in prison, particularly in those circumstances, is about as depressing as you can get. We're all different in many ways. Some people get depressed over petty things because that's the way they are — you know, sensitive. Others need to take a lot more before they get depressed. But somewhere along the line I think all of us do get depressed. And feeling frustrated and threatened is a form of depression.'

To counter it, he plotted to escape — 'run or be killed' — with another detainee who had been there some time. The date set for this do-or-die attempt was 22 October.

'None of us ever thought we were going to leave that place alive. We all thought we were going to be killed, including one of the trusties — a guy who used to clean up the cells and the compound. He'd been there two years.'

The plan was to overpower the night guards, steal the revolver in the guard room, and flee over the wall. There was a car outside belonging to one of the new inmates.

'We planned to jump in that and drive like hell to one of the beaches on the island where the trusty knew someone with a dhow which could take us to Tanga, the nearest point on the mainland,' recalls Amin.

But with that inevitable implication of forewritten destiny, it was not to be. On 19 October he was ordered to wash his clothes — unchanged since his imprisonment. The trusty told him it meant one of two things. 'I was going to be either shot or released.'

In the event he was asked to sign a statement in Swahili denying that he had been ill-treated and on 21 October he was taken to the airport and put on a plane for Dar es Salaam. In twenty-seven days he had lost twenty-eight pounds in weight.

How seriously the Americans took the affair — and the Soviet presence in the Indian Ocean — can be gauged from the fact that they contrived to have a CIA agent board the same plane. The quiet-spoken American managed to seat himself next to the still shocked photographer and spent the short twenty-five-minute flight gently quizzing him about his ordeal.

Long before he recounted his experiences to CBS executive Bill Small in Washington, the news chief had read a secret State Department report, and already knew that he had been made to strip naked in the noonday sun almost daily, and forced to take pills.

In a confidential memo to Gordon Manning in CBS's New York office, with a copy to Patricia Bernie, Small joked: 'I assume this treatment to be the Zanzibar equivalent of physical therapy.' More seriously, he added: 'During the last four weeks I have been in daily touch with the State

Exultant after his October 1966 release from a twenty-seven-day incarceration in the infamous Kilimamigu terror prison in Zanzibar, Mohamed Amin leaves the East African Airways Fokker Friendship that carried him to freedom — twenty-eight pounds lighter in weight.

Opposite: Associated Press correspondent Dennis Neeld (left) an old friend, and a Visnews contemporary in Kenya, Ray Robinson (centre) were among those who welcomed Mohamed Amin to Nairobi after his ordeal on Zanzibar.

'I can't remember ever crying before, but I did in that terrible place'
27 DAYS IN A ZANZIBAR PRISON CAMP

By Mohamed Amin

IN JULY last year I photographed Russian instructors training the Zanzibar Liberation Army at a secret camp to prove how the Communist grip on the once tranquil spice island had tightened.

For about 20 minutes I took pictures freely. The Army apparently mistook me for an official government photographer. Then suddenly I was surrounded by soldiers and told to hand over my film. I had just changed the film in my camera so I gave them the new rolls and kept the exposed ones in my pocket. They seemed satisfied and let me go.

Last September, I was assigned to cover the visit of President Nasser to Zanzibar, and when I arrived at the airport aboard a Press plane everything looked normal. But as I walked across the scorching tarmac towards the airport building with other photographers, a well dressed African pulled me aside and said: "Can I have a word with you?" This was the start of 27 days of fear and humiliation which I suffered in a Zanzibar detention camp.

Three Africans hauled me to a car waiting outside the airport and I was driven to the camp outside Zanzibar town. As I hold a British passport, I asked to be allowed to contact the Canadian High Commission in Dar es Salaam which is looking after the interests of British citizens following Tanzania's break in diplomatic relations with Britain.

Sixteen POST, 18 December, 1966

I WAS A PRISONER ON PARADI

● One of East Africa's leading journalists, Mohamed Amin, barely survived his September assignment to Zanzibar.

● A 23-year-old freelance photographer and journalist from Tanzania tells here how he was held in a detention camp on the island of Zanzibar for 27 days and frequently stripped, beaten and humiliated by guards.

The photographer, Mohamed Amin, a Kenya-born British citizen who is now in London, said he was thrown into the camp for taking pictures of Russians instructing Zanzibar soldiers.

His story is the latest in a string of tales of ill-treatment of prisoners on Zanzibar, one-time paradise island 20 miles from the Tanzanian mainland which is now in the grip of a ruthless military government.

Although Zanzibar is theoretically a partner with Tanganyika in the federation of Tanzania, the island is ruled by Sheikh Abadi Karume and his Afro-Shirazi party (the only legal party) and he refuses to surrender authority to President Nyerere in Dar-es-Salaam.

Zanzibar joins the Government in its hostility to Britain (diplomatic relations were broken off over Rhodesia) but Zanzibar has shown a bigger swing than Dar-es-Salaam towards the Communist bloc.

Several hundred Russians, East Germans and Red Chinese are on the island, which can now be regarded as a real fortress off the coast of Africa.

Story and pictures by MOHAMED AMIN

IN JULY this year I took pictures of Russian instructors training the Zanzibar Liberation Army in a top secret military camp, to prove to the outside world how the Communist grip on the once tranquil spice island had tightened.

I believe the Army mistook me for an official Government photographer. Then, suddenly, I was surrounded by soldiers and told to hand over my film.

Cuban style

I had just changed the film in my camera so I gave them the new rolls and kept the exposed ones in my pocket. They seemed satisfied and let me go.

Two months later I was assigned to cover the visit of President Nasser of Egypt to Zanzibar.

As usual, guards dressed in Cuban-style uniforms and clutching Chinese and Russian automatic arms, stood around the hangar, which contains an ancient biplane — a gift from the Russians to First Vice President Karume of Zanzibar.

As I walked across the scorching tarmac with other photographers, a well dressed man pulled me aside and said: "Can I have a word with you?" This was the signal for a 27-day period of fear and humiliation which I

had to endure in a Zanzibar detention camp.

I was hauled off and bundled into a car waiting outside the airport by three more men. They drove to the camp, near a prison outside Zanzibar town, and handed me over to the guards.

There, I asked to be allowed to contact the Canadian High Commissioner in Dar-es-Salaam, which is looking after the interests of British citizens following a break in diplomatic relations with Britain last December.

The guards refused, and I was hustled into a dark cell at revolver point. There I found an African who told me he had fled from Rhodesia, and had taken a boat to Zanzibar from Beira.

On reaching the island he had reported to the security police but had been sent straight to the prison camp, and had been there for six days when I was seized. He was still there when I was eventually released.

One guard gave me some cushions to rest on, but in the early afternoon a rough bearded man, I later learned was named "Yusef,"

burst into the cell. He ripped and threw a filthy tattered sheet to me. "That's all you get in this place" he shouted.

At about midnight Yusef returned, and ordered me to pick up all my camera equipment. I thought this was the end and feared they were going to shoot me.

I was taken into a tiny room and was told to write a list of everything I had with me. Then I was marched into another room and stripped of my clothing. My shirt and trousers were eventually handed back, but everything else was taken.

Crying

When I was returned to my cell, the Rhodesian had been removed, and the most fearful period of my detention began.

My cell was about seven feet square, with only one small ventilator, and a wooden door with a peep-hole.

There was no bed and I slept on the grimy concrete floor with that disgusting sheet as my only protection from hordes of mosquitoes. These mosquitoes dominated the

nights, and days.

Days ran and nights I seemed to ing even w

I can't bering cr But I did rible plac my fists because seemed se Every r

A RED
E ISLAND

• Some of the Russian guns in which the army uses in training, are quite old, but still in working order.

early, it must have been around 5.30 a.m. I was released from my cell for five minutes to go to a wretched lavatory. But I was not allowed to bath, or clean my teeth, for the 27 days of my detention.

During the day when I wanted to go to the lavatory, I had to knock on my door for the guards to fetch me.

Sometimes they didn't bother. Twice I had to use my cell.

They brought food twice a day — ouji (a flour porridge) and beans, full of dirt, at 7.30 in the morning and ugali (a flour and maize mixture) at 3.30. But I did not eat anything for 13 days.

My drinking water came from the lavatory

flush. There were no taps in the camp. I was forced to wash dishes and sweep my cell.

Once, I refused to sweep the cell, so the guards stripped me and beat me with a broomstick.

At other times they made me roll and crawl naked. It was usually at mid-day when the temperature

was as high as 100°F and the floor burning. They used also to humiliate me and other detainees, by making us dance and sing naked.

After 16 days like this, I was transferred to another cell in which were two Arabs and two Africans.

One of the Arabs had been held for ten months because he said he was not in sympathy with the Zanzibar Revolutionary Government. The other, a former employee of Radio Zanzibar, had been there for eight months after security police searched his home and found a gun.

Television

The two Africans did not know why they were there. They had been detained for six months.

Several times I was interrogated by Africans who were trained by East Germans on Zanzibar. They asked me about the photographic agency I ran in Dar-es-Salaam, and where I sent my material.

When I told them that much of it went to television stations and newspapers in

London and New York one of the questioners shouted: "So you have been spying on Zanzibar for those British-ers and Yankees!"

I was asked how many pictures I had taken in Zanzibar and how they had been captioned. The guards screamed at me: "Tell the truth or we will kill you".

I was punched for refusing to take a tablet given to me by a man in a torn white uniform, who they said was a doctor.

As the end of October approached, my situation was becoming desperate. I had lost more than 28 pounds in weight because I could seldom bring myself to eat the revolting camp food.

Then, on the 25th day, I was at last seen by the officer-in-charge

at the camp, I was told to sign some sort of statement, written in Swahili, which I did not understand. However I signed.

Two days later, I was taken to the airport and put on a plane for Dar-es-Salaam. But, on arrival at the Tanzanian capital, I was served with a deportation order and put on another aircraft for Nairobi.

Later I learned of the tremendous pressure that Western television stations and newspapers, for which I worked, had put on Tanzania's President Nyerere to obtain my release.

The Columbia Broadcasting System of America had been particularly active, cabling President Nyerere almost daily, and sending representatives to

the State Department in Washington and to the Commonwealth Office in London.

Several of my friends in Dar-es-Salaam, who were working to secure my release, complained about the Canadian High Commission. But they seemed to be more interested in keeping the peace with the Tanzanian Government than carrying out their duty to me, as a British citizen.

Such a place could not exist on mainland Tanzania. President Nyerere would never allow it. But he still has no control whatever over affairs on the island.

The Revolutionary Council still rules by force there, and the masters are the Chinese, Russians, and East Germans.

of the Zanzibar Army parade beside their Chinese and Russian heavy machine guns during training in a secret camp on the island.

Department, berating officials high and low for not getting Mo out of prison. State Department people here were somewhat shocked by the ferocity of my attacks on them, for apparent temerity in the face of a delicate diplomatic situation on Zanzibar.

'I assume that Pat Bernie will be in touch with Mo and I am curious as to whether pressures on State were helpful or whether he was released apart from that, because of his own efforts or those of the Canadians, representing the British.'

In fact his release did come about because of the tremendous pressure CBS exerted on the American Government and Tanzania's President Julius Nyerere. CBS lobbied the State Department in Washington daily for action, and the Commonwealth office in London almost as regularly.

Amin remembers that several friends in Dar es Salaam complained about the Canadian High Commission, which seemed to be more interested in keeping the peace with the Tanzanian Government than carrying out its duty to a British citizen.

But his ordeal was not yet over. In Dar es Salaam an immigration officer handed him a deportation order and escorted him to a Fokker Friendship bound for Nairobi where he was met by a member of the British High Commission and sympathetic reporters from the *East African Standard* and the *Daily Nation*.

He did not want to talk. Before leaving the airport he rang Dolly in Dar es Salaam and told her to put together some clothes, collect his cameras and fly to Nairobi. Relatives wanted him to stay with them but he checked in at the New Stanley Hotel. He was still recovering from shock and needed time to think. 'I just wanted to be alone.'

That night in his hotel room he received a call from President Nyerere's press secretary, Hesham Mbita, to say the immigration officer at Dar es Salaam airport had made a mistake. 'I should have been allowed forty-eight hours. He asked me if I would like to come back for forty-eight hours.

'I told him, "not at the moment — I'm not well." But my main fear was that perhaps he meant they had made a mistake in releasing me.' Next morning he met Dolly at Nairobi's Embakasi Airport, still uncertain, knowing only that a major but unplanned change in his life had taken place.

Checking with his Tanzanian contacts, he found that the forty-eight-hour offer was genuine and he returned to the capital to wrap up his affairs. Waiting for him was a cable from New York:

Mo welcome back stop We salute your courage in enduring long confinement stop Happy you are well and relieved to know CBS news is back to normal strength in Africa.
Manning

Amin assigned the running of his business to Bahadur Khaki, Dolly's brother, and two days later, on 26 October, returned to Nairobi on a five-day visitor's pass. Under East African Community rules, a deportee from any one of the three countries — Uganda, Kenya and Tanzania — was automatically prohibited from the other two countries. Each day he visited the Kenya Immigration Office in Jogoo House, Harambee Avenue, Nairobi, to plead his case with Kenyan officials. They gave him no firm answer.

But then it was back to covering news. The trouble-ridden Organization of African Unity — OAU — was holding its third Heads of State summit in Addis Ababa and he flew there for CBS News. The atmosphere in the Ethiopian capital was tense. A group of Tanzanian students on their way home from China marched down the broad wide streets of Haile Selassie's imperial capital in Red Guard uniforms and Mao Tse-tung badges, shouting communist slogans. When he moved into the middle with his cameras he immediately became the target of the mob. By his side was his great friend, Associated Press photographer Dennis Royal. They first met when Amin was a cub in Dar es Salaam. The mob set about them, calling Amin an 'enemy' of their country.

Within hours, two CBS executives in New York sent him another cable:
> Many thanks your great efforts on our behalf but please take care of yourself stop You more important to us than story.
> Segal/Vanbergen

He had a strong case to be allowed to stay in Kenya. His birth in Nairobi in August 1943 automatically entitled him to live in Kenya under Section 18 of the Immigration Act, which also exempted him from the need to obtain a work permit. As usual, he won. On 11 January 1967 his passport was endorsed with the Kenya Residents Certificate: 'Valid for the life of holder of this certificate'.

Now he settled in to a new life based in Nairobi where veteran cameraman Ray Robinson worked for Visnews and Mohinder Dhillon for CBS and other strings. Within days, he was drawn into this cameraman's ambience and had a desk in Dhillon's office. It was agreed he would not encroach on either Robinson's or Dhillon's territorial rights. Kenya was their preserve. But elsewhere he felt free to operate as both stringer and competitor, which he did with such a degree of success that it provoked enmity similar to that which had arisen in Dar es Salaam.

Typically, he also ensured that his lucrative strings in Dar es Salaam were still serviced. Dolly's brother Bahadur shot the film and took the stills while she did the paperwork and accounts.

On 24 January he was in Bullo Howa on the Somalia side of the Kenya border filming Kenyan refugees seeking sanctuary from maltreatment by Kenyan and Ethiopian soldiers. They claimed their troubles stemmed from the running battle the two countries were having with a group of ruthless brigands who operated from a base in Mandera — deep inside Kenya's desert territory — where they ran the Northern Province People's Progressive Party, which sought alliance with Somalia. Known as the Shifta, these were ruthless killers and robbers. Troops were said to have carried out reprisals on the civilians who fled across the border.   73

His film made the CBS prime time bulletin and his stills were splashed across half a page of *The Times* of 30 January under the heading 'Troubles in the Horn of Africa'. Days later, at the Namanga border, he filmed the beginning of what seemed likely to be a major confrontation between Kenya and Tanzania after Kenya tightened up travel regulations following Nyerere's nationalization of banks. These stories were far too close to the border for the comfort of the official Kenya stringers.

He was rapidly becoming as familiar around Kenya with his battery of cameras as he had been in Tanzania. His energy and range were phenomenal. He spent his spare time documenting nature in the wild. Often, with monumental and uncharacteristic patience, he would study an animal for a whole day, rewarded by a growing understanding of its movements and behaviour. One picture sequence of a lioness and her cheeky cub, taken in Nairobi National Park in February 1967, was of such beauty that *The Times* of London used three photographs across more than half a page.

The day these appeared, however, he was far from his new home — in the front line of the violence and guerilla activity that was turning Aden into a charnel house. A general strike had provoked riots and unrest. Sixteen people were killed and sixty-nine, including British soldiers, injured.

All through the action, at the shoulders of the British troops, he was shooting colour and black and white, stills and cinefilm, simultaneously and at the same time dodging grenades, bullets, booby traps and tear gas.

In Aden and Djibouti, with Dennis Royal, he was again trying to draw the line between the 'acceptable' and 'unacceptable' risk. They often nearly failed, becoming an ironic illustration of what frontline photographer Mathew Naythons — who has worn body armour to undertake his assignments on more than one occasion — meant when he said: 'When I get hit, I hope it's because I'm unlucky, not stupid. I'm never worried about the bullet with my name on it. I'm worried about the one that says, "To Whom It May Concern".'

Between February and April, Amin was virtually resident in Aden and neighbouring territories. From Aden he braved a 120-mile journey along the heavily-mined route to Taiz, across the border in Yemen, to interview the leader of the freedom movement, Abdulla al Asnag.

Another world scoop, in Aden, was his UPIN film of two men being beaten to death. UPIN's weekly log for 5 March 1967 reported: 'Mohamed Amin has produced some first-class coverage out of Aden this week, including coverage of a hysterical crowd beating two men to death during a funeral ceremony.'

In mid-March he pulled out of Aden for a week to team up again with Royal in Djibouti, covering the referendum to decide whether French Somalia should retain its link with Paris. The French had declared that only 39,000 out of 125,000 people were qualified to vote. When the result of the referendum — in favour of retaining French ties — was announced, rioting broke out. On 18 and 19 March French troops sealed off the African sector with barbed wire after eleven Somalis were killed and twenty more were injured in a twenty-minute battle.

It was during this battle that he ran, literally, into the man who was to play a large role in his life during the 1970s — bearded Paul Toulmin-Rothe. 'I was running through the street towards the riot and he was running away. We both came around the same corner and crashed into each other. He told me: "Go the other way. Turn back. Follow me. It's dangerous back there".'

Amin ignored him. Royal was not far behind. During the battle the two photographers were so intent on capturing the action that they did not notice the hand grenade that rolled near them. In the blast, shrapnel caught Amin in the knee and Dennis in the groin.

'Dennis went down with total fear in his eyes,' he remembers. 'He thought he had lost everything which made life worthwhile. Then he realized it wasn't perhaps as bad as he thought at first and got slowly to his feet and warily unfastened his belt, unzipped his fly and dropped his trousers to examine the damage.

'I took a picture of him at that point but his relief at finding that the wound was only a minor one stopped him losing his cool. In fact, later when I gave him a souvenir print of that picture he roared with laughter.'

It was the last time they worked together. Royal met his death early in the 1970s, during a peacetime NATO exercise, in a helicopter that crashed.

It was in Djibouti that BBC veteran Ronald Robson also first met Mohamed Amin. 'For the television news correspondent life was a lottery,' says Robson, who joined the BBC in 1954 as foreign correspondent and war reporter for both radio and television news, and who filed reports from India, South-East Asia, the Far East, Middle East, the USA and Africa.

'If the Fates decreed that the correspondent should be blessed with the most dramatic story of the day in his territory, it all meant little if the camera team failed to capture the best scenes or produce sound on an exclusive interview, or refused to move because it was time for a cooked meal, or turned out to be incapable of grasping the significance of events as they happened, or were slow or "bloody-minded".

'The joy of working with Mo was that he was always good — and amenable, dependable, fast-moving, cheerful and courageous; with news sense, picture sense, personal contacts of considerable value, and a burning determination to make the most of any task.

'I'd heard nothing very reassuring about Mo when I was told that he'd be working on the referendum to be held in Djibouti on whether that Territory should remain linked with France, and that I should be ready to script any of his film for use by the BBC.

'Amongst other things I was told that Mo was a "bit of a cowboy", a slick operator who was out to make money and thought nothing of working for two agencies at the same time, as he was entirely a freelancer, and felt limited only by whatever he could physically accomplish.'

He'd also heard that Amin mounted two cameras on a bar with a central sighting device to shoot film simultaneously for two separate customers while using a still camera — on the same bar — to shoot pictures for newspapers.

'He sounded,' adds Robson. 'a real man of action.

'Events in Djibouti were to confirm this. Mo was always in the thick of it. Drums of petrol were set ablaze to impede the soldiers in one riot. Mo was there being singed. Some rioters are content to simply throw stones which is bad enough. In Djibouti the Somalis went one better and used slings of the kind used by David against Goliath and there was a plentiful supply of ammunition in the form of large smooth beach pebbles the size of bread rolls. A stills photographer of my acquaintance had a nasty facial injury from only a glancing blow from one of these missiles, his spectacles smashed, and was lucky to escape concussion or worse.

'Mo decided to capitalize on his brown skin. There was no percentage in remaining on the receiving end of the barrage of stones thrown with such vicious velocity from slings.

'He crossed the lines and filmed from the viewpoint of the slingers whose targets were white faces. This was a bright idea — until the French forces decided it was time to open fire.

'A French rifleman tried to draw a bead on a slinger out to Mo's right. The slinger ran across stage, as it were, passing Mo. The rifle's muzzle swung with him.

'When the trigger was pressed the target had just passed beyond Mo's left shoulder.

'He never stopped filming. He didn't even duck, although a fraction of a second's difference right then in the timing of the shot could have ended a promising career. The French troops were professionals. Mo had taken a calculated risk.'

That performance won him the Visnews Film of the Month award: 'Assigned to the difficult Djibouti story, he maintained a flow of excellent material on the build-up to these important elections, polling day scenes, and the riots which followed the result. He was injured in the process of covering the demonstrations — though fortunately not seriously.

'Most of his stories were accompanied by wild sound tracks and his efforts were a model one-man operation.

'He took pains not only with the camera, but in writing his "dope" sheets, and overcame a problematic shipping situation, with the help of some detailed pre-planning in London.'

One incentive for him remaining so long in the war zone was the £50-a-day darkroom allowance he drew from United Press International. With characteristic prudence, he invested most of the first day's

Man of action Mohamed Amin: with camera bags and typewriter at his feet, the young cameraman holds a sten gun as a British helicopter in Aden prepares to take off on patrol.

allowance on the acquisition of a set of plastic chemical baths, an enlarger, chemicals and a red bulb. Each day, for an hour or so — remembering his experience at the *Nation* newspaper in Dar es Salaam — he transformed the toilet in his hotel room into a makeshift darkroom.

He remembers best the time he covered 'Mad Mitch' retaking Aden's strategic Crater area when the Major, bagpipes swirling, marched into the enemy outpost at night with little more to protect him than pure guts. Amin marched by his side filming this act of bravery.

Aden represented the nadir of intransigent British policies in the 1960s. On 20 June 1967, 400 freedom fighters took control of the Crater area of the protectorate which contained the commercial and residential capital of the country.

But Lieutenant Colonel Colin Mitchell of the Argyll and Sutherland Highlanders was determined to recapture it with the minimum loss of life. His bravery and that of his men on that day, 3 July 1967, captured the hearts of the British public and earned the admiration of fighting men everywhere, winning the officer the name, 'Mad Mitch'.

He was media conscious and before the attack briefed the British Press corps, including Stanley Bonnett of The Associated Press and the *Daily Telegraph*, Stephen Harper and Terry Fincher of the *Daily Express*, Anthony Carthew of the *Daily Mail*, Barry Stanley of the *Daily Mirror*, John Dodd of the *Sun* and Mohamed Amin who, apart from taking stills for UPI, was shooting film for CBS. 'Mad Mitch' told them: 'We're going into the Crater.'

He was piped into battle. 'It is the most thrilling sound in the world,' he wrote in his autobiography, *Having Been a Soldier*. 'In an Internal Security operation against a lot of third-rate, fly-blown terrorists and mutineers in Crater on 3 July 1967 it seemed utterly appropriate.'

It also required steely nerve on the part of the correspondents. Moments after 'Mad Mitch' ordered the advance the enemy opened machine-gun fire. 'Everyone bit the dust,' he recalls, ' — with a few notable exceptions.' Mohamed Amin was one.

Walking unprotected alongside his Land Rover 'Mad Mitch' continued to lead his 'B' Company into the heart of the Crater. The correspondents, he reported, were 'utterly co-operative and friendly and shared the experience in every sense'.

It was Amin's film that the world's viewers saw. 'World reaction,' noted Mitchell, 'had been immediate and intense.' But the BBC and ITN crew only flew in from London the morning after the attack.

It was also Amin's UPI stills that occupied many of the front pages of the British and world Press.

To many people, photographing and filming wars and riots must seem a desperate way to earn a living. But Amin has a buccaneer's love of action and movement. During the next three months he took himself time and again to the limits of endurance and danger, almost like a game

of Russian roulette. He was a member of a unique group of adventurers, reckless yet caring people, whom *Time* magazine would honour years later in a tribute headlined:

'Freezing moments in history — Photojournalists aided by television have come into their own again.'

Walter Gerald Clarke, quoting former Associated Press, now *Time*, photographer Eddie Adams — 'a powerful picture reaches into your heart and just rips it out' — wrote that despite the wonders of television the still news photograph retained its special magic. Clarke also quoted Harold Evans, then editor of *The Times*:

'It is still sometimes thought that the arrival of the moving picture made the still image obsolete. I believe, quite to the contrary, that the still image has never been more powerful. It is a moment frozen in time: it preserves, forever, a finite fraction of the infinite time of the universe.'

Mohamed Amin agrees. 'Filming is actually quite easy. With film you can build a story around an event even when you miss something and still have a very good story. With stills, and particularly on a news story, you've got to get the right picture and often there is just that one right shot. And either you get it or you don't.

'A very simple example is somebody arriving, coming down the steps of an aeroplane, being welcomed and they embrace each other or kiss or shake hands or whatever.

'That's your normal conventional photograph which you have to have. If you don't have that on a movie film you can still cut it in such a way that it looks like a reasonable story. So I find that to do stills requires more talent than to do film.'

Clarke said the status of the photographer was changing. 'Good photographers are among the last survivors of a more swashbuckling era of journalism. As the news has become more complicated, a good reporter does much of his best work at his desk, sifting through piles of research to understand, and make understandable to his readers, the likes of SALT and MIRV and the skirmishes of the Battle of the Budget.

'A photographer, on the other hand, must be in the heat of the action, whether it is a war or a natural disaster — or a budget meeting. That kind of involvement requires a special temperament. Occasionally, photographers are a little crazy, and almost always they are obsessed. Often too they are pushy and, by some standards, obnoxious.' He might have been writing a thumbnail sketch of Amin.

'You don't actually break the door to get into a conference,' says Amin, 'but take an OAU conference for example. It's not an assignment I like because there's a lot of mental strain. The actual story and getting it out is maybe five per cent of all the effort you put in. Ninety-five per cent is hassling people, and talking your way into the conference centre. The majority of my colleagues are told "Wait and we'll call you" — and they'll wait.

'Many will wait forever. They never call you; because that's the way it works; because the guy who's told you he'll call you has gone off. 79

'It's less trouble for him not to call you. That way he doesn't have to explain to anybody why you're in the conference hall. If he stops you, he gets away with it because he hasn't created any scene. But if he lets everybody in there's a possibility of a scuffle between the media and somebody's going to get upset — and *he's* going to get into trouble.

'So if you just quietly sit there and don't fight for what I'd say is your *right* — I mean you are doing a job, and have a *right* to be in the place — you lose.

'When I'm talking to people and getting into those areas I am doing what is right. One year covering the OAU conference we were the only crew covering the airport arrivals of Heads of State. There were about fifty crews but they weren't allowed in. That's ridiculous.'

Photographers, says Clarke, are frequently required to 'display a special kind of old-fashioned bravery and daring that is rare nowadays. More than thirty cameraman died during the Vietnam war — history's most photographed conflict.'

The shell which took cameraman Neil Davis's life in 1985 did not stop his NBC camera. It kept running as it lay on the tarmac in Bangkok, showing his own body being dragged away. It was shocking, akin to the moving images of death which Amin recorded in Aden and Djibouti early in 1967.

He has always calculated what Clarke calls 'the acceptable and the unacceptable risk', nowhere more so than in Aden and Djibouti when he used his burly frame, taking more than a few bruises in return, to stand at the elbow of marksmen searching out snipers, walk behind the tanks, or run with the rioters. It depended on where he could get the best picture.

Only in more recent years have quality newspapers and magazines paid proper attention to pictures which is a predictable reaction to the relentless pressure of television news coverage. Clarke cites the example of the chief of the South Vietnam police whose execution of a Viet Cong prisoner was shown on an NBC news film. It did not shock viewers as much as expected. He notes that Eddie Adams, then working for The Associated Press, had tagged along with the NBC crew and that it was Adams's single picture, described by his desk colleagues in AP as 'the greatest picture of the Vietnam War', not the NBC movie, which shocked the world.

Much later, Clarke noted that Nakram Gadel Karim amassed something like US$50,000 from a single roll of colour transparencies recording the sequence of President Sadat's murder. Sebastiao Salgado Jr. earned a fortune estimated at over US$150,000 for his sequence of the attempt on President Reagan's life.

By comparison, the money that Mohamed Amin earned in Aden, through tireless exploitation of every medium, was petty. He sold his own prints to local sources. The rest were fed round the world through United Press International.

5   Black Jack and the Congo

Good cameramen, Tom Hopkinson believes, are like good racehorses. 'It's essential to know their individual capacities and disabilities. One man will persevere against every obstacle, but has no talent for an emotional subject or situation. Another will be excellent on a story that involves women and children, or the countryside, say, but useless on rough and tumble stories involving riot and bloodshed.'

By general consensus Mohamed Amin is an exception to this rule. He is one man who can handle any assignment. Intelsat's Peter Marshall, who used to be general manager of Visnews, can think of only half a dozen cameramen with *all* the qualities the job demands at its highest level. Three worked for Visnews — the late Neil Davis, Austrian-born Sepp Riff, now based in Vienna running his own business, and Mohamed Amin.

'Like these two, Mohamed Amin possesses a wide range of skills and qualities which single him out. These are skills and qualities which are known only to his colleagues and which go beyond the better-known and well-publicized exploits; they are sustained day in and day out, year upon year, on what would often seem to be the more routine assignments which make up a working cameraman's year.

'First among these is an indomitable determination to seek out the real story in any situation, with journalistic perception of a high order. Secondly, the cameraman's readiness to go anywhere, at any time and to ask questions later. Thirdly, the technical and creative skills to shoot the pictures and record the sound to the highest technical quality, even when under stress or in personal danger. And fourthly, the logistical skills and ingenuity necessary not only to get to the story, but also to maintain contact with base and get the coverage back.

'In addition to these qualities, I should also add his personal charm and sincerity which provide an additional passport in themselves; and a sense of compassion, which is often the dimension which makes a good, professional job into something memorable and moving.

'Those who know and have worked with Mo Amin will recognize this range of qualities, and will probably think of others not mentioned. But for me, they are the important ones.'

Not long after his return from Aden, Amin himself made a little bit of history by using his ingenuity. But it was not a positive contribution.

In 1967, at Formosa Bay, near Malindi, on Kenya's north coast, the   81

Italian Government built the San Marco rocket pad. The first launch was set for the first half of the year and CBS assigned Amin to cover it. He took Jitty Singh, a Nairobi technician, as his soundman.

The launch was a joint Italian, American and Kenyan project. The US space agency NASA seconded their information chief to take care of media arrangements. He and the photographer clashed immediately. The American told him:

'You can't go on the control rig. You'll have to film from the shore.'

Five miles lay between the beach and the rig. Amin was incensed.

'That's no good.'

'Well, you can't go on the rig. The noise will blow your ears off. But you can get film from us if you need it.'

'Where will you be?'

'On the rig, of course.'

'Are your ears made of steel or something?'

'No. I'm just used to noise.'

'So are we.'

Amin seethed. Nobody was going to thwart him on his home ground. He told Jitty to be ready to get up early.

'I figured the American wouldn't get up too early to go to the rig so as soon as it was sun-up, Jitty and I went out to the rig in a dugout canoe. The rig people sent down a basket affair which we climbed into and they hoisted us up.

'We found a spot on top of the control tower next to the public address system. The countdown was played over the loudspeaker, so as to give people their cues for the various phases of the run up to the launch.

'But Jitty was having trouble. The sound quality was not good and the countdown was not clear. So I told him to wire straight into the public address system which he did — disconnecting the speakers.

'It was very close to liftoff. The countdown was at about eighteen, rocket up and all systems go. The controller had no option but to put the launch on hold.

'Jitty and I cottoned on very quickly what was wrong and he quickly changed the wiring back the way it was. But too late. By the time the launch control were satisfied everything was working as it should they'd missed the launch "window". It was several days before there was another.'

There was more drama on the way home. Amin, always reckless on four wheels, had a head-on collision in a brand-new hire car — ironically with the San Marco Land Rover.

'My right leg was broken in two. I was taken to the only hospital. The doctor was a German. I was bleeding very badly and he was holding half my leg in his hand. It was fastened to the rest of my leg only by a shred of flesh. But he insisted that I paid before he operated.

'I pleaded with him, promising that I would pay his bill as soon as I recovered. But he insisted on money up front. I had just come from Aden

Leg smashed in a head-on
collision, the young photographer
was soon back in action — irked
by the boredom of convalescence.

and all I had was about two hundred dollars, so I gave him that and he agreed I could pay the balance later.

'He then stuck a pad of cotton wool full of chloroform on my face and I passed out. In fact, he did a very good job. The next day I was flown back to Nairobi and admitted to the Aga Khan Hospital where Dr Yusuf Kodwavvwala took over and treated me from then on.'

He was immobile for months. Inactivity irks him. Even on holidays he works. 'I spend three days in Maasai Mara. Sure, terrific holiday, but you know I come in with sixty rolls of film. Every one of those pictures I can actually sell. That's not the motivation that gets me there. I go because my family wants a holiday. I say: "Fine! I'll come along with you, but I can't go without my cameras", because that would just bore me to death. . . . I enjoy the trip probably more than them because, you know, they've seen a lion — they don't want to see another lion; but I do, because I just enjoy the animals.

'At the same time I photograph them. But I don't photograph them thinking that I'm going to make some money out of this. I photograph them because I enjoy doing that, like a lot of tourists. They take pictures. They don't get any revenue from them, but nevertheless they enjoy doing that. But I can also put those pictures to a bloody good use because I have the infrastructure and the resources to actually make something out of them.'

Thus, during his convalescence, he occupied himself filming and photographing the peoples, animals and landscapes of East Africa, the region he believes the most beautiful place on earth. As his leg healed he also began to learn to fly at Africair, the light plane charter company run in Nairobi by the father of his instructor, Alex Boskovic. He mastered all the principles of powered flight except one.

'He may have a private pilot's licence but he has yet to master the most basic rules of navigation,' says Roy Lipscombe. 'For instance,' recalls Ronald Robson, 'while he was still qualifying for his full licence he got lost on a cross-country solo flight to Naivasha from Wilson airport in Nairobi.'

His instructor saw him off on this, his first cross-country solo flight — to Naivasha and back — involving only about twenty-five minutes of flying.

'He instructed me to turn back as soon as the airstrip at Naivasha came in sight but as it was a nice clear day I decided to land. Feeling very pleased with myself, I parked the aircraft, switched off, got out and walked around the aircraft. Then I got back in and took off.

'After gaining height, just as I was lining up to head towards Nairobi, the clouds broke and the heavens opened. The rain was so torrential I could see nothing.

'As it was all visual flying, I had no idea what to do. Where I went wrong was in deciding, without looking at the map, to head towards Lake Naivasha and then turn and leave the mountains — Longonot and Susua — on my port [left] side and then turn to port and head for Nairobi.

'But when I turned to port I made the mistake of staying on the course that I had initially plotted from Naivasha — not taking into account the extra distance that I had covered to avoid the mountains.

'When I had been flying for about an hour I realized that I was lost. I came down low to see if I could spot a familiar landmark — a road sign or anything else — and I flew for some distance only fifty feet off the ground but there was nothing that I could recognize.'

It was just a few huts and a lot of bush which was no help at all. When he gained height he called up the Eastair regional air traffic control centre in Nairobi.

'I had not wanted to do that in case it went down on my record and created problems when I went to get my pilot's licence. They were unable to help so they called Nairobi approach at the airport who were also unable to trace my plane.

'Eastair gave me a frequency for Nairobi radar who told me I was too low to be seen on their screens. Would I please gain altitude so they could identify the plane and my position.

'When I became visible on their monitors they told me I was over Magadi and heading for west Tanzania. They guided me back to Wilson where I landed with just a small margin of fuel left. Immediately, my instructor refuelled the plane, climbed in and said: "Let's go back to Naivasha and you can tell me what went wrong". So we did another flight to Naivasha while I pointed out what I had done.'

Some weeks later he had his pilot's licence.

He reckoned that the ability to fly would make him more mobile and he would save on air charter. For instance, in October the television news spotlight fell on Rwanda, where about 100 European and 2,500 Katangese mercenaries, who had mutinied from Mobutu's Zaire army under the command of the legendary 'Black Jack', Jacques Schramme, had fled across the border near Lake Kivu. They were being held in a makeshift, but heavily guarded, camp.

With Rashid Diwan as soundman, he and Robson flew by light charter plane to Kigali, the Rwanda capital. But security was tough. The mercenaries' arrival had created a crisis in Central Africa and newsmen were not allowed near them. Amin returned to Nairobi on 8 November, travelling back to Kigali next day without Robson.

He hired a Land Cruiser and decked it out in the insignia of the Red Cross, who were running the camp, providing food and care for the mercenaries. At the camp gate the ploy worked, but a little further on he was pulled up at gun point by a senior officer. Asked to identify himself he said he was from the Red Cross Press. The bluff almost worked but in the end he was ordered to turn around and drive out before he got any film. Next day the team were back in Nairobi. Three days later, on 13 November, they returned to Rwanda to film the arrival of the OAU delegates and the talks held in the President's office to end the crisis.

Finally it was agreed that the European mercenaries would be released, but only if they signed a pledge never to return to Africa. Amin knew he had to get film of Black Jack and his men, and as the talks ended he heard that the OAU Secretary-General, Diallo Telli, and the Rwandan Foreign Minister were to fly to the camp in a Rwandan army helicopter. He pleaded with Diallo Telli to let him fly in the helicopter, even offering to sit on the floor. But the pilot was adamant. He had enough power to carry only himself and his two passengers.

Arguing that if the world saw the conclusion of the deal, Amin said it would be an excellent public relations exercise for the OAU but without him and his cameras it could not happen. He also pointed out that while there was no chance he would be allowed into the camp except by helicopter, the foreign minister would certainly be able to get in by road. As usual, he was convincing. Apologetically, the secretary-general turned to the foreign minister, shrugging his shoulders. The minister withdrew.

Minutes later, the cameraman was filming the motley group listening to Telli outlining the terms of the agreement on top of a hill overlooking Lake Kivu only ten miles from the East Congo border, while dozens of top European cameramen and photographers waited in Kigali.

Taking close-ups of the legendary Schramme, then thirty-eight, who said he would retire to his home town of Bruges, Belgium, he also shot still pictures on the brace of Nikon cameras carried around his neck. These made magazine and newspaper spreads in many countries. And, once again, he won the Visnews Film of the Month award:

'He went in with the OAU delegation and his 600 feet with COMMAG sound was a remarkable atmosphere piece. It showed how the defeated, disarmed and dejected mercenaries still retained enough independent spirit to jeer at their armed guards and argue with the OAU officials. We serviced a four-minute cut story from this coverage.'

It was on this assignment that he observed to Rashid Diwan — in his native Punjabi, which he thought was gibberish to Robson — what he actually thought about the BBC veteran. In line with many of his remarks it was not altogether flattering. He was shattered to hear Robson respond in fluent Punjabi. Until then, he didn't know that Robson was an ex-Indian Army officer.

Yet, despite his success, he was still haunted by the 1966 Tanzanian deportation order. On 12 December he drove to the Uganda capital to cover a regional Heads of State summit in Kampala.

'While I was waiting for President Nyerere to arrive I met Tanzania's minister for home affairs. He greeted me very warmly and asked where I had been as he hadn't seen me for months. Clearly he didn't know about my deportation fourteen months before and as he was in a very good mood and so pleased to see me I seized the opportunity to seek his help. But as soon as I told him about the deportation he got up and walked away. I immediately knew I was in trouble.' Within minutes he was back in his car, accompanied to the Kenya border by Ugandan security men where he was told never to return. Uganda was simply complying with the East African Community charter: deportation from one country was endorsed in the other two.

But his success had become an embarrassment to his Nairobi rivals and one more such incident, they started to think, would surely compel even Kenya, his birthplace, to evict him.

They had reason for jealousy. By now, he had made his mark not just in television but in the offices of such prestige news magazines as *Time* and *Newsweek*. One of his strengths is that he is as sensitive to the good 'soft' picture story as he is ruthless in hard news gathering.

In January 1968, for instance, there were protests in Tanzania about the indecency of Maasai dress. The warriors were told: 'Wear trousers or go to jail'. *Newsweek* noted that the Maasai warrior's normal garb — 'a skimpy robe elegantly draped to leave the left buttock bare' — struck the somewhat puritanical Tanzanian Government as 'a positive disgrace to the image of the 20th-century African'.

His picture of dancing, semi-naked Maasai warriors illustrated the story, together with a wry footnote by the late Kenya Maasai leader Stanley Oloitipitip who said the Tanzanian order was 'psychological castration'.

Around this time he was contracted as cameraman for the Paradise Films production of the Swahili movie *Mrembo* — a saga which ended months later with sparks flying between producers and stars, and eventually in litigation. Despite this, with his highly developed sense of publicity, he thoroughly enjoyed all the fireworks. In my daily column in the *Nation* at that time, I wrote that the producers should consider themselves lucky to have him as 'he completes films under gunfire if necessary'.

More important than *Mrembo*, however, was his film for America's National Educational TV network, *The Brave Boys*, a ninety-minute story showing the adventures of two American youngsters on safari in Kenya. It won critical and professional acclaim.

Ronnie Robson was a great admirer of his versatility. 'Add to his ability, his news sense, cheerfulness and generosity and his peculiar "luck" and it's not hard to see why he's always been a favourite for any correspondent to team up with.

'It was in 1968, I think, that the Channel Two service of the BBC was first transmitted in colour. Men already in the field were asked in advance to prepare news film "specials" in colour to act as a kind of "stockpot" or reserve of items to see the colour news service through its early days.

'We did have one long running "news" story in Kenya at the time. It was the Presidential Commission on Marriage and Divorce, which ploughed on doggedly holding hearings in the capital and all over the provinces. The main interest, in tribal society, centred on two main topics — the desirability or otherwise of female circumcision, and the desirability or otherwise of polygamy.

'As the commission would still be running when the colour service opened, I decided to use it as a peg for a "stockpot" contribution. Female circumcision, I divined, might not exactly make family viewing — but polygamy? Maybe something could be done on this — its social effects, economics, statistics, and so on.

'Mo came up with a "contact" in Senior Chief Njiri, then 105 years old. I won't pretend to remember the exact numbers involved but the old chief had over the years taken something like fifty-five wives who had borne him something like ninety-five sons and well over 100 daughters.

'These in turn had married and produced countless grandchildren, and there were great-grandchildren — in fact the old man had populated a whole area around Fort Hall [Murang'a]. The old boy wasn't finished yet, either, by the look of it. His youngest son was only two-and-a-half years old.

'The senior chief was a well-known character anyway. He'd been appointed a Commander of the British Empire for his services during the Mau Mau campaign before Independence, and proudly wore this and other medals on his monkey skin cloak.

'Mo managed to gather together most of the surviving wives, and sons and daughters and their offspring from far and wide on one day in the old chief's kraal.

'Of course the film was anchored on an interview with the old patriarch, still very lucid and sensible. It turned out that he was against polygamy. When asked why, he simply looked at me with pity and then with his hand indicated the mass of humanity around him.

'Mo filmed it beautifully. We couldn't have covered it without him because he set up the meetings and the arrangements and had the necessary personal contacts.

'It was a winner — but it never got into the start of the colour film news service. It was rated so good that BBC's Channel One used it immediately — in black and white.'

The year before, when filming the referendum in Djibouti, Robson realized the extent of Amin's talent with film. 'We were in a remote stony desert region where the nomads had to leave their weapons in one room before marking their ballot papers in another room, and I had the chance, undistracted, to see how he set about capturing the atmosphere quickly and economically for the purposes of a news film report. From this first time out with him I felt that I was on a "winner" and resolved to benefit from his services as often as possible.

'Some cameramen with whom I was expected to work failed to produce useable material. There were various reasons ranging from being too slow to making basic technical mistakes, perhaps under pressure of events, to using completely inadequate or unsatisfactory or faulty equipment. Mo used the best equipment he could get hold of, kept it in working order, and seemed to use it as swiftly and as naturally as he used his eyes.'

His photographs demonstrate his ability to extend his visual narratives from the moving picture to the still picture. Almost unique among television cameramen, he learnt his craft as a stills photographer, an

88

Mohamed Amin's first news report in colour, on a 105-year-old Kenya chief with more than fifty wives, was slotted in as a 'softie' to hold in reserve for BBC-2's colour service when it was finally launched in 1968. But news executives rated it so good it was shown in black and white on BBC-1 long before BBC-2 came on the air. Amin's black and white magazine feature of the old chief, from Murang'a, also went around the world, illustrated by several pictures including this one of the Chief being saluted by some of his children and grandchildren. He had ninety-five sons, 105 daughters, and countless grandchildren and great-grandchildren.

apprenticeship that gave him additional grounding for the challenge of filming subjects and stories that move across the frame and through time on the screen.

'When the Kenya Government implemented laws to "Africanize" jobs in the late 1960s, the majority affected were Asians,' Robson continues. 'This led to an extraordinary exodus of people in two separate waves. Mo was invaluable with his contacts in the Asian community and as a team we "scooped the pool" in coverage.

'It required hard and fast work. Mo himself was not affected by the order, but he had that degree of empathy which resulted in telling footage.'

He also filmed the Asian exodus for a *World in Action* documentary for Britain's Granada Television, screened on 4 March 1968 to an audience of more than eight million viewers. Producer Mike Murphy wrote: 'Thank you for some magnificent pictures, especially the airport material. We ran one piece — the men who had overbooked seats — for about three minutes without having to make a single cut. You had more or less edited it in the camera.

'I certainly would be delighted to work with you personally again, and everyone here at Granada who has seen the quality of your work says the same. So I think if you are available you are likely to become our regular in Africa — but God knows when we'll be back.'

Not long afterwards he flew with Robson to the Indian Ocean island of Mauritius for the Independence celebrations to make a news feature film on the island's political make-up and economy, as well as cover the celebrations.

The BBC man remembers a 'particular manifestation — small in itself — of "Mo's Luck" or sixth sense, call it what you will.' One item on the programme was a display by motor cyclists. Most of the international camera crews either ignored it completely or took just a token shot or two.

'Then,' says Robson, 'as the cyclists were carrying out the "cross-over" manoeuvre — when fast-moving riders dash along the diagonals from corner to corner of the field, missing each other apparently by inches — Mo suddenly put up his camera for one pair who hit each other with dramatic results in the centre of the field.

'As far as I know nobody else got the shot (or cared much). But what was it in Mo that caused him to know it would happen? Similarly, spectators had crowded onto a certain roof. Mo focused and filmed just as some of them fell off.

'I'm convinced that some cameramen have a special faculty. It's not purely luck. It has something to do with instinct, probability, and a very special power of all-round observation and deduction.

'I don't believe that cameramen have to be born cameramen. They can be made into good cameramen. But a few have something extra. Mo has always had that bit extra.'

Certainly Amin is only too well aware of mortal danger. He's been close to death many times, mainly in Africa. 'And that's how I've gone on for years,' he says. 'If there were bodies lying in the street, I just filmed them. If people were being beaten up, I just filmed them. There were all sorts of officials performing these acts, beating up people or shooting them. . . . In many of these situations — and I can think of lots of them — I should long have been dead.

'But what I say to myself is, "Well, I'm in this situation and I will cover the story as best I can". At the same time I'm looking around to find out how I'm going to get out of there. There's no point in getting shot in your back while running. You just cope the best you can.

'In many situations — and I've been shot at and arrested many times — you can actually negotiate your way out. That's quite important. If you run, you're more suspect.

'Sometimes you change sides. I've changed from one side to the other when it looks as if there is a better chance of getting out alive from the other side.

'A number of times in Aden in 1968, I changed sides — either from the British to the Arabs or the Arabs to the British. When I was on the wrong side I just worked my way to the other side, and got away with it. Sometimes it has come to my mind that if I get out of this alive I just don't want to know these things again. Fortunately — or unfortunately — memories are short. You get out. You've got a good story. Everyone's happy. You get a few hero-grams. The story's well used. You forget about it.

'When I spent twenty-seven days in jail in Zanzibar, the only thing that was going through my head was

"I'm not going to get out of here alive"; and

"If I do there's no way I'm going to do this job again".

'But the day after I was released I was actually shooting a story. So memory's short. Once I was out I was quite happy to go back to what I was doing before. This is not something you develop. You either have it or you haven't. If I were to stop doing news, I think I should probably feel miserable.'

Calculating the risk was uppermost in his mind in the late 1960s when he made several trips to cover the Biafra war in Nigeria, West Africa. Few internecine struggles in history equal the horrific violence of this conflict which ran its course from 1967 to 1970.

In the autumn of 1968 he had just returned to Nairobi from filming the battles taking place on the Nigerian front line when he met his close friend Priya Ramrakha, a gifted photojournalist working for *Time* magazine, who had been in the Biafran jungle strongholds.

Priya said he was going back, this time on the Nigerian side. Amin suggested they travel together — first to Biafra, where he had never been and Priya knew the score, then to Nigeria where Amin had the experience. They flew to Sao Tome, the little island off the West African coast where the arms planes supplying the Biafran secessionists were based.

Biafran secessionist forces of Odumegwu Ojukwu search the Nigerian jungle, rooting out and killing federal troops as Mohamed Amin records in still and cinefilm the West African tragedy of the late 1960s.

But hanging around for transport, impatient to be back in action, Priya could wait no longer. He flew to Nigeria.

Amin, however, continued to wait in Sao Tome until the night he boarded one of the Biafran DC-3s and, with all lights extinguished, flew at tree-clipping height over the West African jungles. Coming in to land, the Biafran forces of Odumegwu Ojukwu lit paraffin torches lining the landing strip which was just a clearing in the jungle. He went forward to the front line areas with the supplies and shot several news films and many photographs.

When he returned home to Nairobi that Saturday in October 1968 he was just hours ahead of Priya who arrived in a Pan Am jet. But his friend was in a coffin. He had been caught in the crossfire of a Nigerian ambush which trapped the Central Government's own forces.

'I could have been with him,' Amin says today. 'Like any newsman I think the important thing when you take a story on is that you've got to be first — whatever situation you're in. It's a tremendous achievement to actually come out with the first pictures. That really is the satisfaction you get.

'To come out with other people at the same time is a kind of second best. To come out a day later you might as well not go. Because who cares?

'In many ways it's getting more difficult to get the top story. In the early 1960s you could actually drive into countries, go across without a lot of hassle, and cover a war and come out with your story. In the Congo, you either locked in with the rebels or went in with the mercenaries, did the story and came out.

'Now with the kind of wars that are going on in Africa it's more and more difficult and a bloody sight more dangerous to calculate your risk of coming out. And when you put yourself in a position like that it needs a helluva lot more planning and thought. But when you come back with the first pictures I think that gives you a lot more satisfaction now than it did ten or fifteen years ago.'

Yet despite his immensely high professional profile — he believes in publicity with all the fervour of a Hollywood mogul — Mo has always kept his private life to himself. When he married Dolly on 16 October 1968, however, it was more than a desire for privacy. He didn't want his parents, strict, orthodox Sunni Muslims to find out.

'I married somebody outside the religion. But somebody I loved. It was immaterial what religion she was — it made no difference whatsoever.

'Dolly had come up to see me from Dar es Salaam and we decided it was time to get married. But my parents wouldn't allow it. I knew that. So I told her, "It's got to be done quietly."

'I had to find an Imam, a priest, who didn't know any of my relatives. The only one I could find was an African from one of the Nairobi mosques. We were married at my flat in Mf'ang'ano Street, in the centre of Nairobi, on a Saturday afternoon. All we needed were two witnesses. Photographers Afzal Awan and Azhar Chaudrey, then chief photographer of 93 the *Nation*, were my witnesses.

'It didn't take long but the Imam wanted to know why there was no party. I hadn't planned one but I sent David, my house servant, down the road to buy some sweetmeats. Then I left. I didn't have time for a party. I had a news assignment that afternoon.'

He was determined to make his freelance news, feature, and television picture agency the best in Africa and was prepared to achieve this, as I would discover, with a fair amount of ruthlessness.

His rivals did their best to forestall him, generally without much luck. But they came close to bringing him down when, on 26 October 1968, he was sent by CBS on an urgent assignment to Uganda. Several people knew about it, among them his closest friends and rivals.

As he boarded the Uganda-bound plane two of them made telephone calls to Bob Astles, then Uganda's director of information. As soon as the cameraman landed he was escorted into the Immigration Office by a Mr Oyengo who wrote on page 17 of his passport: 'Refused facilities in Uganda'. He was put on the next flight back to Nairobi.

He had no notion that it was his rivals who had shopped him. Indeed, his mind was busy working out which one of them would be able to take on his assignment. Never one to leave anything to chance, however, and realizing that the inscription on page 17 would be damaging evidence at Nairobi Airport, he carefully tore the offending page out along the seam, and passed uneventfully back into Kenya — the missing page unnoticed by the Kenya immigration officers, now accustomed to his frequent trips.

Telephoning around from his office he was puzzled when his colleagues refused to undertake the Uganda assignment. He finally passed the job on to another cameraman whose office was just round the corner.

That evening one of the senior editors on the *East African Standard* rang to question him about his 'deportation'. Amin denied it.

'Why did you come back from Uganda then?'

Thinking fast, he replied: 'Because I was pulled off that story to do another in Ethiopia.'

It didn't satisfy the journalist. The story — a small three paragraph item: **Cameraman told to leave Uganda** — appeared on 28 October. A bigger story — **Nairobi man told to quit Uganda** — appeared in the *Uganda Argus* on 29 October.

By then Amin knew what had happened. One of the *Standard's* photographers told him that while the senior editor was on the phone talking to him, two of his rivals were in the *Standard* office insisting that he had been deported.

When he confronted them they reluctantly confessed. He was furious. 'I'll take every job from you if I have to do it for free, until you come crawling on your knees for forgiveness.'

For the next ten years they had nothing to do with each other. And he was busier than ever.

But then, as others also learned, he was not a man to cross.

6 Assassination of Tom Mboya

There were no daffodils — the Welsh national flower — for the 1969 investiture of Prince Charles at Caernarvon Castle as Prince of Wales.

And as Kenya is a land of flowers, one reporter, with a Fleet Street man's guile, thought what a nice tabloid story it would make for the London *Daily Mirror*, one of the world's largest selling newspapers, if the prince were to receive a gift of his national flowers from a young African girl in Kenya, which is a Commonwealth country.

Buying four dozen daffodils at Nairobi's city market, he drove to a friend's suburban home where the Kikuyu house servant had a pretty five-year-old daughter. Replanting the cut daffodil stems in the friend's lawn, he photographed the little girl plucking them out again. The girl's mother then got her daughter to write a simple note to Prince Charles. It said she had been so upset to hear about the shortage of daffodils that she was sending him some from Kenya.

Feeling pleased with himself, the *Mirror* stringer wrote a 500-word story, selected the best negatives, and sent them in an air-freight package to the newspaper. Along with the now wilting daffodil stems, he put the girl's letter in another package addressed to Prince Charles, and went to the airport crew area where a BOAC VC10 captain agreed to deliver the package of flowers to Buckingham Palace.

The stringer assured the *Mirror* news and picture desks that it was an exclusive story but he did give it to the *Nation* which ran it on page three the same day the *Mirror* collected the negatives and story from Heathrow.

It didn't cross his mind that you never serve notice of an exclusive in the making to Mohamed Amin. At that time in particular Mo had an almost pathological compulsion not only to be first with the television stories but any news story. Nobody, but nobody, was allowed to beat him on his own patch.

Because of space problems London told the stringer that they hadn't been able to use a picture, but the story was on page one. Then they rang again to ask what the hell was the *Daily Mail* doing with the same story — and a virtually identical picture.

After reading the story in the *Nation*, Amin simply went along to the *Nation* and bought a print which he radioed to the *Mail*. He paid £1 for that print — and sold it for £30.

Lesson Number One!

At that time, however, most of the stories out of Africa were dramas or tragedies. One was the continuing agitation to rid the region of its Asian minority — many of them second and third generation East Africans — which culminated in the mass expulsion of Asians from Uganda in 1972.

In Kenya, new trade licensing laws — effectively prohibiting merchants who had run their shops for as long as half a century or more from continuing in business — were announced. The first victims, around fifty families totalling some 500 people, booked passage for India aboard the SS *Kampala* departing from Kilindini docks, Mombasa, on 10 January 1969.

'There's racism in every society,' says Amin, 'but it's nothing to do with colour. There are various backgrounds, clans, castes, and communities, and all that, which all boils down to some kind of racialism.

'If you look for it, there's plenty of it around. In many instances people get treated badly — I've seen it happen — because they suck up to others. You know, they get themselves into a position where they get treated roughly.'

His film sequence of the first Asian exodus closed with a long slow 'pan' of the sad and haunted faces taking their last look at East Africa from the top deck. It reminded him of his own decision, made four years earlier in 1965, to remain. The one-way ticket to Karachi had never been used. No matter what happened he never intended that it should. He was where he wanted to be, where it was all happening.

Always unhappy without action, he was delighted to cover a professional parachute jumping contest in Nairobi early in the new year of 1969, but found the student riots at the end of January more challenging. Over a thousand Nairobi University students were evicted from their halls of residence following a boycott. Kenya's tough old founder-leader, Mzee Jomo Kenyatta, closed down the university and ordered in the riot police. Several students were beaten up in a mêlée, which Mo filmed.

In February he shot a remarkable story about Richard Amiani, a thirty-two-year-old humanitarian who had spent six years travelling almost 10,000 miles a year through remote areas of Kenya, performing literally thousands of eye operations. He followed that with another story about the blind — the ascent of Africa's highest mountain, the 19,340-foot-high Kilimanjaro well inside Tanzania, by a group of blind students from the Outward Bound Mountain School, Loitokitok, on the Kenya side of the mountain. Despite his prohibited immigrant status in Tanzania he followed the climbers to the peak. That news film was seen around the world while still pictures were published in major magazines in Europe and America, including *Ebony*, America's largest selling Afro-American magazine.

He was now regularly making half-page spreads in *The Times* of London, too. One, of cheetahs all over a tourist's car in Nairobi National Park, illustrates Gerald Clarke's point that 'only someone with a special eye can catch those odd and revealing juxtapositions that give meaning to the obvious and the jejune'. In February, it was an ostrich courtship ritual which commanded half a page.

But when that appeared Amin was in Dhaka — then Dacca, East Pakistan — with the BBC's India correspondent. They were reporting the aftermath of Ayub Khan's resignation as President and the imposition of martial law — more pictures which made *The Times* and other major newspapers around the world.

Back in Kenya he filmed the five-day, 3,500-mile East African Safari Rally. To find the most dramatic pictures and the best early morning or late afternoon light, he often set off at midnight, not returning until ten or eleven the next evening. Yet to him, these exhausting days were times of recreation compared to his usual routine.

After the rally, he joined a Flying Doctors' mercy flight from Nairobi to Moyale, on the Ethiopian border. A seven-year-old boy had been snatched from his bed by a hyaena.

His film of the rescue made two minutes on CBS news. It was his last story for the American network which had fostered his career for more than seven years. American interest in Africa was waning, only to revive in any depth fifteen years later when his Ethiopian famine coverage, shown on the rival NBC network, once again turned eyes and hearts towards the so-called Dark Continent.

Indeed, the story he shot for Visnews only three days after the Moyale story could have been a preview of his 1984 film in Ethiopia. Drought and famine had afflicted Kenya's Maasailand and the seasonal rains, due in March, had failed. He flew out to one of the worst-hit locations, Selengai, with Flying Doctor pilot Dr Anne Spoerry. He also filmed President Kenyatta laying the foundation stone for Kenya's satellite communications headquarters in Nairobi, another pointer to his own future although, at that time, he had no idea of it. In between all these stories he was also busy filming the Swahili language movie, *Mrembo*.

This role came to an abrupt halt at midday on Saturday 5 July 1969 with another astonishing instance of 'Mo's Luck'. 'I was at home in my flat in Mf'ang'ano Street, a few hundred yards from the Nairobi city centre, when a friend rang to tell me Tom Mboya had been in an accident.' Minister for Economic Planning and Development, Tom Mboya was the rising star of Kenya politics, considered by many a likely successor to President Mzee Jomo Kenyatta.

Grabbing his equipment, Amin ran downstairs, leapt into his car and drove to the scene of the assassination. Minutes after the assassin had gunned Mboya down, Amin was photographing the body which was sprawled in a pool of blood in the doorway of a pharmacy. He didn't even have time to load his Bolex.

When an ambulance pulled up he followed inside. Asked by the driver where to go, he shouted 'Nairobi Hospital'. As the ambulance turned the corner he was trying to load a reel of cine film into his Bolex. But the door swung open and he had to throw his take-up spool on the floor to hold on and avoid being thrown out.

'One side of the spool bent and I thought, "What the hell do I do now?" I hadn't got anything else. I broke off the damaged side and placed it in the camera, hoping the camera lid would hold it in place and started filming as the ambulance sped to the hospital. Luckily, it worked. I certainly couldn't have reloaded because half the spool was missing.'

Inside the ambulance, Amin filmed and photographed as medics and Dr Rafique Chaudry fought to save the victim. At Nairobi Hospital, Mboya was wheeled into the intensive care unit. But too late. As Mboya's weeping younger brother, Alphonse Okuku, and another cabinet minister, James Osogo, entered the room a European doctor pronounced the pioneer trade unionist and freedom fighter dead.

This exclusive film — shot with a make-shift spool — led television newscasts in many stations around the world. His stills were used in newspapers everywhere. In the *Sunday Nation*, his picture filled the front page under the heading:

KENYA WEEPS

Reuters reported:
Mohamed Amin, a photographer who arrived at the scene shortly after the shooting, accompanied the body to hospital in the ambulance.

Amin said: 'The Asian doctor, who had tried to revive Mboya, was also in the ambulance and oxygen was administered all the way to the hospital, two miles away. The ambulance driver was going as fast as possible but I saw him literally trying to push the ambulance along faster. He was very distressed,' said Amin.

'When the ambulance arrived there was panic. Only a nurse was on duty and she did not realize at first it was Mboya. She immediately rushed around summoning doctors.'

Amin said Mboya was taken into casualty and few minutes later a European doctor arrived.

'This doctor examined Mboya with a stethoscope and then walked away. We knew then Mboya was dead.'

'Some have confused Mo's hard work and intuition with luck,' says John Platter, former United Press International bureau chief in Kenya. 'As he repeatedly triumphed at what is surely the most difficult of all aspects of a cut-throat business — being first and best — people would marvel at "Mo's Luck". Sometimes they suspected more than luck.

'When, on that Saturday, cameras at the ready, he was in the Government Road [now Moi Avenue] drugstore a few minutes after Tom Mboya was shot, my London UPI picture department was incredulous.

'"Mo must be in with the culprits," they gasped. "He's got a Mafia network setting things up."

'As usual, his radiophotos were flawless — and first. I could only gasp

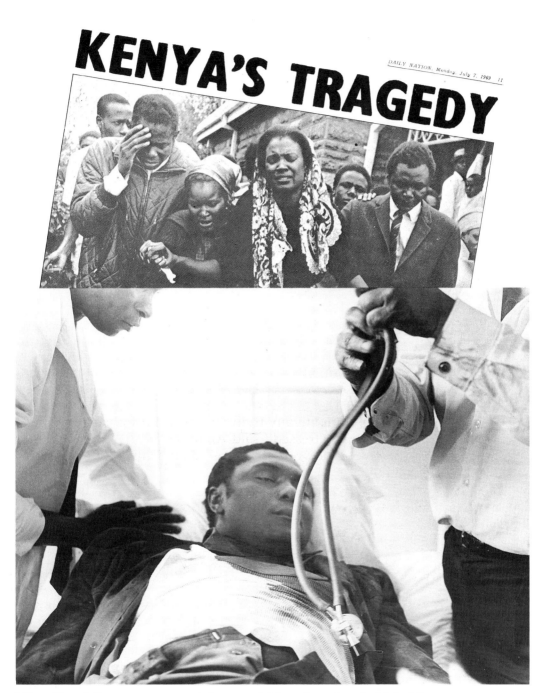

KENYA'S TRAGEDY

When Tom Mboya was gunned down outside a drugstore in Nairobi's Government Road (now Moi Avenue) on 5 July 1969, Mohamed Amin was at the scene within seconds. His dramatic picture of the slain Kenyan minister being declared dead minutes after his arrival at Nairobi Hospital was carried by newspapers around the world.

myself, and admit his omnipresence was quite uncanny.'

The film had such immediacy and impact it earned him the 1969 award of British Television Cameraman of the Year in the hard news silent category and brought him his first Visnews contract. 'Once he was appointed a permanent staffer,' says Ronald Robson, 'his international stature grew even faster.'

Mboya's death sparked the most critical period in Kenya since Independence, a crisis made more serious because Kenyatta was still recovering from a near-fatal stroke suffered the previous September during one of his increasingly frequent rest and recuperation visits (known euphemistically as 'busy working holidays') at the coast.

George Githii, editor-in-chief of the *Nation*, a former private secretary to Kenyatta, had courageously published his own story about Mzee's 'mild indisposition'. It resulted in Githii being tossed into exile at Oxford University to work on a doctorate thesis and in the *Nation* offices being raided by Kenyatta's European-run Special Branch.

Now Mboya, a member of the Luo tribe, rival to Kenyatta's Kikuyu, was dead and Kenya was smouldering. For months, Mohamed Amin's cameras recorded the aftermath.

The day after the assassination, the script to his next report began: 'Sadness and tension mark procession of mourners as body of Tom Mboya lies in state.' It went on, 'Violence broke out when a young Kikuyu boy tried to enter the grounds of Mr Mboya's house. The Luos quickly began to beat the boy and then ejected him from the grounds. . . . On Saturday night there were disturbances in Nairobi and other Kenyan towns as Luos and Kikuyu tribesmen clashed. . . .'

The Kenya Government declared five days of mourning. Flags came down to half mast as people queued outside the National Assembly in Nairobi to sign the book of condolence.

While President Kenyatta held an emergency cabinet meeting at his private home in Gatundu, thirty miles outside Nairobi, Amin filmed a clash between steel-helmeted riot police and Luo mourners in Nairobi city centre. Then, talking his way through the heavily guarded gates at Gatundu, he filmed the unique emergency 'Privy Council' meeting held under a mango tree in Kenyatta's garden to discuss plans for Mboya's State funeral.

Next day, at Nairobi's Catholic Holy Family Cathedral, the courtyard and the church were ringed by riot police and heavily armed troops wearing gas masks. Fighting broke out with the arrival of the hearse when the crowd milled around Mboya's widow, Pamela. Shortly after, President Kenyatta arrived and the crowd became more violent, throwing shoes at his Mercedes saloon during the last few yards of its approach.

Reprisal was swift. Tear gas was fired into the crowd and inside the cathedral. Kenyatta's dignity was immense. While most coughed wretchedly and tried to clear their eyes, he could be seen sitting impassively, head held high, unblinking. Amin filmed it all.

The Rank Organization's 1969 British Television Cameraman of the Year Award, presented to Mohamed Amin for his dramatic film of the minutes after Kenya's Economic and Planning Minister Tom Mboya was shot down in a Nairobi street.

From Nairobi he travelled for five days with the funeral cortege to Lake Victoria through crowds of hostile and impatient Luos, estimated at around a hundred thousand. The cortege stopped at Kenya's third largest town, Kisumu. When he reached there his Land Rover had holes as big as a man's fist from the rocks thrown at it by the mobs lining the route.

Three days later Tom Mboya was laid to rest on Rusinga Island near Homa Bay on the mainland. Six hundred crack troops of the paramilitary General Service Unit, Kenya's own Special Service commando group, were deployed on the island as Mboya's long-time political opponent in Luoland, Oginga Odinga, arrived in full tribal costume to exploit the occasion.

Before the month was out another Luo, Joseph Odero-Jowi, thirty-nine, was sworn in to succeed Mboya and two other Luos were promoted to important positions — thirty-seven-year-old Robert John Ouko moving from the Civil Service to become finance minister to the East African Community and John Okwanyo, forty-one, becoming an assistant minister for foreign affairs. But the die was cast.

In the next few weeks Kenyatta appeared at a series of mass rallies intended to condemn tribalism and unify the nation — one in the heart of Kambaland, another at Mombasa, one in Nairobi and another at Kiambu, not far from where Kenyatta had been arrested by the British in 1952.

By August, an unknown thirty-two-year-old Kikuyu, Nahashon Isaac Njenga Njoroge, had been held for the slaying. When his trial opened on 1 September he whispered 'not guilty' to the European judge, Mr Justice Simpson. But he was convicted and hanged. Among those who assembled the case against Njoroge were the head of the Kenya CID, John Bell, State Prosecutor John Hobbs and government pathologist Martin Rogoff — all Europeans. The killer's motive remained a mystery.

Kenya was in a ferment. On the back of the murder of his political rival Oginga Odinga was building discord and Mohamed Amin's sensitive news antennae were twitching with all sorts of vibrations. He foresaw a showdown between the Luo leader and President Kenyatta.

'Which played a bigger role in Mo's success?' asks Platter. 'Intuition or hard work? One incident in particular tends to favour the work angle. He listened, always listened, researched, mulled, waited — then pounced.

'It was in September or October 1969, just after his return from Addis Ababa, that he picked up a confidential tip. He was passing my office in Nation House and put his nose around the corner. He whispered the information. What did I think?

'Kenyatta would change his schedule during a visit to Kakamega and make a surprise swing down into Kisumu, in Luoland, volatile then in the long Mboya assassination aftermath and the perennial Odinga pot-stirring. It would be the grand old man's first real visit to the sugar-cane country and mosquito-laden lakeside since Independence.

'Mo said he would keep tabs on his informant. Until then the presidential trip was billed as just another "Hurrah Harambee" [Pull

Together — Kenya's national motto] outing to peaceful Abaluhyaland, which we could all leave to the Kenya News Agency and the Voice of Kenya.

'However, a hospital built with Russian money garnered by "Double O", Oginga Odinga, was due to be opened, probably by Mzee himself. This was pure Kenyatta-style — to tweak Odinga's nose in his own backyard and show both the Luo and Moscow who was the boss. The last minute diversion had possibilities, Mo thought.

'Without alerting "hackdom" we sped off from Nairobi a few days later well before dawn and breakfasted at the Tea Hotel in Kericho, then still a thriving colonial relic.

'We caught the Mzee and his entourage at Kakamega. Lots of harmless jollities in the little showground there. Mo and I felt rather sheepish pretending to cover the innocuous festivities. He took a picture of me laughing beside a witch doctor got up in colobus monkey skins and clanking warthog tusks. The bourgeois, uncomprehending white intruder beside impenetrable mother Africa.

'At the last moment, the tour to Kisumu was announced and, sure enough, the convoy of Mercedes and Land Rovers swung round and headed down the escarpment to the provincial lakeside capital.

'The afternoon clouds had built up over the lake by now. An offshore wind awaited us and so did thousands of Luo people gathered outside the hospital. Odinga was waiting, too, in his beaded, coloured cap and knee-length gown with the Mao collar. His guest was the Russian ambassador, but not to worry. In Kenyatta's Kenya, the communists couldn't be too choosy.

'Kenyatta and Odinga smilingly exchanged pleasantries through clenched teeth as they took their seats on the dais.

'Loudspeakers were set up along a perimeter fence about a hundred yards away so the swarming crowds could hear Kenyatta from the hospital's front entrance.

'But several hundred locals seemed to have barged in and clustered around, mingling with VIPs. The paramilitary GSU guarded the exit where the mobs had set up an ominous chanting in Luo. Not quite the usual welcome for the travelling President.'

Mohamed Amin remembers that they were shouting 'Dume, Dume' the slogan of Odinga's Kenya People's Union opposition party, the KPU. As the chanting continued, Kenyatta inspected a guard of honour lined up outside the hospital and then walked towards the red-carpeted entrance where microphones for the public address system had been set up.

'At this point,' says Amin, 'all hell broke loose.'

John Platter remembers: 'Within a few feet of the President, people began smashing each other with broken chairs. Odinga and the Russian ambassador fled into the hospital.

'Mo, as usual, was already filming and photographing, close enough to have to wipe the flecks of flying saliva off his lens. Then pandemonium. 103

'Kenyatta's bodyguard immediately surrounded the President. Neither they nor he panicked but they began to let fly, firing outwards from the encircled President and moving him to safety.

'Mo somehow gained the protective inner circle, next to the President, and I followed. He was filming the carnage until an official, berserk with rage, spotted him and shoved a pistol into Mo's face, twisted his shirt and shook him. "Open that camera! Give me that film!" he shouted. Unfussed, Mo obliged. He surrendered his film.

'But he was far too old a hand to have been beaten like that. Seconds after the first shots were fired and the bodies began to fall, he had changed his films, and kept on changing, simultaneously handing me the exposed reels for safekeeping. Naturally, I ducked behind someone during this scene. I didn't want to be seen as the plumber's mate just then. But my pockets contained yet another Mo Amin scoop.'

In the midst of all this Kenyatta reached the microphone where he began to speak. Odinga and the other guests came out from hiding to take their seats. As the President spoke, medical orderlies were carrying the dead and wounded on stretchers before him into the hospital.

'Odinga sat opposite Kenyatta,' recalls the photographer, 'and they exchanged words. Kenyatta was very angry. He was mad.'

Remembers Platter: 'Kenyatta reciprocated the Luo jibes and launched into them in his raunchiest, anthropological best. . . . The mobs were incensed. That only made Kenyatta angrier and even richer with his taunts. Odinga butted in and, I think, tried to grab the microphone.'

The battle resumed.

'We disentangled ourselves from the mad mêlée and my only problem was persuading Mo to leave the battlefield. By now the GSU and the presidential bodyguard were literally shooting a pathway out of the town. Dust and the crowd's jeers enveloped the scene.

'We retrieved my car and weaved into about sixth place behind the President, again photographing the shooting and the wild Luo crowds being "taught their lesson". Even two policemen, trying to hold back the mobs, were shot. One in starched khaki, his head partly severed, reeled over into the curbside to the left of us.

'Mo was leaning out of the window furiously trying to record the mayhem and wanted me to stop. GSU gunfire crackled from both in front and behind, and we'd have caused awful problems if we'd blocked the "getaway" of the official vehicles behind.

'"Anyway, it's my damned car," I had to say finally, "and it's not insured for this sort of thing."

'We sped away into the night, preparing to break another world story with eyewitness accounts and a batch of exclusive Mo wirephotos. The casualties: fifteen killed, more than eighty treated for gunshot wounds. Has any hospital ever had such an opening?

'How — among all the international photographers based in Kenya — was Mo once again *alone* on the scene? No Mafia setup. No luck.

'It was straightforward planning, foresight and hard work. He'd sniffed out a possibility and while others were content to dismiss a routine presidential trip and take off for a weekend at the coast, Mo was ready to rise with the sparrows and head the other way.'

At the end of October Kenyatta named December as the month for the first general elections since Independence, proscribed the KPU, Odinga's opposition party, placed the leaders, including Odinga, under house arrest, and made a sentimental return to the place where he held his last rally before he was arrested in 1952.

In the aftermath of this turbulence, three British newsmen employed by the Kenya newspapers, the *Standard* and the *Nation*, were deported. Mo's luck held. He was left untouched. Slowly calm returned to Kenya.

There was a sequel to the elections. Old ministers were ousted and in the wake of the Mboya tragedy, that shrewd and canny statesman Jomo Kenyatta used the occasion to give his country a new sense of direction.

He announced the new cabinet line-up to a Voice of Kenya — VOK — camera crew sitting in the garden of his Gatundu country home. But he gave his Press secretary, Kinyanjui Kariuki, little time to alert the world Press and the VOK team were all alone.

Amin heard the announcement on the midday news bulletins and rang Kinyanjui to ask why he hadn't been told.

'I had very little time, Bwana, to organize anything. You know how it is.'

'Can we get the Old Man to do it again?'

'No chance at all.'

But the photographer refused to be beaten.

'Come on, Kinyanjui. This is important news. The rest of the world should know.' He was filming many stories a month for Visnews and thought this would be simple.

Finally, Kinyanjui suggested he should drive over to Gatundu to discuss the situation. When he arrived, however, Kinyanjui was quite adamant that Mzee Kenyatta would not repeat the announcement for the Visnews camera.

Mzee's close friend and aide, Mbiyu Koinange, who was in the garden, spoke to Amin demanding to know what he wanted.

He explained.

'Why weren't you here this morning?'

'I wasn't told.'

Koinange reprimanded Kinyanjui and then asked the cameraman whom he represented.

'He was pretty impressed. He said: "You should be here all the time" — with a pointed look at Kinyanjui.'

The presidential confidante said Kenyatta was asleep but he would wake him and tell him of the Visnews man's request.

'He came back looking pretty sheepish. Then Kenyatta came out. He'd obviously been woken up and was in a real temper. He went for Kinyanjui who explained that he hadn't had time to gather the international press.' 105

Above: Guns out, President Kenyatta's bodyguards surround the Kenyan head of state after riots broke out during an exchange of insults with Luo leader Oginga Odinga at the opening of Kisumu's Soviet-built hospital in 1969.

Below: Kenyatta's bodyguard and police hurl chairs at threatening mob.

Then Mzee noticed a cabinet minister hanging around in the drive some distance away. Told the minister's name — he was short-sighted — he waved him over with his fly-whisk and demanded to know what the minister wanted. When the minister had finished his explanation Mzee dismissed him — with a blow across the face from his fly whisk.

Now the doyen of African statesmen turned to Amin, who was trying hard to vanish.

'How do you want me to do this?'

The soundman was also trying to shrink into invisibility — inside a clump of rose bushes.

'I was beginning to wish I hadn't bothered,' remembers Mo, whose camera was set up facing the table at which the Old Man was now seated.

'I told him: "Do it as you like sir."'

Kenyatta became even more angry.

'How do you want it?'

'Just as you did it this morning, sir.'

'Do you want it in Swahili or English?'

'In English.'

'Very good.'

The President visibly relaxed. 'He was a tremendous professional,' says Amin. 'He went straight into it like a veteran broadcaster and started with a real introduction.

'All good things come to an end and my first government has ended. Now it's time to announce a new cabinet.'

Kenyatta finished the preface and then named the cabinet.

'I'd only gone with one reel. Just enough to get the cabinet. But Mzee gave the names of the assistant ministers and then the permanent secretaries. My reel had long finished but I wasn't going to say stop. Not after what I'd seen. I kept my eye behind the viewfinder and the motor on.'

Just before Mzee began speaking Amin had noticed a VOK crew setting up their camera. When the Old Man finished and went to resume his interrupted sleep, he asked Kinyanjui what the crew were doing.

'I thought they were here this morning.'

They had lost their film. Changing magazines after the morning announcement, the cameraman had placed the exposed reel on the roof of the Presidential Press Unit car but was called back to take some more film. Thinking the film was in the car, the driver drove off, back to Broadcasting House in Nairobi. Halfway between Gatundu and Nairobi, negotiating a roundabout, the film can slid off the roof and rolled into the gutter, the lid breaking loose — and the precious film spilling out like a long snake.

The camera crew certainly could never have explained that to Mzee.

This was the year Amin met Christopher Rawlings when the BBC producer was preparing to shoot the *Search for the Nile* series — at that time one of the longest and most costly in television history. With six one-hour episodes, it would take long months to complete.

Rawlings planned to shoot the film in Uganda but President Milton 107

Obote and his ministers rejected the scripts. When Obote met Rawlings he told the producer that there had never been any slavery in Uganda nor any Kabaka — the traditional monarch of the Buganda. Therefore the BBC would not be allowed to film.

A Hollywood producer at the same meeting was looking for some pretty shots of the Nile for his feature film. When he, too, was told that he could not film in Uganda he exploded: 'Well, screw you. We'll build our own Nile in Hollywood — bigger and better than yours.'

Rawlings's alternative location was Kenya, where Amin confirmed that almost every locale in Uganda could be matched. Rawlings was impressed. He hired Amin as production manager. The move from news and documentaries to an ambitious film-style feature series was a major step which Mo took in his stride.

'In the BBC series, the actor playing the English explorer Samuel Baker, who was the first European to discover Lake Albert, found the lake 500 miles east of the real location — from the top of Central Island in Lake Turkana [Rudolf].' Amin remembers. 'In fact we shot a lot of the series around Turkana, including the slave caravans. We used areas along the Kenya shores of Lake Victoria, too, of course.

'There were two BBC film crews shooting major specials — Rawlings and Tony Isaacs' team which was producing *The British Empire*. They were deadly rivals.

'For our series Chris created a huge thatched palace of the Kabaka, on the shores of the lake. The idea was to present it to the locals after shooting had finished.

'Isaacs heard about this magnificent set. It was just a facade. But he thought it would be very useful for his series, too. So he chatted up the locals to get them to agree to him using it. When Chris heard of this he was furious. So instead of handing it over to the locals he had the palace burnt down.'

One event hard to rig, however, was Speke's discovery of the Nile. To film this vital sequence in Uganda Mohamed Amin agreed to drive in together with the actor playing Speke and one make-up girl.

The actual falls where the Nile tumbled out of the lake are no longer visible. The Owen Falls Dam, built in the 1950s, caused the waters of Victoria to obliterate them. Nonetheless, a little way downstream, there's a similar series of cataracts where they filmed the sequence.

The crew booked in early in the morning at Jinja's Crested Crane Hotel and the make-up girl set about creating Speke, the bearded giant, from the clean-shaven young actor. Receptionists and guests were astonished to see Mohamed Amin and the girl leave the hotel with an entirely different companion.

When Speke first set foot at the source of the Nile he carried a rifle. But the wooden gun provided by the BBC's props department had been confiscated at the Malaba border so in the finished series this element of authenticity is noticeably absent. Instead, Speke carries a stick.

7 Idi Amin's Coup

Today's young cameramen, brought up to film with electronic news gathering equipment — ENG — where footage costs no more, be it ten or 100 feet, could learn a lot from Amin's generation of cameramen. Their instinct for composition has always been allied to an admirable sense of economy.

'In the late 1960s, when I was manning the newsdesk at Visnews and directing the assignments of cameramen,' Peter Marshall notes, 'we were still making the transition from the thirty-five-millimetre cameras inherited from the cinema newsreel crews to the new, lightweight sixteen-millimetre equipment. And it was still a black-and-white world.

'The introduction of colour was the next big step, and it was the cameramen in the field who had to make the major adjustment. By the early 1970s it was becoming possible to visualise the possibilities for TV news which were going to emerge with the growth of communications satellites.

'We could only begin to imagine the concept of a portable satellite uplink, transmitting those pictures direct to London for redistribution to the rest of the world.

'Together with satellite transmission came the electronic news camera, ENG, removing the need to process film before the pictures could be edited and supplied to the broadcasters. Again, as with the arrival of colour, it was the cameraman who had to learn new skills.

'The effect of these technological developments,' adds Peter Marshall, 'is to shorten the time between the coverage of a news story and its appearance on the screen of the viewer at home, whether in West or East, South or North. Distances are no longer the governing factor.

'In consequence, the cameraman's responsibilities become even greater, year by year. Once there were always hours, if not a day or two, before the world saw the pictures of a momentous or controversial story, and this provided time for assessment and consideration; perhaps for subsequent editing in the light of new developments, or even political reactions.

'Now, there may be no time to search through the footage for the second "take". No time for uncertainties about identifying personalities and locations.

'It is in the challenging and exciting environment of television news development that you recognize the true talent of cameramen such as Mo.'

Yet Amin has no doubt which medium he thinks most challenging. Not television.

'If I had the choice I would still prefer stills because there is more to it than just taking pictures. You come back from an assignment, you process the film, you do the selection, the cropping and the prints and if it's for news use you wire the pictures.

'Most of my filming is for news but I would say that about 90 per cent of the time I don't see the results because I am out in the field doing the shooting and I have to get the film out as quickly as I can.

'With satellite we sometimes have time to edit ourselves which is a lot of fun. But often there is no time or the editing equipment is not available locally. So we just transmit it raw and then the editing is left to people in London or New York. And we have to trust them. Generally they do a very good job although there are times when they don't quite do what one wants them to do.

'But that's because when you are on the scene yourself you have conceived the story in your own mind while often the person sitting in New York or London doesn't quite grasp the story because he is just doing a mechanical job. He is cutting one story after another and he just follows your guidelines.

'So generally I like doing stills very much but it doesn't really worry me which assignment I get. And when I shoot film I always take stills. I have never travelled on any assignment without a stills camera.'

'In the very early days of photojournalism,' Gerald Clarke observed in *Time*, 'picture takers often trailed behind writers like baggage carriers in the African bush' — hardly a simile for Amin's latter-day role in Africa.

'I always felt a great deal more comfortable', Platter recalls, 'when Mo was on a story with us. If he was there, things were always likelier to happen and yield copy; if he wasn't, things had a habit of happening elsewhere, and you could be scooped. Usually by Mo.

'In any contretemps, we courageous scribes would push him to the front to argue it out with fuming political worthies, fiery soldiers, grieving relatives, and rioting mobs. He was usually up front anyway. And he would usually win them over, with a mixture of humour and pretended innocence.

'His relentless desire to complete any assignment well, and of course therefore lucratively, meant he needed little prompting. And what he may have lacked in formal academic grounding was more than compensated by his innate political savvy, as indispensible to a successful international cameraman as to an international autocrat.

'Yet it was always useless to try to engage Mo in any heavy political discussions. These were meaningless — and unprofitable — trifles. He abhorred violence and injustice, but talking wasn't going to help.'

Says Amin: 'I used to go in cold and just do the job and come out cold. You have emotions and all that, but so far as the work and my own personality were concerned it did not matter. It had nothing to do with me;

it was an incident that happened and I just recorded what happened. I could do nothing for it; the fact that it happened had nothing to do with me.

'I just never interfered, never tried to stop anything, because it was not for me to do that. If I had actually tried to stop some of the things that I actually saw I could have been killed because I was dealing with people you couldn't negotiate with; because when they're killing people there's no logic any more. There's no sense. Interfere with that and you yourself go. Covering wars and things like that, I was just doing a job. It's not my world.'

Adds Platter: 'He wasn't a participant, he was an observer. He has that particular cast of mind, even "distinction of mind" — to use an Elspeth Huxley phrase from her book, *Out in the Midday Sun* — peculiar to so many East African personalities.

'Mo is an adventurer. It must be in the Highlands air. In common with the earlier British pioneers, affected by that heady atmosphere, or something else indefinable about East Africa, Mo was, and remains, oblivious to danger and discomfort. He has a job to do and if possible it should be done with *élan* — and it has to be lucrative.'

Harold Evans, former editor of *The Times*, comments: 'When I hear snooty remarks about photojournalists, I think of one of their greatest achievements — objective presentation of war and its consequences. Their pictures have told many truths, and they have been prepared to risk everything to capture an image and hold it fast forever.'

By the 1970s, Amin had done that many times, and on a scale and frequency which have led friends and critics alike to believe his life has a kind of inevitability.

'Go in with all your options open and hope that luck is on your side,' says Amin. 'Certainly it's been on my side in many situations. I believe quite strongly that a lot of things happen because God wants them to happen.'

The first months of 1970 were routine enough, with coverage of an eye operation in Nairobi's Kenyatta Hospital early in January, a royal visit by Denmark's King Frederick and Queen Ingrid, a shantytown blaze started by Nairobi City Council workers to clear an illegal slum and, in February, a visit by US Secretary of State William Rogers.

Then he talked his way into filming a secret Palestinian Liberation Organization — PLO — terrorist training camp in Jordan, and shooting stills for United Press International. It became an acid test of his faith in destiny. The training camp in rocky hill country was close to Israel and one day he joined one of the PLO patrols that went across the border. 'It was,' he recalls, 'one of the most frightening days of my life.'

Well into Israel, the patrol spotted a schoolbus on a hillside and opened fire. Israeli guards immediately returned the fire. 'Those guys don't miss,' says Amin. 'I thought: "This is where I'm going to buy it", and I got down on my belly and crawled through the bush. I crawled like hell. I ripped all

Mohamed Amin's 1970 pictures from a PLO terrorist training camp in Jordan included some of young women being indoctrinated in the arts of guerilla fighting and sabotage.

This picture, with Amin at the centre of a group of dedicated PLO guerillas, was taken for his personal album.

my clothes and bloodied all my hands but eventually we were back in Jordan and they weren't following.

'That's the only time I can remember being totally shit-scared.'

As usual, more or less the next day, it was back to the same kind of calculated risk that, in retrospect, he so enjoys.

The non-Muslim population of southern Sudan had been fighting a secessionist war for thirteen years. With veteran Nairobi-based reporter Henry Reuter and BBC Television reporter Peter Stewart, a ruthless veteran of Fleet Street tabloids like the *Mirror*, he planned a long trek through Uganda and Zaire and across the Sudanese border — into the Any'anya 'freedom fighting' group's stronghold deep in the trackless wilderness.

His contacts in Nairobi arranged the visit. It involved a dangerous five-day trek in sweltering heat, with a column of newsmen and porters that stretched several hundred yards.

Friction arose between Stewart and the cameraman over the heavy equipment which Amin had to carry and Stewart's provocative sneer earned him a right-handed punch from Mohamed Amin. They never spoke again, addressing their remarks to each other through Henry Reuter.

'I was particularly impressed,' recalls Reuter. 'Not only was he carrying a great deal more weight, with all those cameras around his neck, but he also never stopped hurrying from one end of the single-file caravan to the other end to film or take stills. He must have covered three times the distance that the rest of us did. I saw total and complete commitment and dedication.'

The march ended at Bungu. A collection of small, thatched huts, scattered about a clearing hacked out of the jungle, had become the 'capital' of the self-proclaimed Nile State, with its own Parliament.

Amin's film, edited into two news reports of around six minutes each, was unusually compelling. The first dealt with 'Africa's longest and most forgotten civil war'. The second drew comparisons with the widely reported Biafran conflict, and the fact that thousands were dying in the unreported strife between Black Christians and animists of the South and Arab Muslims. He showed the guerillas in training and the treatment of wounded soldiers. But the only real action Amin saw himself was his own, uncharacteristic and unplanned contact with Stewart.

On his return to Kenya, however, he found compensation by covering army training in Ngong Forest near Nairobi. He was drawn by the fact that the soldiers taking part used live bullets.

By way of total contrast, in May the reigning Miss World, Eva Reuber-Staier, visited Kenya. He covered the visit extensively. His working day rarely allowed him, or those associated with him, time to go home. Work frequently ended past midnight and he seemed not to have heard of weekends. To him, days off, if he thought of them at all, seemed to indicate lack of strength, purpose or character — or all three. 113

In a long trek through the game-infested country of eastern Zaire and southern Sudan, Mohamed Amin led a group of newsmen to the bush headquarters of the rebel Any'anya freedom fighters to report a forgotten thirteen-year-long rebel war against the forces of the Sudanese government controlled from Khartoum. A member of a guard of honour, armed only with wooden sticks, collapses as the 'President' of the rebel 'state' inspects the guard.

The BBC's Peter Stewart, left, with Mo and Henry Reuter, right, watched by members of the Any'anya freedom fighters: their long trek through wild country ended with the cameraman and Stewart refusing to speak to each other.

Evidence of the momentous change in global communications was taking shape at this time in the form of Kenya's new satellite ground station at Longonot, thirty-five miles north-west of Nairobi on the floor of the Great Rift Valley, one of the oldest and greatest geological wonders of the world.

He went to film progress on the ground station and persuaded a Maasai, spear in hand, and dressed in scant toga, to pose with the station in the background. Then, using his VW as a kind of motorized sheepdog he herded up giraffes so that he could film them in front of the satellite dish, little knowing that one day the station would transmit his own news coverage around the world.

The last line of the Visnews script to his film said: 'All forms of international communications will be handled by the station — telephone calls, telegrams, telex messages and radio pictures.' No mention of television news. The most he hoped for then was to send his still pictures through space.

But if technology was swiftly changing the face of the world, old and unreasoning prejudices still prevailed.

Britain was beginning to renege on its commitment to certain groups which claimed citizenship, and laws were passed which created a class of 'stateless' British citizens. Although holding British passports, they were not allowed to enter Britain. Amin was no exception. His passport was endorsed: Holder is subject to control under the Commonwealth immigrants act.

Britain underlined the point on the day his son Salim, also British by law, was born — 6 June 1970 — by returning thirty-four Asian citizens from Heathrow to Nairobi. The minute they landed, the Kenya Government declared them Prohibited Immigrants. Amin's footage showed the plight of these first victims, shuttlecocks in Britain's sorry game of racial politics.

A few days later he covered a similar story in Nairobi. The City Council cracked down on 3,000 Asian traders who the year before had been ordered to sell their businesses to indigenous citizens. He filmed the inspectors checking shops, the shuttered windows of empty stores with 'For Sale' signs and headlines warning against non-citizen businesses.

Earlier in the year, while he was in Jordan, his brother-in-law Bahadur, who was looking after the Camerapix office in Dar es Salaam, was tragically killed in a road accident. To replace him, he hired Paul Toulmin-Rothe, the former British naval commander he had first met in Djibouti.

They had met again in October 1969 at the funeral of assassinated Somali President Abdirashid Ali Shirmarke. 'Paul had been planning to go on leave at the time but Prime Minister Mohamed Egal asked him to stay on for the funeral. On the same day, soon after the funeral, Paul asked Egal if it was all right for him to go on leave. Paul caught the same flight as I to Nairobi.

'Early next morning he called to tell me that there had been a military coup in Somalia. Siyad Barré, the army chief, had seized power. Paul was not at all fond of Barré — he didn't like or trust him one bit — and decided never to go back to Somalia.

'So he stayed in Kenya and one morning about two years later walked into my office asking for a job.

'I told him I could give him a job as a cameraman based in Dar es Salaam. And Paul said, "Well, if you're willing to teach me I'd be happy to go to Dar es Salaam".

'So I taught him how to load and film and sent him off.'

Three weeks later, on 25 January 1971, while Ugandan President Milton Obote was still in the air, en route home from Singapore and the Commonwealth summit, he was overthrown. The East African Airways Super VC-10 which was carrying him was diverted to Nairobi.

Kenyatta, who had already crossed ideological swords with the deposed politician, swiftly issued instructions: get him out of Kenya. Closeted secretly in Nairobi's Panafric Hotel, where they occupied the entire top floor, Obote and his entourage were only in Nairobi for five hours, but Amin's film showed the security network at the Panafric Hotel and Obote's 'ministers'. Because of heavy hotel security, however, he missed their 'escape' from the hotel through the kitchen. Hurrying to the airport, he filmed the plane leaving. But what he did not film was the briefing given to EAA's Captain Colin Skillett by Vice-President Daniel arap Moi.

'You will fly them to Dar es Salaam.'

'And if Dar doesn't want them I bring them back here?'

'No! Take them anywhere but don't bring them back to Kenya.'

'And if we run out of fuel?'

'That's your problem. Just be sure you don't bring them back.' In Dar es Salaam, Paul Toulmin-Rothe filmed Obote saying: 'There's no question of any takeover.'

Recalls Amin: 'As soon as we did Obote's departure I dashed off to Wilson Airport to charter a plane. But the pilot wouldn't take off without clearance from Kampala. Idi Amin's troops had shelled Entebbe Airport bringing down half the airport and killing two people, one of them a priest. Naturally, the pilot was quite nervous.

'At the charter company I booked a call to the Command Post in Kampala — hoping to talk to an officer who would give us permission to land. If I recall correctly I was with John Osman of the BBC.

'While we were waiting for the call to go through — it took at least thirty minutes or so — I tried to persuade the pilot to take off but he was adamant.

'When the call came through a soldier's voice said: "This is the Command Post Kampala".

'I said, "This is Mohamed Amin. Can I speak with General Amin?"

'There were a couple of clicks and then a voice came on the line: "This is General Amin." I was surprised. You don't usually get straight through to the top man — just like that — anywhere in the world. I was expecting to talk to an aide or secretary.

'I had given the operator my name without really thinking about it. But I'm certain he took me to be a relative.

'Anyway, I said, "Sir. My name is Mohamed Amin. I'm a cameraman and a newsman — and we'd like to come to Uganda to record the events of the last few hours."

'He said, "You're welcome. Everything is fine here and people are very happy that I have taken over."

'I said, "That's very good, sir. However, we need clearance from the control tower at Entebbe as our pilot won't take off without it."

'He said, "Give me the registration number of your plane", which I did. I think it was 5Y AKT, or something like that, and he obviously wrote it down and said, "There'll be transport to meet you."

'When we landed at Entebbe the plane was immediately surrounded by troops. They searched us very thoroughly, including my equipment, and then took us to the presidential lounge. All the walls were pockmarked with bullet holes and bullet-ridden pictures of President Obote were lying on the ground.

'Eventually the transport arrived. In fact, it was an armoured personnel carrier which had been sent by Idi Amin. It was sweltering, almost unbearably hot. I'll never know why he sent an armoured personnel carrier. The drive from Entebbe to Kampala normally takes about twenty-five minutes but it took us about ninety — by which time we were roasted.

'We were taken straight to the Command Post on one of the hills on which the capital stands and up to a balcony on the first floor where I put my camera on the tripod and lined it all up — waiting, I hoped, for Idi Amin to turn up.

'Sure enough, after a little while, this huge figure walks out of a door and I start rolling the camera. Then he says, "I'm very sorry gentlemen. I'm not going to talk to you as Tanzania has just invaded me. Therefore I have to go to the front line to command my troops."

'And he disappears. This story, of course, led the world's television news bulletins because up to this point nobody knew how much truth there was in this, but here was the new Head of State making a statement on camera which was accepted as a true story.

'By now it was late evening, so we went to Entebbe to ship the film and then returned to spend the night in our hotel.

'Next morning I heard that Idi Amin was going to take the salute at a parade to honour the soldiers who had helped him take over the country, including the tank battalion, which had about half a dozen tanks.

'In fact, the tanks wouldn't start. They had to be pushed one at a time to get them started.

Mohamed Amin's poolside picture of a jubilant Idi Amin after his overthrow of Milton Obote gave the world its first glimpse of the macabre clown who had entered the world's stage.

'The parade took place in a dusty open field and as the tanks rolled past we were all covered with dust, including Idi Amin. After the parade I saw him get into the driver's seat of his jeep and I walked over, introduced myself and asked him where he was going.

'He thought for a second and then said, "I'm going for a swim", so I said, "Can I come along with you?"

'I jumped in the back and filmed him as he drove to the Apollo Hotel which soon afterwards he renamed the Hotel International. Obote's middle name was Apollo.

'I followed him to the swimming pool. When he came out of the changing room in his swimming trunks I realized what an enormous, truly enormous, man he was.

'There were lots of young girls around, and they were all very friendly with him. Obviously, he was a regular visitor. I took some pictures of him with the girls and then some film and pictures of him in the pool, which again made headline coverage around the world.'

But when he was having a shower he called the Nairobi newsman over to say:

'Look, I saw you taking pictures of me with a lot of prostitute girls but please don't use them. I didn't want to upset the girls which is why I didn't stop you but please don't use the pictures.'

After that the two talked in general terms. 'For some reason he really took a liking to me and it was from this contact that I became one of the few people allowed in and out of Uganda freely.

'In fact, during the last two years of Idi Amin's rule I was the only cameraman allowed in. I can't explain why but I think initially it was probably because we had the same name.'

A macabre clown had entered the stage of world politics — and, at first, the world laughed, entertained by Mohamed Amin's film and picture coverage of this seemingly benign gangster.

Perhaps as reprisal for his work in hustling through Kenya's security network to film Obote's departure, twelve days later the photographer was punched and harassed at Nairobi Airport when Prince Charles and Princess Anne arrived in Kenya on 6 February. The Visnews log notes laconically:

> Cameraman Mohamed Amin, assigned to cover the arrival of Britain's Prince Charles and Princess Anne at Nairobi Airport at the start of their two-week visit to Kenya on Saturday, reports that Kenya Police were "very rough with photographers". It seems they man-handled cameramen and smashed the main set of lights. It would appear to have been a much tougher assignment than had been anticipated. Nevertheless, Amin got his story.

One problem was the large Press party which followed Charles's progress. In particular, everybody wanted to go to far-off Lake Rudolf — 500 miles from Nairobi in the far north, now called Turkana and known as a 'Cradle of Mankind'.

Opposite: Nominated on a 'pool' basis as the sole photographer-cameraman to cover the visit of Britain's Prince Charles to Kenya's blistering northern deserts, in 1971 Mohamed Amin truly became a Photographer Royal.

Overleaf: From Amin's portfolio of nubile Turkana maidens.

Opposite: Mohamed Amin's pictures of the British heir to the throne with Kenya's colourful northern peoples included this Turkana chief.

Above: His pictures of Princess Anne holding a young leopard cub in Nairobi National Park's animal orphanage appeared around the world.

But Charles was to pilot his own plane — one of the Queen's Flight — from Nairobi, which meant that the news 'pool' system was invoked: out of the battery of the best of Britain's Press photographers and television cameramen only one was allowed on the flight. The work of the 'pool' man would be used by all the papers — and all the television networks. Alone among all this talent, only Mohamed Amin had the qualifications to meet both requirements. The unknown young Asian from the Eastleigh quarter of Nairobi had come a long way.

Prince Charles spent idyllic days in the remote wilderness studying its phenomenal bird life. With the birds and more than 2,000 square miles of storm-tossed water set in the centre of a 100,000-square-mile desert, this astonishing inland sea is a unique resort. Mohamed Amin truly became a Photographer Royal.

Within a week of the royal visit, the Archbishop of Canterbury, Dr Michael Ramsey, visited Kenya, Mrs Miriam Obote and her children arrived to take up residence in exile, there was the State opening of the Kenya Parliament – and then Amin was back in Uganda.

Still working on *Search for the Nile*, the producer wanted him to film the river itself for the titles and continuity sequences. As none of the episodes had yet been shot within sound or sight of the Nile both felt the series would be incomplete without actual film of the world's longest river.

I drove from Nairobi with Amin. At Jinja, after we turned left down a dirt road, seven soldiers suddenly ran out from an acacia tree at the side of the road and blocked our way. One jabbed his rifle barrel at the door, chipping the enamel just beneath the window of my Vauxhall Victor.

'Get out, you pig.'

As I opened the door he cracked me across the head with the rifle butt. When I stumbled he jabbed me in the ribs, knocked me down, kicked my knee from under me, and put his foot on my chest. Then he placed the barrel against my neck and began squeezing the trigger.

Suddenly he jumped to one side and cracked the butt against Amin's chest. He had seen what was happening and had come out from the passenger side. His action saved my life. Drunk, the soldier now forgot all about me and started threatening him.

Hands up, Mo talked swiftly in Swahili, and slowly the tension eased. The soldiers checked the car boot, taking no notice at all of the half-a-ton of film equipment inside, declared us worthless 'Kenya pigs' and waved us on.

Amin took over as driver and drove on down the dirt road. After a few minutes I told him:

'Okay. Let's turn around and go back.'

'Back where?'

'Nairobi.'

'You must be crazy.'

'But surely you can't want to stay?'

'Why not?'

'Because the bastards will kill us.'

'Come on, Brian. These guys are just drunk.'

He pulled up overlooking a series of cataracts where he had filmed 'Speke's discovery', got out, opened the boot, took out the tripod and his Arriflex and began filming as if he were on a fishing holiday in the Scottish highlands. Much later I learned that the blow on his chest had badly fractured two ribs.

Two days later, I stood with him and an Acholi game ranger at the top of Murchison Falls. When he went off to photograph and film the scenic falls the ranger told me of massacres in northern Uganda by Idi Amin's troops and pressed on me a hand-written list of hundreds who had gone to their deaths. Weeks later, I was able to verify it.

That night we stayed at Para Lodge, downstream from the falls, and next day went close to this magnificent spectacle in the lodge's motor launch. It was an experience from a time removed. Elephants balanced with uncanny sure-footed ease on narrow ledges, invisible to the eye, carved in the walls of the cliffs lining the falls, more like mountain goats than five-ton herbivores. Spray shrouded everything. Slowly the launch drifted away from the eddies and back downstream — hundreds of crocodiles basking on the shores and sandbanks, slithering down to the water as we glided by. Here was magical footage for the Nile series.

That afternoon we motored down to the shores of Lake Albert. For me, these were all the faraway and remote places I had hungered for when I was in Britain. It was enchanted country. Beyond Lake Albert's shimmering waters we could make out the foothills of the Ruwenzoris, the fabled 'mountains of the moon.'

Later, Amin set up his tripod about thirty yards from a herd of elephants while I kept the engine running. As the elephants cropped the grass and came nearer and nearer, stately and graceful despite their size, he kept filming and I switched off. They came to within three or four yards before turning from his perfectly still silhouette. The only noises were the rumbles of their stomachs, the chaffing of the grass as they moved through it, and my rapid breathing.

As they ambled away, he slowly panned his camera after them, kites soaring high on the thermals above the lake, its waters glinting silver through the heat which made all the images shimmer.

I thought, 'He sees all life through a lens, as removed from conscious reality as if he were watching a movie.' Perhaps that's why so many of his kind die at work.

Next night at Chobe Lodge, near the Karuma Falls Bridge, the Acholi barman asked me to wait until the others had gone to bed. Each night, upstream on the bridge over the Karuma Falls, he told me, hundreds of Acholi and Langi were being machine-gunned. Later, by the light of his lantern I saw the bloated corpses floating in a Nile backwater, while, from far away came the sound of machine guns.

124   In the morning the bridge pavement was covered with what looked like

tar. I thought it odd. I had never seen dried blood before. An old English rigger who lived in a caravan a few hundred yards from the bridge told us: 'They're killing thousands. Every night. At first I couldn't sleep but now it makes no difference.'

My story appeared on the front page of The Observer on 14 March 1971; mine because Mohamed Amin's only fear was that he wouldn't get back into Uganda if it carried his name as well.

'I have to come back,' he said.

He did. Many times. Towards the end, at considerable risk.

8   Bloodbath in Bangladesh

Most people who meet Mohamed Amin expect the kind of five-star conversation you might have with a Hollywood star or an international celebrity. But unless you have something to offer in exchange the conversation is usually brief and forgettable. He dislikes small talk at any level. Celebrity hunters usually cross him off their list as a 'bore'.

But professionals who work with him, or against him, rate him at the opposite end of the scale. When it comes to shop talk they spend hours in conversation.

'I really liked and admired him, as a mate and a pro, and still do,' recalls John Platter, 'always acknowledging, however, that we parted company as businessmen. While he also relished the commercialism, we purist hacks grandly eschewed the dreary penny-collecting side of journalism — in favour of distinguished pauperism.

'And, of course, as an employer himself Amin never underworked or overpaid anyone. But at least he drove himself as hard if not harder.

'I do not have to guess at his present circumstances — the flood of documentaries, books, and everything else spells tycoonery with which I am sure he is very comfortable. He deserves it. His talents and restlessness destined him for it. I can't think of any of his contemporaries who would resent it.'

Adds Roy Lipscombe on his friend of twenty-five years: 'As I remember it, Mo had precious little of anything in the early days . . . perhaps an elderly Bolex mute camera and a couple of stills cameras. I shall be interested to see how much he has amassed from various enterprises around the world since then . . . that's if he'll ever tell you.'

Recalls Brendan Farrow: 'One day I was ribbing him a bit about his expenses. "A star like you," I told him, "all those awards, all that fame, all those books under your name! You don't need the money." He came back sharply: "Yes, and I didn't get any of it lying in bed or drinking in bars".'

When, towards the end of March 1971 BBC *Panorama*'s Alan Hart asked Mohamed Amin to go with him to cover the East Pakistan conflict, he refused. (After the collapse of the conciliation talks between the East Pakistani opposition and the Pakistan Government, a guerilla war between the Mukti Bahini and government forces had flared into ugly life.)

The East African Safari motor rally, one of the biggest assignments of the year for Amin, was about to start.

'I couldn't do it because it clashed. The rally was a money maker.

'Alan said he understood. But he rang me again the next day and asked me to meet his flight to Nairobi the following morning. I said, "Fine, but please don't travel all this way to talk me into taking this assignment because I cannot go until after the rally which will be too late for you."

'He said, "No, I just want to come to Nairobi to have a chat with you".

'I picked him up next morning. Alan never went up to his room at the Panafric Hotel. He just checked in, dropped his baggage and then took me to the coffee shop where I told him again just how important the rally was. Nothing would persuade me to go. He asked me what kind of money would compensate me. I told him it wasn't a matter of calculating the loss. It was all to do with the contracts and agreements I had that continued each year. I was adamant. But he said, "Well, tell me what would persuade you to do the job? Give me a figure."

'I told him, "This is ridiculous. If you want a figure you'll have to turn it down because it will be ridiculous, so why bother?"

'He said, "No. Go on — give me a figure."

'So I said, "Right. I'll charge you £1,000 a day and I want a minimum guarantee of ten days work."

'In 1971 that was a lot of money. The average rate for cameramen was around £100 or £150 a day. Alan took me up to his room while he called the editor of *Panorama* at his home in London. I think the editor fell out of his bed but Alan persuaded him that it was worth it.

'The deal was that it would be just me and Alan. No soundman, as it was best to keep the number of people to an absolute minimum which I prefer when I'm working in a dangerous situation. It's best not to have anybody else to worry about.

'We flew to Karachi that evening. We wanted to go to Dacca and work on the side of the Pakistan Army. But the doors were absolutely shut. Nobody was prepared to give us any permission so we took a Japan Air Lines flight to Calcutta, one of the most pleasant flights I've had. With Alan you flew first-class all the time.

'We arrived quite late at night. There was a transport strike which apparently was quite common in Calcutta, so there were no taxis or buses. But the JAL crew gave us a lift in their transport, an armoured vehicle they had requisitioned from the airport police.

'Hundreds of newsmen, waiting to go in and cover the rebellion, were staying at the Palace Hotel. We spent the night at another hotel, the Hindustan International. I always prefer to stay away from the pack. You tend to worry about what the others are doing and can't get on with job. You're also influenced by what everybody else is doing.

'Nicolas Tomalin of the *Sunday Times* joined us on the flight from Karachi. As he wanted to stay close to us he also checked in at the same hotel.

'Alan asked me to arrange a vehicle to the border. The strike didn't make 127 life very easy but eventually I found a Sikh who agreed to take us to Banapur. We set off at six in the morning. The border post officials refused to allow us to enter, but after a lot of talking said we could go in without our passports being stamped.

'We refused to accept that. If we got arrested by the Pakistani troops when we were in the country illegally we reckoned we could be lined up in front of a firing squad. At the least, if we were in the country legally we'd have a chance of talking.

'Finally they stamped our passports but, understandably, the taxi driver refused to go with us. We gave him some money and told him to wait, saying we'd be back at any time during the next two or three days. There was no transport at all in East Pakistan.'

In blisteringly hot weather, the roads crowded with refugees fleeing the carnage of East Pakistan, Amin carried his heavy camera equipment for three or four miles, until he flagged down a man on a bicycle rickshaw and persuaded him to take them to one of the main towns in the region, Jessore, about twenty-five miles inside the country.

The sweating coolie was pedalling the three heavyweight newsmen slowly through the milling refugees when Amin waved down an ancient fire engine heading for the border. Speaking Urdu he asked the firemen to give them a lift to Jessore. They refused.

'Then I started negotiating with them to hire the engine but again they refused. Eventually, however, I got them to agree to sell the fire engine for hard currency — about a thousand dollars.'

Hart produced the wad of dollar notes and the three jumped into the antiquated machine. There was little power left in the old engine but since the roads were crowded with refugees it made no difference.

'We passed several massacres — men, women and children slaughtered in their homes. We filmed this gruesome evidence as we drove towards Jessore. It wasn't clear who had done the killing but the locals told us that these people had been killed by the Pakistani soldiers. It was also evident that there was a lot of killing by the Bengalis as well.

'It took me time to realize that this was a war between Bengalis and Punjabis. Since my parents were Punjabis I realized that if I spoke in Punjabi I might get slaughtered too.

'So whenever I was asked where I was from I said Africa — easy enough to prove — and since they had never seen an African before they were quite happy to accept the fact.' He had reason to be wary.

Time, calling the conflict 'A Second Vietnam', said the genocide was 'the most incredible, calculated thing since the days of the Nazis in Poland'. At the end, estimates of the dead varied between 200,000 and one million. An estimated 7.5 million refugees fled to India.

'All along the route', remembers the cameraman, 'the stench of decomposing bodies hung heavily in the air. We saw many, including that of a three-year-old child still clinging to its mother.'

'When we rolled into Jessore we met the rebels who took us to an old two-storey house which was their headquarters, where they had some prisoners, about a dozen West Pakistani businessmen and priests whom I filmed.

'Later, their hands tied with rope, we saw the same group being paraded up and down the streets. They were clutching the Qur'an in their hands. I did several takes and asked the people what they were going to do them. They said, "Nothing. They're our prisoners."

'We then drove around, filming the results of the killings and the destruction of property, houses and shops. About midday we decided to drive back to Banapur with the material that we had and perhaps try another border post farther north.'

What happened next shocked viewers worldwide.

'As we were driving through one square in Jessore we saw a mob killing a small group of people. I filmed this massacre, first from a distance, then closer when I saw it was the same West Pakistanis that we had filmed earlier. They were being beaten to death with sticks, stones, knives — anything. Their bodies were still twitching, the most gruesome thing I had ever seen.

'There was nothing I could do. My policy was never to get involved. Try to interfere and the next thing you know you're being beaten to death yourself.

'But Nicolas Tomalin tried to stop it. It was only then that they realized we were there. One of the leaders walked up to us with a pistol by his side and said, "These people have been killed by the Pakistani Army."

He obviously had no idea we had filmed what had happened. I didn't think we should argue but Nick said he thought they should be taken to the hospital.

'The Bengali asked, "Why? It's nothing to do with us. They were killed by the Pakistani soldiers and they should do something about it."

'Nick was pretty insistent. He said, "Since you had nothing to do with it that's another reason you should take them to hospital."

'This made the guy very angry and he pulled out his gun. "I'm going to kill you if you keep telling me to do something."

'I cut in and told Nick, "Look there's nothing you can do about this so let's get the hell out of here."

'I didn't have any doubts the Bengali could just as easily shoot us. So we got back into the fire engine and drove off.'

This time Hart drove, Amin by his side. What the refugees, filing by on either side, thought of this odd trio aboard one of Jessore's fire engines can only be guessed. But after the horror minutes before, the photographer welcomed the comedy.

'How will you claim for this on expenses?'

Hart paused.

'I'm not sure. I don't think the BBC has bought a fire engine before.'

Near the border they passed the firemen and stopped to try to sell the engine back to them. 'But they were pretty sure that we wouldn't get very

Mohamed Amin's 1971 film and still pictures of sprawled bodies, including that of mother and child massacred in the East Pakistan uprising, shocked British viewers and newspaper readers around the world.

British viewers watching BBC's *Panorama* were witness to this stark massacre filmed in the town square of Jessore by Mohamed Amin.

far.' The newsmen left it at the border and walked across. The taxi was still waiting.

'On the way back to Calcutta our Sikh driver hit and killed a dog,' Amin remembers. 'Alan Hart went berserk. I've never seen anyone so upset. Alan screamed and shouted at the driver for killing the dog. I said, "Come on Alan — what's a dog after the massacre we've just seen. You weren't that upset then." But he wouldn't calm down. And I thought, "Oh well. That's an Englishman. Killing people may not be distressing but never hurt a dog."

'At Calcutta Alan caught a flight to Britain. The film was shown as a special the day he landed since there was no *Panorama* that night. It caused a tremendous outcry.'

Hart, who appeared as anchorman, was indefatigable. As soon as the programme ended he flew back to Calcutta where he was met by Amin. Using a dirt road which bypassed the border posts, the same day they went to Dinajpur where they met members of the Bangladesh liberation army, the Mukti Bahini, whose front line was pockmarked by dug-out trenches, tunnels and guerilla-type hideouts.

Schoolchildren were undergoing training from Sandhurst-groomed secessionist officers in a soccer stadium. Half of the 50,000 fanatical freedom fighters came from the East Bengal Regiment, the paramilitary East Bengal Rifles and the Bengali police.

'After about a week we drove back to Calcutta. To really balance this programme we needed a couple of interviews from the other side, the government and political leaders. We had to go to West Pakistan.

'But we didn't want to take the film with us in case it was confiscated. On the other hand we couldn't ship the film from Calcutta to London because at that time the BBC was banned in India.'

Hart flew to Karachi to set up the interviews, Amin went back to Nairobi to ship the film from there, returning to Karachi on the same flight.

'It arrived early in the morning and the Customs guys told me they couldn't let me take all the equipment into the country without a letter from the Ministry of Information.

'It's routine but obviously I tried to talk my way around it. They wouldn't have it and I told them I had to inform the correspondent with whom I was working who was waiting outside.

'So I was allowed to go out where I saw Alan and an old friend of mine, Ronnie Robson.

'Alan, who was a bit cross, said he needed to talk to the Customs officer himself and came in with me. But the Customs guy wouldn't listen to him either and Alan — because it was late at night I suppose — got very angry and started shouting, "We've come here to interview your fucking President and stop fucking us about", or words to that effect. But they were adamant. They weren't going to let the equipment through until they had a letter from the Ministry of Information. I left the gear at the airport.

'I was in Karachi at the time,' remembers Robson, 'and if anyone should 131 have been browned off it was Mo. He'd had the long flight. He was the one still on the wrong side of the barrier. He was showing no concern.'

In Karachi, Amin went to the Ministry of Information and found a man to go with him to clear Customs. Then back to his hotel where, exhausted, just as he was about to sleep there was a loud banging on his door. There were three men.

'Are you Mohamed Amin?'

'Yes, who are you?'

'We're Special Branch.'

'Come in.'

'Can we see your passport? You're under arrest.'

'What for?'

'We've orders to arrest you. We can leave you in your room, but you can't go out.'

'Immediately, I was concerned that they had been tipped off that I had been in East Pakistan and that it was going to cause me trouble. My passport had at least two East Pakistan entry stamps in it. That didn't seem to worry them, but they asked me to hand it over. I refused. They left me with a warning that the hotel was guarded.

'I immediately told Alan and Ronnie what had happened and Alan said, "That's a great pity." He'd already arranged an interview that day with the [then] opposition leader Zulfiqar Ali Bhutto at his Karachi home. In fact, Bhutto was one of the key men in the talks between the Mukti Bahini and the Pakistan authorities.

'The interview was set for seven that evening. I told Alan that if he could get me out of the hotel it was fine with me. I'd film the interview.'

Down in the lobby Hart studied the layout. The Inter-Continental (now the Pearl Continental) had two entrances on either side of the hotel, both guarded by Special Branch men. There was no way the cameraman could walk out with all his equipment.

'Alan was upset. It was going to be a key interview which would add tremendous weight to the programme. Anyway, he told me, "Keep ready and we'll see what we can do." The magazines were all loaded. All we had to do was find a way out without being seen.

'Sure enough, just before seven o' clock Alan knocks on the door along with two or three guys who looked like kitchen staff and said, "Let's go and do this interview."

'He'd made a deal with the kitchen staff to get us in and out for a sum of money that probably ran into several hundred dollars. We went out through the kitchen door and drove straight round to Bhutto's house.

'Ronnie had gone to see Alan Brown, the British Consul in Karachi, to find out what he could do on my behalf.

'This fantastic interview with Bhutto used up all my four film magazines — something like forty-eight minutes in all. We were very excited about the interview. One of Bhutto's men took some pictures of us. I thought it was for the family album.

The union of British television technicians would never have allowed this — but perhaps none of their members would have volunteered for the assignment anyway. As Mohamed Amin films for BBC's *Panorama*, anchorman Alan Hart (crouching low with microphone) acts as soundman as defecting Pakistan soldiers of the East Bengal Regiment, who joined the Mukti Bahini rebels of East Pakistan, begin jungle training for Bengali dissidents.

The BBC's Alan Hart and Mohamed Amin in 1971 with the future Pakistan Prime Minister Zulfiqar Bhutto, later executed. When this picture appeared in the Pakistani Press the following day, it led to Mohamed Amin's arrest by Pakistani security.

Young Benazir Bhutto in the garden of her family's Karachi home in 1971. Married in 1987, she is now one of Pakistan's leading opposition political figures.

'After we packed up the equipment, we drove to Alan Brown's house to meet Ronnie. I was impressed with Brown. Usually, when you're in trouble — and I'd been in trouble before — the British High Commission's answer is, "Do as the government tells you and don't bother us." But here was a man who was prepared to go out of his way to help.

'He said that if the authorities decided to arrest me, there was not much the High Commission could do. Not only that, under martial law — which prevailed at that time — they could put me in for seven years and there was nothing that anybody could do about it.

'After Zanzibar the thought of going in for seven years scared the hell out of me. So I said, "How can you help?"

'He asked me for two passport pictures — I always carry a dozen or so on any trip — and he said he would make me a new passport. In the meantime if the Special Branch insisted on taking my other passport I should give it to them because once they had it they would relax.

'He said they would almost certainly let me stay in the hotel and that he would try to get me out through one of the land border routes, using the new passport. I thought that was impressive for a British High Commission official.

'On the way back to the hotel the thought of spending seven years in a Pakistani jail kept going through my mind. It was more than depressing. Our contacts in the kitchen were waiting and we went up the service lifts back to our rooms. I took my clothes off and dived straight into bed hoping for a good night's sleep. I hadn't had any for about fifty hours.

'At around four a.m. there was a tremendous banging on the door. I had kept the security chain latched but outside there were five very angry men indeed shouting that I should open the door.

'I said, "Hold on" and I immediately rang Ronnie and asked him to tell Alan and then threw some clothes on because they were still banging and shouting. If I hadn't opened it they would have smashed it down. These five stormed in. They stuck a newspaper in my face and said, "You are a spy. How did you get out of here last night?"

'Before I could answer they opened the newspaper and showed me a picture of myself together with Alan and Bhutto. In fact, I had assumed it was Bhutto's private photographer and that was that. But this guy had been from the newspaper so there was no point at this stage in giving the Special Branch any spiel so I said, "Well, what's the problem? I went down to the lobby to look for your men but there was nobody around and I assumed you realized you had made a mistake in the first place by putting me under arrest since there was nothing I had done to deserve being treated like this."

'They didn't believe me. They called me a liar because they said their men were at the doors all the time.'

Robson vividly remembers that phone call. 'Mo just had time to say: "The heavies have come for me." Then the phone went dead.

'In the past he and I had shared some "in" jokes about what was apt to happen to bandits, *dacoits*, or other miscreants captured in the old-time Punjab. They were crude jokes which featured greased canes and hot chillis.

'More seriously, we'd had time to discuss certain implications of his being uncovered as the cameraman who had illegally taken the massacre film in East Pakistan.

'Pakistan, then, was effectively under military dictators. Those in charge were frustrated and exasperated with the East Bengalis, with the Mukti Bahini, with India and its role in the problems, and certainly with the international news media from whom, they felt, they'd received unsympathetic treatment.

'Now they had their hands on a representative of this breed — and a prime one, of Pakistani stock and connections, which meant there were undertones of "treason" although he didn't hold a Pakistani passport. But surely the old Raj wouldn't worry or hurry too much over a subject from East Africa who was not "British-born".

'No doubt Hart had been recognized anyway, and resented, but it would have been a different matter entirely coming down on him. Mo was easier meat.'

Robson says he, too, developed a high regard for the British diplomatic presence in Karachi. 'They appreciated the situation instantly. It was a matter of urgency to make consular representations at once, and I pressed particularly that there should be insistence that a fully-fledged diplomat, not merely an official, should be allowed to be present at the place where Amin was to be interrogated.

'In some countries, for example, if an enthusiastic interrogation has led to visible injury, even if the authorities can be brought round to accepting that in a particular case it would be prudent to allow release, there's already something to hide — and the victim may simply vanish. There are various ways of persuasion, or of applying pressure, of "leverage", of "calling in favours" — even of bluff.'

Amin remembers: 'In the meantime, as the argument went on, Ronnie came along and the Special Branch told me they were going to take me away. They allowed me to finish dressing and Ronnie insisted that he would come with me.

'He said, "If you go on your own these people are going to treat you like one of their own and beat the hell out of you, but if I'm there they might feel a little concerned."

'Just as we were leaving Alan also came down and said, "I want to come with you, but I'll stay here and make all the right noises and see what I can do."

'I was interrogated for several hours. Most of the things I was asked were totally irrelevant. At the end of it all I had no idea what they were talking about. They were asking me where I went to school, where I was born, what I studied and nonsense like that; and why was I actually working for the BBC.

'The Pakistanis were not happy with the BBC. This went back to the 1966 war with India when the BBC — wrongly — ran a story that Lahore had been taken. Pakistan never forgave the BBC for that and because I was working for the BBC and able to speak all the languages in Pakistan they were very concerned that I had been brought there by the BBC to dig out information that they could not dig out themselves.

'I told them that I was only a "technician" who did what he was told, but they didn't believe any of this.

'Sometime in the afternoon — I think it was around four o'clock — somebody high up called them and told them to put me on the plane. It was the best thing that could have happened. The thought of spending seven years in a Pakistan jail had been firmly fixed in my mind right through the interrogation.

'I went to the airport with the Ministry of Information officer who had put up the bond for the equipment. And it was the same Customs officers who had been there when I arrived.

'Quite obviously they had complained that Alan had been very rude to them. But since they did not know his name they had used mine. I knew that they were going to take the film off me but I was determined to do everything to hang on to it.

'In fact, after the interview I had actually marked four new cans of unexposed film as "Exposed Films" marked "Bhutto Interview One to Four". I was hoping they would take that and not the reels in the magazines which were the actual film I used.

'They went through every item on the list. I decided to create a distraction. I told the Customs officer what a bastard he was and how very wrong it was to report me when I had said absolutely nothing to them to complain about. They were obviously scared, I said, of reporting an Englishman and had put it all on me.

'He was startled. He tried to make excuses and I said, "I don't give a damn. Do what you like." At this point they were just counting the films. Four rolls were missing from those on the import list. I said they were in the magazines. The Customs officer said, "What makes us think they are not the exposed rolls?"

'So I manufactured another outburst and said, "I don't give a shit because you're not going to believe me. After what you did yesterday you're capable of doing anything. You want to confiscate the cameras. You want to confiscate the films. You want to confiscate the magazines — well help yourself. You're obviously a bunch of rogues anyway."

'At this stage I felt that they were rather ashamed of what they had done and that it was very clear to them that I was not at fault on this.

'They sort of apologized again and told me to cool down and ordered a Coke for me and they were very pleasant, obviously trying to make up for what they had done.

'In the meantime the officer said to me, "Do you mind opening the gate of your camera?" I was not sure what he was trying to get at but I opened the gate and the last foot of film was still threaded in. You couldn't tell whether it was at the beginning of the reel or the end — but it satisfied him.

'He said, "That's fine" and then he explained that he had been taken for a ride by another cameraman before and obviously if there was nothing in the gate it had been run through and was exposed. He didn't worry about the other magazines. He believed me.

'Instead they took the four new rolls which I had marked. I was promised that those would be sent to the Pakistan Ambassador in London who would have them processed and view them. If there was nothing against the government, nothing offensive, then the film would be handed back to the BBC. But if there was anything offensive it would be edited before being handed over to the BBC.

'I made a strong protest saying it was against the freedom of the Press. But obviously I wasn't going to win on that.

'I then joined Alan in the departure lounge and with a thumbs up indicated that we still had the film. He said, "Please buy yourself a present from the duty free shop — it's on the BBC."

'I decided to buy a Zenith radio which I had always wanted. It was priced at a thousand dollars. I assume the BBC paid for it since Alan picked up the tab. I think that was my bonus for the grief which Alan's behaviour had caused.

'We were put on a flight to Nairobi, and Alan took the plane from there to London with the film and immediately began to put together the fifty-five-minute *Panorama* special on East Pakistan.'

Later the four confiscated rolls arrived at the Pakistan High Commission's London office where they spent £250 having them processed. The entire staff sat around a screen with a hired projector ready to censor the film. But, of course, there was nothing on it and the following day *Panorama* was broadcast.

In Nairobi the Pakistan High Commissioner rang the cameraman demanding a meeting. He was refused. Finally, he said, 'Can we meet on neutral ground?' They lunched at Marino's, an Italian restaurant in International House in the city centre.

'He accused me of taking the side of the Bengalis while I told him that I was not in the business of taking anybody's side. I was in business to do a job as a reporter and to report what I saw and what was the truth.

'I was shocked that as a high commissioner he was not in the picture about what was really going on in his country. He then asked me not to publish a series of reports in the *Nation* on the situation in East Pakistan.

'Apparently my Pakistani darkroom operator was the source of this information. He had described the pictures and the kind of story I was writing.

'I told the high commissioner it was none of his business to tell me what I should be doing. We parted on very unfriendly terms with each of us paying our share of the bill for the lunch.'

A little later the envoy rang his office with an unsubtle reminder: 'Your parents live in Pakistan, don't they. . . . ?'

At once, Amin rang Kenya's foreign minister, Dr Njoroge Mungai, and told him of the implied threat and assured him: 'None of this has anything to do with my parents.'

He received another call from the high commissioner, more conciliatory this time. 'Mr Amin, you don't have to tell the foreign minister of everything we talk about.' His parents went unmolested.

Months later one of the BBC storekeepers rang Hart.

'Do you remember when you were in East Pakistan, Mr Hart?'

'Yes.'

'It's about this fire engine you bought. It's on our inventory. Do you think we could have it please?'

At home in Kenya Mohamed Amin watched the unfolding years of his young son's life and absorbed himself in his passion for wildlife with his close friend, Masud Quraishy. Sometimes they drove more than two hundred miles before dawn, and then followed one animal for hours. 'Never hurry' is his advice about filming animals. 'Patience and dedication are needed at all times.'

It was about this time that his first book, *Tom Mboya: a Photo-tribute*, was published. Albeit unknown to him, a new direction in his life was taking shape.

Then, in January 1972, he was assigned to cover Britain's Pearce Commission that was touring Rhodesia to assess the acceptability of a proposed Anglo-Rhodesia settlement.

He took Paul Toulmin-Rothe with him as soundman, and scored his own little victory over Rhodesian racism. His first clash was at the Customs. Paul knew nothing about the sound gear as, typically, he had been given just two hours instruction before leaving and was technically ignorant about the equipment.

'The white Customs officer refused to talk to me. He was only interested in talking to Paul and asked him all sorts of technical questions about the equipment which Paul couldn't answer.

'Paul looked at me and explained to the Customs man that he was only a soundman and that I was in charge of the team. Obviously racialism was deeper than I thought. Not only would they not to talk to me, but, they wouldn't even look at me. So I answered the questions while the Customs officer continued to look at Paul.

'Then we got a taxi and drove off to Meikles Hotel. I told Paul to go and check in while I sorted out the equipment and paid off the taxi.

'When I arrived at the check-in desk they were horrified to see my colour. Although apartheid was never spelt out in Rhodesia it existed, and quite deeply at that time. Paul got a call every day asking him to tell me to move to another wing. Paul kept explaining that there was no way that I was going to move. In fact, that I was in charge of the operation, but it made no difference. They didn't stop asking. 139

The story the Pakistan High Commissioner to Kenya tried to gag after Mo Amin's return from East Pakistan.

ABOVE: Young Bengali men train in the football stadium in Dinajpur, to meet an expected attack by West Pakistan soldiers. **BELOW:** A "Bangla Desh" unit commander briefs his men on an impending attack by West Pakistan soldiers.

Ins

AMIN writes: "P
other assignments
the Kabaka's fur
the East Africa
Rally, I reluctant
to cover the East
conflict for *BBC*
ma when they s
man, Alan Hart
robi to persuade
. "On Tuesday, I
Alan and I flew
cutta, the nearest
East Pakistan. It
possible to fly
because of a to
down by the We
tan authorities
and journalists.
"We arrived in C
a moment when all te
were staging a strike
of the Bengalis in E
tan, and it was on
long argument
persuaded a taxi dri
us from the airpo
town.
"We were also ac
by Nicholas Tomal
Sunday Times.
morning at 3 a.m.
car to take us to
border post at Banap
Indian Customs and
tion authorities clea
"We walked across
separating India
Pakistan and met
Customs and Immig
cials who were in
the 'breakaway'
They allowed us in
identified ourselves
men.
"We walked for
miles carrying our
before we caught

ABOVE LEFT: The corpses of local businessmen slashed to death by East Pakistanis, putrify in the market square in Jessore, East Pakistan's second largest town. **ABOVE:** Women and a three-year-old child slain allegedly by West Pakistan troops.

LEFT: A villager in East Pakistan carts his wife and children off to safety across the Indian border.

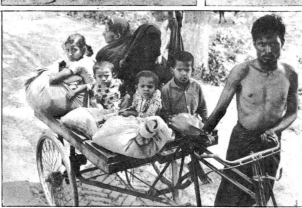

140

ide East Pakistan

A VILE, nauseating stench of putrified human flesh decomposing ismchly in the open greeted the "infiltration" into battle-torn East Pakistan of Kenya news photographer, **MOHAMED AMIN.**

He was one of the first Pressmen to enter the country ravaged by a bloody civil war which threatens to separate East Pakistan from its Western half.

In this exclusive account for the NATION, Amin of Camerapix reconstructs the moments of terror and horror that he faced in recording for "BBC Panorama", a sequence on sound film of the conflict.

After his ordeal in the East, he later flew to Karachi where he was detained and interrogated before he was granted an interview with the West Pakistan leader, Mr. Bhutto. He filmed the interview with Mr. Bhutto for the BBC.

Of the East, Amin says:

MOHAMED AMIN

"Atrocities were being committed by both sides. Unfortunately, because of a total clamp down on news by the West Pakistan authorities, I could only associate with the 'Liberation Front' which afforded me unrestricted movement within their captured or defended grounds."

drawn rickshaw.

"The rickshaw took us to a village where we persuaded an ambulance driver to take us to the nearest town. He gave us a lift in his ambulance flying the *Bangla Desh* flag (banner of the secessionists), to Jessore, East Pakistan's second biggest town, which is 25 miles from the Indian border.

"All along the route, the stench of decomposing human bodies killed in the conflict, hung heavily in the air. We saw a number of bodies including those of women and a three-year-old child still clinging to its dead mother.

"On the outskirts of Jessore there was a village which was completely burnt down allegedly by the West Pakistan forces, the previous night.

"We entered Jessore and called at the East Pakistan Rifles Sector Headquarters, which was manned by Bengali soldiers who deserted to join the secessionist cause.

"I saw hundreds of young men carrying sticks, knives, pangas, crow-bars and other improvised weapons, pouring into Jessore while at the same time a number of elders with their women folk and children were fleeing to refuge in other quarters.

"In Jessore, then, there was no sign of the West Pakistan troops. We were told that the nearest troops were three miles

down the road in a cantonment.

"At the East Pakistan Rifles Sector Headquarters we saw a dozen prisoners who we were told were Punjabis working as businessmen in Jessore. They were being paraded in the street outside the market.

"I shuddered at the sight, being a Punjabi myself. However, I was fortunate in escaping recognition as I spoke several languages and avoided any conversation in Punjabi.

"We were told to move from the area, but 30 minutes later we stole back to witness the brutal killing of these prisoners in front of the market. They were killed by a wild mob armed with knives, sticks and shot guns. We were shocked and helpless to do anything.

"Later in the afternoon, after that sordid public execution of the businessmen, we returned to Calcutta.

"Our second excursion into East Pakistan, took us along a battered track to the small town of Dinajpur, without having to go through any border posts.

"At Dinajpur we met the leaders of the *Mukti Fauj* (Liberation Forces) who gave us a 'briefing' on what was happening in their area.

"The next morning the *Mukti Fauj* took us to the front line, which was pockmarked by dug-out trenches, tunnels and guerrilla type hideouts.

"The troops that had deserted from the Central Government Forces had brought along their weapons with them. They were quite heavily armed with a lot of ammunition including anti-tank rockets and machine-guns.

"We were also shown some Chinese machine-guns which the soldiers claimed they captured.

"They told us that the West Pakistan force which was in a cantonment ten miles from Dinajpur, had three Chinese tanks and was intending to attack.

"In Dinajpur, life seemed normal. Shops were opened in the morning but closed in the afternoon when people who did not want to be caught in the fighting, left for the villages.

"The large football stadium in the town had been converted into a training camp where Sandhurst-trained officers were shaping 300 juveniles into soldiers.

"We stayed in Dinajpur for four days before returning to India. After crossing the border we were arrested by Indian Police but after two hours of questioning they released us. We drove to Calcutta where I caught a plane to Nairob' to have my films flown out to London.

"I then flew to Karachi to balance my story by getting an interview either with President Yahya Khan or Mr. Bhutto.

"I had just arrived in Karachi when Special Branch police detained me for several hours demanding an explanation of why I was filming in Pakistan.

"After satisfying them and being released I was granted an interview for the BBC, with Mr. Zulfikar Bhutto, leader of West Pakistan's majority People's Party.

"Mr. Bhutto, the former Foreign Minister, told me that he urged his Government to ease martial law restrictions and called for the restoration of political activities to help overcome the gravest crisis in the nation's 23-year history.

"Mr. Bhutto expressed concern over martial law regulations prohibiting political leaders from addressing public meetings. He pointed out that he told President Yahya Khan of the need for active association of the people in overcoming the critical situation.

"But, he also bitterly criticised foreign interference in what he called 'attempts to bring about the disintegration of our country' and stressed that unity must be maintained at all cost."

ABOVE: A Bengali soldier tries out an anti-tank rocket captured from the West Pakistan troops during fighting to restore order in East Pakistan.

BELOW: Former Pakistan Foreign Minister, Mr. Zulfikar Bhutto, the leader of West Pakistan's majority People's Party, is pictured relaxing with his family in the gardens of their home in Karachi.

'I noticed at breakfast and dinner in the dining room that there were no other non-whites there. Everybody looked at me. I thoroughly enjoyed that and I went in to that restaurant a lot more than I normally would have done — just for the hell of it.'

There was little else to 'enjoy' during this assignment. For three days, with Paul, he filmed riots in the shattered streets of Gwelo and other African townships — the worst Rhodesia had experienced. Then 8,000 Africans marched towards the centre of the European area of the city — to be met by a wall of armed, steel-helmeted police, backed up by troops with light machine guns and automatic rifles. As the crowds pressed in he stood with the government forces shooting film of the angry masses. Tear-gas exploded all around and rioters were arrested.

Martin Bell, who travelled out with his own BBC crew, abandoned them to stay close to the Visnews ace. Like many before, he quickly discovered that Mohamed Amin could get into places nobody else could and grab the story that meant the most. He was prepared to visit the black townships where the European crews refused to risk their lives. Bell was out of the same mould. He wanted the truth — and to be first.

In his autobiography, *A Sort of Life*, Graham Greene notes that all writers need a little ice in their hearts. The same applies, more so perhaps, to today's television news cameramen. Without it, their life — ever on the brink of madness — would be unbearable.

Later they were caught amid flying stones and gunfire in Salisbury's African ghetto, Harare. Senior Visnews film editor Al Wells cut two minutes of typical, centre-of-the-fray Mohamed Amin footage: fire engines racing to a burning vehicle, stones raining down, bystanders bleeding onto their sheets and victims being lifted into ambulances, looted shops and banks.

The empathy between film editors and cameramen is remarkable. Though they rarely meet, each is dependent on the other. Few television news film editors can boast Al Wells' experience. He has been cutting stories for more than thirty years; some of the most dramatic and explosive stories of the last three decades and during this time has often been first to see Mohamed Amin's coverage. After screening hundreds of hours of his film and video footage Wells is in no doubt.

'It's a joy to work on his material. If we had 800 feet of film, which is twenty minutes worth of material, coming in from Mo, it would be very difficult to edit down to three minutes. Every scene would be a vital part of the story.'

9   Uganda's Asian Exodus

As well as his commercial acumen John Platter also remembers Mohamed Amin's warmth and generosity. 'On a personal level he was always terribly generous. He introduced me to the delights of Tandoori chicken and other fiery eastern delicacies, both at his home and at the many restaurants he frequented. He always liked a good meal and was always eager to be host. He rarely remembered a debt, which was among the most endearing of his many natural and social graces. And he had humour. He played many a practical joke. He enjoyed watching the fear play across an adversary's face as he was informed of some fictitious scoop. But he would right matters instantly. It was this easy manner too which made him as acceptable — for purely professional purposes — to murderous villains like his Uganda namesake as to the high and mighty.

'I hope that he hasn't lost that malleable versatility, because along with his pluck and intuitive savvy, it's what has made him today's superstar.'

You have to be black, brown or yellow to know the meanness of racial prejudice. But Amin has never let its shadow darken his sunny nature: either, as in Salisbury, Rhodesia, turning the tables on it or at least finding in it a good yarn. But when 'Field Marshal' Idi Amin Dada 'VC, DSO, MC, CBE', showed his true colours, there was nothing to laugh about. Calling his troops together at Tororo Barracks, close to the Kenya border, he told them that God had visited him in a dream with the divine instruction to expel the entire Asian population from Uganda.

Hours later, Uganda television cameras swept over delegates at a co-operative conference in the Kampala OAU Conference Centre and Idi Amin's bulky frame filled the screen: 'Asians came to Uganda to build the railway. The railway is finished. They must leave now.'

He gave them ninety days.

'I attended a luncheon which Idi Amin threw for the Asian leaders and various ambassadors and high commissioners,' Mohamed Amin recollects. 'The British High Commissioner Richard Slater was there. Apparently, at a meeting with Slater before this, Idi Amin agreed to withdraw the ninety-day deadline.

'At the luncheon, however, Amin made a statement directly opposed to this understanding and there was a heated exchange between the high commissioner and Idi Amin which I filmed. The envoy virtually accused Idi Amin of misleading him.

143

Above: Despite an agreement between Idi Amin and a visibly upset British High Commissioner Richard Slater, the Uganda dictator repeated his ninety-day ultimatum for Asians to leave the country in 1972 at a luncheon for the diplomatic corps based in Kampala. From this moment, relationships between the British government and the former colonial army sergeant began to deteriorate.

Ever the astute publicist, despite his threat to execute author Dennis Hills (right), Idi Amin culled massive coverage when he agreed to a stay of execution following an appeal by British Foreign Minister James Callaghan — and, holding his son Moses, posed happily with the two Englishmen.

Above: Idi Amin welcomes Mohamed Amin as the Uganda leader prepares for an interview. In August 1972 the dictator revealed to his troops at Tororo that God had appeared to him in a dream ordering him to expel all Asians from the country.

'But Idi Amin had obviously made up his mind that he was going to expel the Asians.'

Queues quickly formed outside the British High Commission in Kampala as Idi Amin, wearing the uniform of a paratroop general, gave vent to more vitriolic anti-Asian sentiment at a mass rally of university students.

'While I was there we also filmed long queues of Asians at the British High Commission getting their passports sorted out and a number of stories around Kampala of traders packing up and selling, even giving away, their belongings.'

On 31 August 1972 the first Asians to leave Uganda passed through Nairobi airport's transit lounge. Once again the cameraman's coverage touched hearts. Most of those expelled had been subjected to rigorous and embarrassing searches by Customs officials at Uganda's Entebbe Airport. Money and jewellery had been blatantly stolen under the pretext of 'confiscation'.

The paranoid psychotic, who was to dominate world headlines, had replaced the imagined genial clown. Idi Amin's antics had repercussions. In Kenya, the already nervous Asian business community quietly started to build more escape routes by sending its scions to Europe, the Americas and Australia to establish new roots, to start new businesses.

In Nairobi the 'For Sale' notices went up again and Mohamed Amin filmed the shuttered shops, the clearance sale signs, the Asian women walking past closed businesses and other familiar scenes. And in January 1973 the Kenya Government, too, set a deadline — 1 June — for 418 Asian traders to wind up their businessess and quit Kenya.

In February he filmed the second of his many Idi Amin interviews. The theme was the personal safety of General Idi Amin.

More routine stories followed: the original James Bond, Sean Connery, in action on the fairways of Nairobi's Muthaiga Golf Club during the Kenya Open Golf Championship; the opening of Hilton's £1.5-million Salt Lick Lodge complex in a private reserve close to Tsavo National Park; Amin's friend, game rancher Don Hunt, trapping eland, buffalo, zebra, leopard and rhino to send by a 'Flying Ark' to Nigeria — a gift from President Kenyatta and the people of Kenya to the West African state; and, in Addis Ababa, the installation of General Gowon, the Nigerian Head of State, as Chairman of the Organization of African Unity at the annual OAU Heads of State summit.

Then it was the twenty-first East African Safari Rally, marked by the publication of his second book, *East African Safari Rally Comes of Age*, under the Heinemann imprint, in the same format as his previous book. The rare copies that now come on the market celebrate both twenty-one years of rally adventure and his flair for telling an action story in a single still picture.

In the first photographic exhibition of his and Masud Quraishy's pictures, he demonstrated the same strength. Formally opened by

Kenya's Minister for Tourism and Wildlife, Juxon Shako, *Wildlife Heritage* was staged at the Watatu Gallery in the New Stanley Hotel. Ever a believer in the power of the media to which he has devoted his life, Mo hired a friend to film the ceremonies which Visnews syndicated around the world.

The exhibition received critical acclaim. 'Magnificent photographs with an impact that no words could ever equal . . . ' was typical of press reviews. Film star Paul Newman, on a visit to Kenya, wrote in the visitors book: 'This show should be taken to Hollywood and staged there!' Other visitors included executives of the World Bank, which was holding its annual conference in Nairobi's new twenty-nine-storey Kenyatta International Conference Centre.

Many of the photographs were taken in Kenya's northern deserts, Mohamed Amin's favourite photographic hunting ground. Lake Turkana exerted an unfailing fascination from his first visit in 1968, pulling him back time and again. He needed no excuse to visit this sere yet stunningly beautiful wilderness; so when it was designated the ideal place for observing the 30 June 1973 eclipse, which subsequently drew scientists from around the world, he arranged to go there about twelve days beforehand to film scientific preparations and local colour.

There was plenty of both. The local people with ages-old superstitions about the bad omens of an eclipse, and a way of life as near to untouched primitive society as any in Africa, were vivid counterpoint to the eighty American scientists, sponsored by the National Science Foundation, who set up workshops and astronomical laboratories on the lake shore at a cost of about US$600,000.

Mo agreed to split costs of the essential four-wheel drive vehicle with Ray Wilkinson, John Platter's UPI replacement. Afzal Awan arranged for them to hire his hunter cousin, Mohamed Bashir's Toyota Land Cruiser.

Mo's office major-domo, a remarkably hardy character of Nubian stock, was also in the party. Saidi Suleiman is a veteran of bush life who can conjure up five-star dinners in the middle of nowhere — an invaluable asset to Amin who likes his food.

'Since the hire was on a daily basis, we didn't want to take the car the night before so we agreed to pick it up at four in the morning when we were ready to leave,' Amin recalls. 'But when we arrived at Bashir's house the vehicle wouldn't start. The battery was dead. So we gave it a push-start and then loaded all our stuff, including a tent and supplies and set off.

'Just down the road, from the top of the Rift Valley escarpment, Ray, sitting next to me, decided to try to get some sleep and leaned against the door which immediately fell off. There was a sheer drop at the side — and we nearly lost Ray down the escarpment.

'I stopped and picked up the door. We couldn't replace it because the hinges had gone. Then, at the bottom of the escarpment, we had two punctures in the space of as many minutes.'

When, after several hours, they arrived at the very last outpost of civilization, Maralal, at the foot of the Matthews Mountain Range, too late to reach the lake the same day, the Cruiser was in a state of collapse, and the battery so anaemic it could barely raise enough power to light the indicators.

He went straight to the only garage which was run by an Asian called Bola who took one look at it and handed Amin a set of tools. 'You'll need these,' he said.

'I was surprised,' remembers Saidi, 'that the Boss did not turn back long before — and even more surprised when we made it to Maralal. It was late in the afternoon but after stopping for a cup of tea we drove on.

'We'd only gone about twenty miles however when the fan belt broke. There was no spare and it was impossible to walk back to town because of the wild game and the Samburu.'

All the land, from Maralal to the lake shores, is home to these fierce and proud people, kinsfolk of the Maasai. 'Not,' says Saidi, 'a good place to be left on your own.'

But the party were lucky. A rare car heading for Maralal came by. Mo and Ray thumbed it down, leaving Saidi on his own.

'After they'd gone two Samburu warriors came out of the forest,' recalls Saidi. 'They had the usual shuka [toga-like dress], ochre over the face, hair and body and all the war paint. They were young bucks out for blood having just been initiated and their spears were gleaming.

'They talked to me in Samburu which I don't understand. And they didn't know Swahili or English. Eventually, they just took off and disappeared into the forest from which they'd come. I was shit-scared and very glad when Mo and Ray came back so that we could pitch the tent.'

The tent they were carrying was new to them all. As soon as one pole was up, and they started on another, the first one collapsed. It was dark, too, which did not help as they kept bumping into each other. 'We couldn't switch on the car lights because of the state of the battery,' says Amin.

Eventually, however, they managed to get the tent to stay up. Everybody was exhausted and just wanting to sleep when Saidi's Samburu friends, with what sounded like the rest of the tribe, began chanting war songs in the forest.

'We couldn't tell how far away they were, but they sounded as if they were getting closer and closer. Then somebody said the magic words: "Let's get the hell out of here."

'We just threw everything into the back of the Cruiser and drove through the night until we reached Baragoi where there's a police post and it seemed reasonably safe to catch a little sleep before sun-up.'

The Press camp set up next day by Amin and Wilkinson at Loiyangalani in the grounds of the mission run by Father Joseph Polet was about three miles from the lake shore.

As usual Amin planned a stay of several days, shooting several other stories unconnected with the eclipse including Father Polet's work among 149 the impoverished el Molo and other communities along the lake shore. This tribute to the devotion of a saintly man was sent around the world by Visnews.*

He shot other stories, as well as the build-up to the eclipse, while trying to organize a new battery for the Cruiser. A swap with the battery used by the tourist lodge proved disastrous to both. Another flown in from Nairobi by his friends at Boskovic was slung in a bucket of water during the bumpy flight. 'We never got it. There were so many camps around that it went to the wrong one.'

Later, a BBC science correspondent flew in with Amin's occasional soundman, Saif Awan. Both the BBC and Amin needed to get their film back quickly and he persuaded the Ministry of Defence public relations officer, Daniel Gatangi, to arrange a lift on a Kenya Air Force plane, asking the unsuspecting Saif to drive the Land Cruiser back.

Left on the ground with no other choice of transport Ray Wilkinson was furious. His temper soon worsened when, going down the side of a steep bank to cross a dried-up river bed, the brakes failed. Saif gunned the vehicle up the opposite side, on which both back doors fell off. All the equipment slid out. Slowly too, the Cruiser slid backwards, crushing everything, including Wilkinson's personal belongings. Distraught with rage, he grabbed his typewriter, and leaping out of the vehicle, began the long twenty-five-mile hike back to Loiyangalani.

'That was the last I saw of him on that trip,' says Saidi.

'All the traffic was heading to Nairobi,' says Amin. 'Nobody was going the other way. Nobody stopped for Ray. They figured that he either knew what he was doing or was mad. He should have died. The heat out there is around 120°F and you quickly die of dehydration. There's no water. Nothing. I think he thought we were trying to kill him. He didn't speak to me for one or two years.'

Neither did Mohamed Bashir. 'When we got back and gave him his vehicle it was in bits.'

Three years earlier, in 1970, when Enos Nyagah was press attaché in Kenya's Paris Embassy, he met a European film-maker named Christian Zuber, who had filmed extensively in Marsabit before becoming a World Wildlife Fund publicity officer. Zuber and Nyagah discussed the region's rich wildlife, in particular the most majestic of all the species that Zuber had filmed — an elephant called Ahmed.

Zuber had caught wind of a story that two American millionaires had laid bets on which would be the first to shoot this, the last of the great tuskers.

The two wildlife lovers decided to launch a campaign to pressure the Kenya Government to protect Ahmed by encouraging people to write

*A few years later, Father Polet was murdered by Turkana outlaws, not many miles away in the wild country around Suguta Valley.

directly to President Kenyatta seeking his personal support for the elephant.

As a result, Ahmed made headlines as the first wild animal to be protected by a presidential decree. And with the decree came a round-the-clock guard of Kenya's top game rangers.

Now, years after the two began this campaign, Amin decided to safari to Marsabit to film a story about Ahmed. He took Kenya journalist Peter Moll with him as soundman and spent two days on the mountain filming the patriarch of the forest. Its two magnificent tusks, worth several thousand dollars, were reckoned to weigh more than 200 lbs.

Finally the old and, as it turned out, ailing animal had had enough. Irritated by their constant presence, and already sick, Ahmed charged the two and they took to their heels. Amin darted to one side of a giant podo tree, Moll the other. Between them stretched the cable fastened between the Auricon recorder which Moll carried around his neck and the camera which Mo carried.

Amin kept running, but Moll found himself stopped abruptly by the cord.

'I was certainly not going to retreat,' says Mo.

Moll came round the tree like a whiplash only inches from the lunging tusks.

The film was sent to London by air freight and processed and edited the day that Ahmed died. Shown by Visnews-subscribing stations around the world it served as an obituary to this mammoth of the Marsabit forest. The impulse which led Mo to film Ahmed just before its death is typical of countless instances which have persuaded people that he has some kind of sixth sense.

Perhaps another was the assignment in November 1973 when Visnews sent him on a week-long journey through Ethiopia, an all too tragic rehearsal for the story that he would film in 1984.

An estimated 100,000 people had already died when the world's attention was drawn to the drought which had begun years earlier. For two years, said David Nicholson's script to Amin's report, the people dug into their grain reserves, then began slaughtering their cattle.

> This year, as the drought continued to suck the land dry, they began selling their farms and homes for food. Finally, they began the long and pathetic march to the relief centres.
>
> But although the disaster was growing to massive proportions there was apparently no plea for international aid from the Ethiopian Government. The Ethiopian Government has now denied it deliberately kept the famine a secret for political reasons and has claimed its pleas to the world were ignored . . . '

As the commentary went on, it became distressingly like that which would follow in the 1980s.

> Since then relief workers have reported horror stories of whole villages dying of malnutrition and disease. In one village, 212 children 151

out of 250 are reported to be orphans while in another at least a third of the current survivors will still die despite medical aid.

Poor communications are a major hindrance and only a small proportion of the starving population are receiving the vital protein and vitamin supplements . . . and pessimistic officials now estimate that another £11 million is needed over the next six months if a major human tragedy is to be averted and the majority of victims survive. . . .

The words could have been laid over the horrifying report that he was to film eleven years later.

Al Wells remembers: 'He shot 400 feet on his first report and this story was wanted for the Eurovision exchange out of London. Everyone in Visnews HQ was very excited, but time was against us, what with Customs clearance at Heathrow, and developing the film.

'The processed film was given to me at 15.55. Eurovision started at 16.00 and everyone was in a panic. The pressure was on. It was my job to make sure that this story got on air. But not 400 feet — that was much too long for EVN.

'I just cut the first 200 feet from the 400 feet roll — I didn't even look at this last 200 feet — and put that into Eurovision.

'Everyone said the coverage was first class although it was unedited. This is what I mean. How can one thank a man like Mohamed Amin for a job more than well done.'

World reaction to this 1973-74 tragedy set the stage for the crisis which brought down the Royal House of Ethiopia, whose Emperor Haile Selassie claimed a lineage going back three thousand years to the House of Solomon and a blood line traced to Sheba.

But Selassie remained in power long enough to visit Kenya and share the spotlight with his old friend Kenyatta on 12 December 1973 when the country marked Ten Great Years of Uhuru (Independence) — the day Amin launched his photobiography of the Kenya leader, published by the East African Publishing House.

Selassie's days were numbered, however, and in March 1974 Amin was in Addis with John Bierman, the BBC reporter, to cover events which precipitated the Emperor's overthrow.

Years before, Bierman had launched the *Nation* newspaper for the Aga Khan and had frequently used Mo's picture material, particularly that of the Safari Rally. Now they worked together reporting a student boycott of the new government which Selassie had appointed to forestall his downfall.

Amin was known to His Majesty. 'One of my earlier documentaries, *To Build A Nation*, was made for the Ethiopian Government. It was commissioned by the prime minister and the Cabinet as a present for the Emperor on his eightieth birthday.

'We travelled the entire country using helicopters and planes. I remember landing in the Danakil Depression, when it must have been

140° Fahrenheit under the shade of the wing of the DC-3.

'Nobody was there and we hung around for a while and then saw a mirage in the distance that gradually transformed into a truck.

'There were half a dozen Danakils armed to the teeth in it. They didn't know what we were doing there but they drove us through this fantastic landscape to a huge sulphur mine. When we got into an office I was desperately thirsty. There were diesel barrels filled with water, but you could see the scum and it smelled so bad it was undrinkable.

'I decided to have a shower instead. It was an open shower and I went under it fully clothed. It was so hot that as soon as I walked out of the shower I was bone dry.

'My soundman collapsed while we were filming. Our pilot also got very edgy. He was waiting at the plane and he finally took off and flew very low over us to tell us to get back to the airstrip. It was his way of saying "Get the hell out of there."

'We were supposed to film at some other place but none of us was fit enough. Instead we flew to the nearest city which was Asmara. When we got to the hotel I remember I drank twenty-six large Cokes one after the other and I was still thirsty. We were pretty well totally dehydrated. I think another hour and we would have passed the point of no return.

'It was decided – despite our protests that it was not a good idea to have a two-hour-long documentary – that the commentary for the Amharic version would be done by the Emperor himself.

'We were to film the Emperor recording his commentary. We went to the palace and set up the mikes and cameras. I asked the staff if I could put a neck-mike on the Emperor as that would produce a better sound quality but they were horrified. "Absolutely not. That is totally forbidden. The Emperor has never been touched and it will not be allowed."

'There was not a lot I could do, so I set up the other mikes. But I kept the neck-mike handy because I was going to ask the Emperor myself. Physically he was short and skinny, but he radiated power.

'When he was on his chair looking all grand and ready to go I approached him, bowed and said, "Your Majesty. Can I please put a microphone around your neck as it will give a better quality of sound?"

'He was a bit stunned but extremely friendly and said: "Would it give better sound?"

'I said, "Yes it would" and he said, "Fine".

'So I undid the neck button of his shirt and fixed the microphone. The security guards were absolutely furious but there was nothing that they could do as I was dealing with the King himself.'

Now, as the storm clouds gathered over Addis Ababa in 1974, Amin recorded a sadder occasion. They were in the Emperor's office on 5 March to film his nationwide address on television, and his pledge to write a new civil rights constitution for his troubled kingdom. A few days after this Amin filmed what was effectively the Emperor's last public appearance: it was an elegy for a deposed monarch more eloquent than words, the lone,

Filming *To Build A Nation*, commissioned by the Ethiopian government to commemorate Emperor Haile Selassie's 80th birthday in 1972, Mohamed Amin and producer Keith Hulse travelled the length and breadth of this vast country in the air force's veteran DC-3s in the company of Tafari Wassen (right), who later became head of information at the Relief and Rehabilitation Commission.

During a visit to Ethiopia in the 1960s Emperor Haile Selassie's palace lions gave scope for imaginative pictures.

In a more sombre mood, in 1974 Mohamed Amin filmed a final elegy for the deposed monarch as he made his last public appearance and disappeared to die a lonely death.

frail and tiny figure with his pet dog at his heels walking back to his palace to vanish forever from public sight.

By September, when the Emperor's whereabouts and health had become a mystery, the political situation in Ethiopia was sad contrast to the ebullience in Kenya. There, in the second general elections since Independence, in which opposition leader Oginga Odinga was again banned from standing by the ruling Kanu Party, three cabinet ministers, including Foreign Minister Dr Njoroge Mungai, were ousted by voters. Stomping through the country with his familiar limp, Amin recorded this demonstration of democracy on film throughout the month-long campaign leading up to the polls.

The limp is his most distinctive physical feature. Many people believe he was born with it but in fact it was caused by one of his many car accidents.

'The National Youth Service was building this major road all the way from Nanyuki to Moyale on the Ethiopian border with American equipment,' Amin explains. 'The embassy was interested in some pictures, so I borrowed one of their vehicles, a four-wheel drive Wagoneer.

'Just as I was leaving, Paul Toulmin-Rothe, who was still in Dar es Salaam and had done a story on the diamond mines in upcountry Tanzania, arrived. He had hitched a lift on a plane to Nairobi.

'I asked him to come along. We were also with the *Der Spiegel* correspondent, Peter Seidlitz, and his wife Janice.

'When we got close to Isiolo I wanted to do some tracking shots of the new road so I asked Paul to drive while I sat on the bonnet. He did that, and then I took the wheel back. Paul kept insisting that he wanted to drive, but I'm a rather nervous passenger.

'He was so insistent however that finally I gave in. He drove some distance overtaking a couple of other cars and then skidded. On slippery murram [red soil] the worst thing you can do is brake. But Paul just hit the brake very hard indeed and we rolled several times. I was thrown out of the car unconscious.'

The next thing he remembers was lying on the side of the road looking up at Paul who was very shaken.

'Mohamed, Mohamed. Don't worry, I'll look after the office.'

'Paul, where are we?'

'Don't worry Mo. I'll look after the office.'

'Yes, Paul but where are we?'

'We were going to Moyale.'

'But who was driving?'

'Don't worry about that. It'll be all right. But please I have to tell you something. Please say you were driving.'

Slowly, the memory returned.

'But Paul, it was you who was driving.'

'I was driving. But please don't tell anybody. I don't have a licence and I've never driven before.'

Mo thought, 'God, this is a nice time to tell me.'

Soon after, he was taken to the mission clinic at Laisamis. They radioed a doctor in Moyale who drove four hours through the night to Laisamis as Paul sat next to Amin in the clinic flicking mosquitoes away with a fly whisk.

'The doctor thought I had a broken leg but couldn't do very much without an X-ray. Next morning the American Embassy sent a Flying Doctor plane to lift us out.

'Apparently, one of the cars passing the crash saw the vehicle and because it had US diplomatic plates they had called the Embassy to say there had been a serious accident.

'I was flown to Nairobi and taken straight to Aga Khan Hospital and they called Dr Yusuf Kodwavwala, who had been my surgeon when I last broke my leg. He was on his way by air to Nanyuki but they were able to contact his plane and he turned back.'

Mo asked to see his X-rays — unusual in Nairobi, but the nurses knew him. He took one look and almost passed out again. The bone was shattered.

'Sister, these are not my X-rays. Can you bring my X-rays?'

'These are your X-rays.'

'No. They can't be. It's not that bad.'

'I'm sorry. That's your X-ray.'

At this point Kodwavwala walked in and after looking at the X-rays, he told Amin, 'You have a problem.'

'Yusuf, you're going to have to do something about this.'

'You have two options. One, we put you in traction with your leg all strapped up and leave you hanging there for six or seven months and hope the bone will join and heal.

'The other option is to cut you up and do what we can. The chances are that if we cannot fix it we'll have to amputate your leg.'

Mo thought about it for a couple of seconds. 'There's no way I'm going to have my leg in traction for six months. The other option is fine, but please make sure you don't remove my leg. Because if you do there's going to be a lot of trouble about it.'

'I'll obviously do my best.'

Next morning he was wheeled into the operating theatre and Kodwavwala worked on him for several hours.

'He put a rod rather like a shish kebab skewer through the bone and spliced all the pieces together with wires. I was in the hospital for two weeks. I should have stayed for six weeks or so, but I got bored and left. I didn't really give my leg a chance to heal. This is why it's an inch or so shorter than the other one.

'Kodwavwala did a terrific job. Since then I've never had any problems with my leg. I've been on mountains up to 23,000 feet. I've done expeditions and many other things and everything has been fine.

'I was out of the hospital but Paul, who suffered no visible injuries,

When he was not filming, Mo absorbed himself in happy hours watching his son
Salim grow up.

Victims of the world's first jumbo
jet crash — the Lufthansa 747
which stalled seconds after take-
off at Nairobi's Embakasi Airport
in 1974. For perhaps the only time
in his life, Mohamed Amin missed
the news of an exclusive on his
doorstep but returned from
northern Kenya in time to film the
aftermath of the tragedy and the
still-smouldering debris.

stayed in for six weeks and Janice, who had no injuries whatsoever, was in for more than two months. She thought some fluid dripping out of her nose was her brains leaking away.

'I visited them regularly on the second floor in a private wing where there was no lift.'

So far Mohamed had never admitted professional defeat. But even the best err. It's axiomatic, of course, for any international newsman to remain in touch with events. Out in the field, Amin tunes to the BBC World Service at least three times a day with almost religious fervour.

Yet in late November 1974, filming a story on the Flying Doctor pilot Dr Anne Spoerry who tended the sick over an area of several thousand square miles, and collecting material for the book *Peoples of Kenya*, he did not for once tune in his short-wave radio at their camp at Alia Bay on the shores of Lake Turkana.

'We arrived very late and we were very tired from hopping around various points on the lake shore filming the Flying Doctor as well as the people. I just went straight to sleep and didn't listen to the radio.

'Next morning we flew back to Nairobi where we were met at Wilson Airport by the wife of one of the missionaries. [Most of the work around Lake Turkana was being done by the missionaries.]

'She offered to give us a ride home. As we were driving along she was saying how awful the accident was. So I said: "What accident?"

'She said, "The crash of the Lufthansa 747 jumbo jet."

'I said, "Oh. Were there a lot of casualties?"

'A number of people had died, but all along I assumed that this must have happened somewhere else in the world.

'It wasn't until we were halfway to my house that she actually said the crash had happened at Nairobi Airport.

'When I heard that I asked her to drop me at my office. In fact, Paul was in the office having just done a second story on the aftermath, and he and I went back and did another story and then on to the hospital for survivor shots, and then the mortuary for bodies.

'Because he just could not look at the dead and the wounded, especially children, still strapped in their chairs, he filmed quite a lot of the carnage looking away from the camera. Even so, Paul did a tremendous job.'

10   Idi Amin's OAU Circus

Mohamed Amin's 'gift of the gab' is spell-binding. People fall to his charm and, in retrospect, often contrary and contradictory logic, as swiftly as he captures them in film through his lens. Most times, however, his line of thought is direct, piercing all hyperbole and hypocrisy. He sets about resolving problems with a powerful will.

When new restrictions limiting his right to enter Britain were endorsed on his new passport, No. 463577, issued on 20 May 1974 by the British High Commission in Nairobi he had just such a problem. In effect, these 1968 laws created first, second, third and ultimately fourth-class citizens. For him, however, the regulations were yet another challenge to be overcome.

'I had what they call a D passport, basically a useless piece of paper. Because it gave no right of entry to Britain it was not accepted by many other countries. You had to get visas for countries which did not normally require them for British passport holders.

'It wasn't just frustrating. It was very difficult to work. Once, for example, I was a guest of British Airways on an inaugural flight to Japan. The Japanese Embassy in Nairobi said that if I had a British passport I didn't need a visa.

'But when we landed in Tokyo all my other colleagues went through and I was held. Apart from the fact that it was embarrassing for me, it was also embarrassing for British Airways. I was their guest in Tokyo.

'I was taken into a little room and the immigration officers got to work with lots of little papers and finally these were handed to me and I was told I had been declared a Prohibited Immigrant for arriving in Tokyo without a passport.

'Since I was only on what we call a "jolly" it didn't really matter, so I said, "What next?"

'They said, "We have to tell you your rights. And your rights are that you can make an appeal. The appeal will be taken to court tomorrow morning and the decision will be conveyed to you."

'They filled in more forms which they finally asked me to sign and I was told by this jolly little Japanese man, "You have now appealed and the result of your appeal will be given to you tomorrow."

'I asked what I should do in the meantime and they said, "We will allow you to go the hotel with the rest of your party, but you are not allowed to leave the hotel until your appeal has been heard.'"

Next morning, while the others went to Kyota, Amin waited for the result of his appeal. About the middle of the day he got a call from the airport to say it had been successful. He could stay in Tokyo — or indeed Japan — for three months.

'I don't want to stay in Tokyo for three months. I only want to stay for two weeks.'

'Well, the judge said you should stay for three months, so we'll give you a three months' visa.'

Because of that passport he was thrown out of Egypt. Travelling on a document which, in effect, had no value, he had problems in a number of other countries, too.

'I even had to have a visitor's pass to enter Britain. It was absolutely absurd. I made a lot of noises and lots of protests but didn't get very far.

'Then my wife's passport ran out. As she was a Tanzanian, it meant that she had to go to Dar es Salaam and wait there two months to get it renewed, which didn't sound like a very good idea. I suggested the best option was that I should try to get her a British passport.

'I told the British High Commission I would like my wife to get a British passport. They said, "Of course. You're British and you're wife is entitled to be British."

A week later he collected Dolly's new passport, a proper one with the right of abode in UK. He went back and saw the immigration officer.

'Look, you must have made a mistake. My wife can't have the right of abode in the UK because I have no rights at all and she's only getting this passport because of my nationality.'

'Well, that's true, but the law is that your dependant, in this case your wife, has the right of abode in the UK.'

It all sounded absurd and he made more protests, but the counsellor said:

'I'm sorry. There's nothing we can do. That's the law.'

Amin protested. He had been British all his life with a useless passport, and here was his wife with the right of abode in the UK. It was ridiculous.

'What about my passport? Don't I get some sort of rights?'

'Look, the only one way you can get permanent residence in Britain is by accompanying your wife. If you are landed unconditionally at London Airport, then you will have the right of readmission into Britain, which means you can go back there any time and even live there.'

'This is ridiculous. I don't wish to go to Britain to live. I'm quite comfortable in Kenya and I would be cheating if I said that's what I really want to do.'

'I don't really wish to hear that. That's the only way around this problem.'

'But if I fill in a form saying all this, you know that it's not true.'

'That's not my concern. That's the way it is.'

Amin filled in the form and they put a stamp in his passport which said, 163

'Accompanying wife for permanent settlement'.

'Salim and Dolly were allowed through without any problems,' Amin remembers, 'but I was marched off to the Heathrow Airport hospital or clinic where they took chest X-rays and passed me as medically fit.'

Another Asian in the waiting room was having problems: nobody could understand him. In Punjabi, he told Amin that he had come to live in England permanently but didn't understand a word of English. All he had was a note which he had been told to hand to officials. It read simply: 'I am going to Bradford. Please show me the way.' In Urdu.

'I think', says Amin, 'that about summed up the tragedy of the whole situation.'

Two hours later he was allowed into Britain, an unconditional right of readmission stamp in his passport. 'And that was that. Now my passport reads, "Holder has the right of readmission" which means I can go in and out of Britain as I like. The only difference between mine and a *British* passport is that theirs is not stamped — while mine is.'

That night in his London hotel room he watched Ludovic Kennedy interview Idi Amin's runaway Foreign Minister Wanume Kibedi on television. Asked how Idi Amin would behave during the forthcoming OAU summit in Kampala, Kibedi replied:

'Well, I think that would be anybody's guess but being an eccentric he will obviously do anything. . . . I can say that as far as his mental strain is concerned he's got this letter which he calls MC and he says this represents Metal Cross which is a rich honour.'

Kennedy: 'Does he have it?'

Kibedi: 'Oh! He just ordered it himself but as far as the people of Uganda are concerned MC stands not for Metal Cross but for Mental Case. That's what he is.'

Watching Kibedi, Mo recalled the conversation he had filmed two weeks before between Idi Amin and Canadian TV journalist Martyn Burke. It provided some revealing passages.

A lot of people say: 'Uganda's a very dangerous place to go. You shouldn't go, a lot of strange things happen there.' This is a feeling that a lot of people have. How do you think this has happened?

Amin: They got these facts from the people whose business was taken away, and some of these people are in Nairobi. Also, most of the headquarters of the British news media, who are against Uganda, are in Kenya. So, those people who are reporting about East Africa are in Nairobi and they are against the Republic of Uganda. They are also very jealous about Uganda's natural resources. We have got the best climate in the world, very good natural resources, and good national parks for tourists. Our people have got enough food and yet people say there is fear to come to Uganda because Uganda is insecure! But now Uganda is going to attract more tourists and I am sure that you find the situation is different. I am supposed to drive with over a thousand guards to guard me, but actually I drive alone. You do not find in Uganda even a single road-block on the

Idi Amin's seven-year rule of Uganda was notable for excesses at every level of human behaviour — especially execution and murder. Public executions were commonplace. As a state of anarchy developed, soldiers like Sabastiano Namirundu were stripped, dressed in a brief apron, tied to a tree and gunned down by their army colleagues.

roads except at the Customs at the border . . . You will be with me in the town and you can tell me where to go and I will drive you. And you will find that everybody likes me and I can eat and drink with the people all because of Watergate. And President Ford has got a lot of problems. It is too early for me to tell you now, because I am still studying his problems, but I have been briefed by American people.

There was a cable which you sent to President Nixon wishing him a 'speedy recovery' from the Watergate situation. (Amin laughs.) A lot of people were not really sure whether you were joking or not. What was the reason for that cable?

Amin: Because he was very sick, he had to be taken to hospital and the people were very worried he was going to die and he might not give the answers on the case of Watergate for the whole world to know. Because nobody knows, the only person who can answer is Nixon. He is the person who started this Watergate affair and if he dies I am sure the whole blame will be pushed on to him. That is the reason why I wished him a very quick recovery, so that he may be in a position to answer all those questions even now.

Often, people are not sure if you are joking or not. For instance, did you really want Scottish bodyguards?

Amin: The officers who promoted me up to the rank of major were all Scottish. General Blair is, I think, now commander-in-chief in Scotland and I would be happy if anybody came from there to be an escort to me or a bodyguard . . . and I will be talking to them about their traditions, because I have been with them for a very long time and they are very brave people in the battlefield. I remember very well that when they were going to war at night they played their pipes and they were very brave. I am very happy to remember what we had with them during the Second World War.

(At Mo's suggestion, and to give a practical demonstration of his popularity and confidence in the midst of large crowds, Idi Amin took his questioner and the cameraman for a ride around Kampala in his Citroen Maserati.)

Don't you usually drive around in an open jeep?

Amin: I drive the jeep, especially when I go to visit the army barracks or when I go to military parades — and also sometimes to get the fresh air.

Most other leaders have security guards. Why don't you have them along with you?

Amin: Because my people love me. They consider me one of their heroes. And I don't fear anybody.

(At this point the car stopped at traffic lights, and the dictator talked briefly with passers-by through the car window. Mo was still filming.)

All the stores up and down this street, were they all Asian owned until two years ago?

Amin: All were Asian stores. Now the owners are Africans. And you find that the town is more beautiful than before and the shops are more full of commodities than before. This is the extension to the post office and this is the Uganda Commercial Bank and that is a shopping centre. . . . Down this street also, down Bokassa Street, there are many shops. One of them belongs to my former wife; she is very rich.

By the way, how many children have you?

Amin: Twenty — and I like them very much.

Is there any place you'd like to stop?

Amin: Anywhere, you tell me. I suggest we go where it is very crowded. You would not think that any Head of State could come here because of security. I want to take you where there are private people, because some of the restaurants here are owned by the government and I don't want that. I want to take you to the ordinary local people.

Are all these stalls owned by Africans?

Amin: Yes, all. They were given to them free of charge.

Idi Amin got out of the car and Mo filmed the large crowd of people pushing forward to shake the dictator's hand. There was no sign of bodyguards or any other security. Idi Amin was completely unprotected in the jostling crowd.

Mo had already established a solid working relationship with Idi Amin, but was always careful to remain detached. It was part of his commitment to what management consultant Sean Hawkins calls 'Mo's own standards'.

'Two major qualities stand out for me in Mohamed Amin's life,' says Hawkins. 'Firstly, he has always been a true artist, in that he has always set his own standards of excellence, and unless he himself considers something to be "really great", all the honours and cheering of the world around him wouldn't convince him otherwise.

'"They think it's great stuff," he has often said in his own blunt manner, "But I know it's crap!"

'Yet each time he *has* achieved a "great" in his own eyes, rather than inflate his ego in any way it always seemed only to spark his creativity and determination to embark on the next project — always to be better and more ambitious than the last.'

This insistence brought him into conflict with publisher John Nottingham of the East African Publishing House over the book *One Man, One Vote*, a photo-record of the 14 October 1974 Kenya general elections. It was supposed to appear within weeks of the polls, but suffered from one protracted delay after another and was not published until a year later. The argument was about delays, not money. 'Money is not so important for me', says Amin, 'as far as my way of life is concerned. Obviously you can't run a business if you're losing money all the time. You have to be realistic from time to time about certain projects that you take on.

'I don't think I would consciously take another party for a ride knowing I was taking him for a ride. But if you just sold something for fifty pence that you should have sold for a pound, you try to make it up on other projects. Sometimes you can, sometimes you can't . . .'

At this time his interest in books was certainly not financial. Amin received the princely sum of 250 shillings for his work. For him, books 167 were fun affairs – and still are.

It was Nottingham of East African Publishing House who approached him to do a book after the murder of J. M. Kariuki, a prominent left-wing Kikuyu politician, as a photo-tribute. Not such a fun book, but he tackled it with his usual enthusiasm and diligence.

A bomb blast at a Nairobi bus depot on 1 March 1975 had left twenty-seven people dead and ninety injured, many seriously. It was the third explosion in Nairobi in two weeks. Minutes after the bomb went off, Mo filmed the devastation and then the victims being treated in hospital.

Only days later the bullet-riddled body of Kariuki was discovered. He had disappeared the day after the bus bomb. Amin filmed the scenes outside the mortuary, and the arrest of students demonstrating against his murder.

The riots got worse. Two days later police had to use tear gas to disperse them. As the riot squad swept through the campus he was in the middle of the action. He accompanied the cortege home to Gilgil where Kariuki was buried on Sunday 16 March.

'I was given old pictures by two of his wives and collected a lot of my own pictures and we were actually in the process of putting it together when, one day, my office door was flung open and in walked two CID guys. One was Sokhi Singh, accompanied by a European.

Sokhi produced his identity card but Mo told him his face was good enough. Sokhi was heavyweight stuff, an assistant commissioner of police.

'Well, can we get to the point? Are you doing a book on J. M. Kariuki?'

'Well, yes, there was some suggestion of doing a book.'

'Are you doing a book?'

'Yes, there's some thought about it. But I haven't done it yet.'

'Well, hand over all the material to us or we will search your office.'

'Have you got a search warrant?'

'That's no problem. We can get one in the next five minutes.'

'Oh well, I just have a few pictures. Can I get them for you from the next office?'

'No, we'll come with you.'

The two counted them and put them in their briefcases.

'We're taking these pictures. You know how to get in touch with us.'

Amin goes on: 'I called John Nottingham immediately to find out how the hell they could have learned about it since only two or three people knew about this project anyway.

'But while I was talking John said, "They're here," and put the telephone down. Obviously they went straight from my office to his. I never saw the pictures again, nor was the book ever finished.'

Amin was filming stories almost daily: the Easter weekend Safari Rally which started on 27 March, a story on an orphaned rhino in the Nairobi National Park animal orphanage, a track and field meet starring Kenya's new generation of track stars, and more big game trapping on the million-acre Galana cattle and wildlife ranch in the arid wastes of Tsavo East National Park.

Then, another distressing preview of the tragedy which was to strike Ethiopia in 1984. Famine again cast its shadow across that country on a scale even greater than in 1973. Half a million people were reported starving to death. It marked, in fact, the beginning of the ten-year-long drought that ended in the calamity that shook the world in 1984. Amin flew to the war-stricken Ogaden region of Ethiopia with the BBC's John Osman, who had taken over in Nairobi from Ronnie Robson.

Once again his shot-list reads all too much like the 1984 famine: 'Emaciated children sitting on mat; mother holds emaciated child; German nurse holding starving child; English nurse holding starving child and handing it to mother; young starving child in nurse's arms; child drinking from mug; children receiving food; young children being given food by nurse; mother and child; mothers waiting for food handout; young child covered in sores and flies; mothers and children.'

The Ogaden, Osman reported, 'is one of the world's vast scrublands. . . At this particular relief camp children are dying every day of sheer starvation.'

The English nurse Amin filmed holding a dying child was Ruth Thomas, future wife of the BBC radio reporter Mike Wooldridge with whom he planned his 1984 Ethiopian famine coverage. Ruth, working with Oxfam, was particularly struck by Amin's sensitive approach to filming the story.

But it was the antics of Idi Amin, rather than the thousands dying of hunger in Ethiopia which occupied the television screens of the so-called developed world throughout this year. In June and early July the dictator was busy preparing the colourful, but bizarre, annual OAU Heads of State summit in Kampala.

'It was a big event from the news point of view. We took over a house, installed our own darkroom and moved staff from Nairobi to Kampala. We had a great number of assignments,' recalls Mo.

During this conference, the Ugandan leader exploited Mohamed Amin's work to boost his own alter-ego. 'Idi Amin used two of my pictures. One of them on a very colourful OAU T-shirt showing Idi Amin in full dress uniform with all his medals.

'He actually pointed it out to me. He was waiting in the VIP lounge at the airport for Heads of State to arrive. I had already seen the T-shirt. Many people were wearing it. It was also on dress material and various other fabrics. I felt I should ask for a royalty.

'When he called me over he introduced me to one of the Heads of State and said, "This is Idi Amin Junior — and this [he thrust out his chest] is his picture."

'At this point I almost said, "Yes and I haven't been paid for it". But I had second thoughts. I think if I had asked for a royalty it would have been a disaster. For me.'

During the fortnight-long prelude and actual summit, which opened in 169

Ex-British serviceman Bob Astles,
a former pilot sergeant who served
in East Africa and earned notoriety
as one of Idi Amin's closest
confidantes, at a press conference
in the gardens of Amin's official
Kampala residence.

Kampala on 18 July 1975, his cameras barely stopped turning. A great deal of money had been spent to spruce-up Kampala and starring in this burlesque mounted on the refurbished stage were a fashion spectacular; a Miss OAU Bathing Beauty contest; an OAU 2,500-mile car rally; the opening of Uganda's new colour television system; the dramatic and unrehearsed overthrow of General Gowon as President of Nigeria; and a stand-up drama turned into macabre farce, the 'Battle for Capetown' involving the strafing and bombing of an uninhabited Lake Victoria Island. As final titillation there was Idi Amin's unannounced wedding to a fifth wife.

Tanzania, Botswana and Zambia added to the theatre by boycotting the event, with Tanzania accusing the OAU of remaining silent when it should be naming Idi Amin a 'murderer, an oppressor, a black fascist and a self-confessed admirer of fascism'.

'This was one of the few conferences that the Libyan leader Gaddafi attended. On the opening day as he entered the conference hall, where the name Libya was written in English on the delegate's nameplate, I filmed him as he crossed out the English and wrote the Arabic script for Libya over it,' recalls Mohamed Amin.

Some Britons emerged without credit from this carnival-style conference. On the eve of the summit, at a reception for the foreign ministers, Idi Amin was carried into the reception on a litter by a group of British expatriates.

'Apparently, this was meant to be a bit of a joke,' says Mohamed Amin. 'But in fact Idi Amin outsmarted the Brits. He planned it very well. He had it filmed and photographs were given to every Head of State and every delegate to show that there had been a turnaround in Africa: that it was now the white man who carried Africans.'

The group, which also prostrated itself in front of the tyrant before carrying him, afterwards accused Mo of rigging the pictures that appeared in newspapers around the world: an accusation reported in the British *Daily Telegraph* and on BBC radio.

Independent examination of the pictures provided definite evidence that Wing Commander James Cobb and his cronies did kneel at the feet of Idi Amin, and carry him on a litter.

Idi Amin was a newsman's joy. Once switched on, he was hard to silence. At an informal Press conference after being named OAU chairman, he rambled on about his brothers and sisters in Tanzania and the need for Arab investment to prop up Africa's economy.

Barely literate sentences, such as 'the most important is the economic... I am now the current chairman of the OAU, I have already won my economic revolution in Uganda . . . I am no longer slave, even my people no longer slaves', ran on like a river in flood. Yet Idi Amin was no lovable clown. Observer and reporter, Mo kept his distance.

On the second day of the conference he picked up a Reuters flash on the Press Room telex — Nigerian President General Gowon had been

Europeans based in Uganda seemed only too eager to pander to the huge ego of the man who overthrew Milton Obote — kneeling in homage before him and his aides to swear loyalty.

Some Europeans, watched by an exultant Astles, even carried the dictator in triumph on a litter into the grounds of his official residence for a cocktail party on the eve of the Kampala OAU summit — then accused Mohamed Amin of faking the picture.

overthrown in a coup. 'I was upstairs just watching the Reuters wire machine. I ripped off the story, went straight downstairs, picked up my cameras and started filming Gowon who was sitting with lots of other Heads of State. I filmed from every angle.'

Pressmen enduring a boring speech from a United Nations envoy watched and wondered as the Nairobi newsman filmed the Nigerian Head of State, close-up, front, profile, back view. 'Then Gowon's foreign minister came over and whispered in his ear. This I filmed, too. Gowon's face dropped and he got up and left.'

Still filming, Mo followed Gowon leaving the conference hall. The cameraman asked if he could have a statement. 'Statement about what?' asked the still stunned leader, and walked on.

'I had the television and stills as an exclusive,' Amin recalls fondly.

Next day Gowon held a Press conference. 'There was a lot of drama about who would be allowed to cover it but eventually we were all allowed in. Gowon's dignity was absolute. He was one of my favourite leaders. There he sat, quoting Shakespeare:

> All the world's a stage,
> And all the men and women merely players,
> They have their exits and their entrances
> And one man in his time plays many parts

'He said he would not answer any questions but wished the new leaders of Nigeria and its people well. This was the most dignified exit I've seen. Most deposed leaders moan and bitch and threaten what they will do when they come back. Compared to all of them, he was great.'

With Gowon's overthrow came a hurried exodus of OAU leaders, many fearful for their own positions, returning to their countries.

As an added attraction, the flabby dictator celebrated his fifth wedding to nineteen-year-old Sarah, a member of his 'Revolutionary Suicide Mechanized Units', his co-driver in the OAU car rally. 'Idi's wedding was actually held on the quiet at his house. It was only when we approached him and pointed out that most of the people had missed the wedding that he decided to restage it in a big hall and invite all the media.'

The second wedding had western razzmatazz. Sarah, decked out in a white gown and veil, cut a three-tier wedding cake. Guests included President Siyad Barré of Somalia, President Nimeiri of the Sudan, and other African leaders. Best man was PLO leader Yasser Arafat, complete with six-gun and holster.

The strategic 'Capetown' exercise ended in pantomime — and murder. The Ugandan Air Force's bomb aiming was so adrift that they missed not only the South African flag, which denoted the heart of the city, but the island itself.

'Some of the VIP guests began to worry they might hit the spectators too,' remembers Mo. Idi Amin grew angrier and angrier. Then the Ugandan invasion force 'hit the beaches of Capetown'. The climax of the landing was the uprooting of the hated South African flag which Idi's

Among the revolutionary leaders who paid court to Idi Amin were Libya's
Moamar al Gaddafi.

Cuba's Fidel Castro was another who called on Idi Amin.

bombers had missed. Even that was farcical. So firmly was it embedded on Ugandan soil the soldiers couldn't budge it.

The enraged Idi Amin issued his orders. That night Brigadier Smurts Guweddeko, Commander of the Uganda Air Force, was relieved of his command. His corpse was found a few weeks later.

Now Mohamed Amin's thoughts turned to the wilderness he loved. His mind was already occupied with plans for an expedition around his favourite stamping ground, Lake Turkana, formerly Lake Rudolf. It had never been circumnavigated by motorized vehicle: the house magazine of Total, the oil company, which sponsored the expedition, explained why:

> There are no roads around the lake and the terrain is daunting — tracks across lava flows, dry river beds, rock fields and mountains such as Teleki's Volcano, Mount Kulal and Mount Lapur. Only four-wheel drive vehicles can negotiate this sort of country. [Lake] Rudolf was 'discovered' by Teleki and von Hohnel in the 1880s. Two other journeys were undertaken by Sir George Dyson and Vivian Fuchs in this century but none of these explorers went all the way round.
>
> Apart from chalking up a 'first' for circumnavigating Rudolf, the expedition expects to collect useful geographical and scientific data and to stimulate interest in the area — and in Kenya — through a well-planned publicity campaign.

In the event, it was another five years before the expedition got underway. But, early in 1976, Amin with Peter Moll was already at work on both a book *People of the Lake* and a television documentary, to be called *Hunters of the Jade Sea*, both based on the lake and the el-Molo people who live around Loiyangalani. The book was to have been published by the East African Literature Bureau, founded before independence by best-selling writer Elspeth Huxley.

There was another instance of 'Mo's Luck' when Amin and Peter Moll went to Loiyangalani to research the el-Molo community. The *In Town This Week* column in the *Standard* reported:

> To get the most out of his busman's holiday he carried along half-a-ton of movie equipment, cameras and sound gear together with a fibre-glass dinghy. He was paddling around in this while Peter and another friend were wading along the shore, neck deep in the Turkana waters.
>
> Mo paddled in and invited them to join him aboard. The minute the two had pulled themselves from the water the dinghy settled with hippo-like dignity on the bottom — putting a twist in the outboard motor, ruining Peter's camera and causing something of a giggle among the watching el-Molo. . . .
>
> A little later, after the outboard had dried out, in the quickly descending dusk of a Turkana evening, Mo was out once more, when the engine failed. A brisk wind began to take him out beyond the spit 175

Idi Amin turned out his youngsters in battle fatigues for the OAU summit rally which was one of the highlights of the 1975 OAU conference in Kampala. At left of picture is nineteen-year- old Sarah, his rally co-driver and a member of his Revolutionary Suicide Mechanized Battalion.

During the 1975 OAU summit Idi Amin married his rally co-driver, Sarah, in a quiet ceremony which he restaged at the request of the media. Best man was Yasser Arafat.

at Loiyangalani and into the deep waters of the lake — abundant with crocodile — nicely whipped up into a brisk chop. Only Peter's quick thinking in hailing a fisheries whaler, providentially close, saved Mo from a certainly most dangerous night out in the wave-whipped, stormy waters of the remote lake. He was towed ashore.

Amin was serenely unconcerned. For years the el-Molo have hunted crocodile, with harpoons tied to long strands of rope. Throughout the filming of *Hunters of the Jade Sea*, Mo stood within four or five feet of these dangerous reptiles.

The biggest news drama of 1976 was however, the Israeli raid on Entebbe, Uganda, to free hostages taken by Palestinian terrorists when they hijacked an Air France jet. The Airbus, carrying 246 passengers and a crew of twelve, had departed for Paris via Athens from Tel Aviv on Saturday 27 June 1976, piloted by Michael Bacos, fifty-two. At Entebbe Airport, outside Kampala, there was a full complement of hostages, 258, including seventy-five-year-old Dora Bloch who had been persuaded to fly to New York for her son's wedding.

Once again Idi Amin starred. The story kept him on the world's front pages but it meant that he had to curtail his usual voluble visit to the annual OAU Summit, in Mauritius, or forfeit the limelight he craved. As outgoing chairman, however, he had to hand over office to his successor: so temporarily forsaking the stage he was strutting at Entebbe the dictator flew to the Indian Ocean island in his personal jet.

Mo, already in Mauritius, was eager to get to Entebbe. When the Presidential jet landed he button-holed two of the men closest to Idi Amin. One was Farouk Malik, Pakistani by origin, who was head of broadcasting in Uganda; the other Juma Oris, foreign minister. He told them that the world's eyes were on Entebbe and he wanted to get there quickly before the OAU meeting ended.

Could he join the flight? Idi Amin agreed.

Next morning he checked out of his hotel, took a car to the conference hall where he filmed some of the proceedings, and then went to the airport. But he felt uneasy. 'I'd been worrying all day from the moment I woke up. I knew the Israelis were too smart and tough to take this lying down and must be planning some kind of reprisal,' Mohamed Amin mused.

'I have to calculate my chances right from the actual start to the end of a story. You have to study the odds. No story is worth getting killed for. You can never be absolutely sure about situations but you can cut down the risk by doing the right sort of planning beforehand.

'There are times that I have not gone into a situation but waited instead for a day, two days, maybe even a week, because I knew it was too dangerous and the chances of going in and coming out with the story were pretty much zero.

'I decided on the way to the airport that Idi Amin's movements were no secret and it would be very easy for an Israeli jet to bring down his plane. I   177

Dominating the world spotlight in 1976 after terrorists hijacked an Israeli jet to Entebbe airport, dictator Idi Amin took time out from negotiations to attend the summit in Mauritius and hand over Chairmanship of the OAU to Prime Minister Sir Seewoosagur Ramgoolam (right) — only to return to the debacle of the raid on Entebbe by Israeli commandos.

reckoned it was an unreasonable risk.

'By the time I reached the airport I'd changed my mind about going but I filmed the President's departure, following him as he walked out to the plane. He was news.

'Just before he climbed the steps he called me over and said, "You're coming with me?" I apologized and told him that I had been asked to stay on for the rest of the conference. He said it was OK and that we'd meet again soon anyway.'

Next morning Mo heard on the BBC's world service of the Israeli attack on Entebbe only hours after Idi Amin's jet had touched down. 'If I'd stayed on that flight I would have certainly gone to Entebbe after the raid, and just as certainly I would have been killed. Neither Idi Amin, nor anybody around him, would have hesitated. That loss of face was his biggest humiliation. Anybody trying to film it for the world to witness would have been dead.'

Danger was at hand, too, in his next assignment. Danish television commissioned him to film an hour-long documentary on the freedom war being waged in Rhodesia from Mozambique. With producer Peter Dhollof and soundman Saif Awan, Amin first went to Mozambique to film refugees and Rhodesian raids on rebel camps.

'I also felt that it was important we should get film of their activities in Rhodesia as it was this that was really the cause of the problem. Peter was unhappy about this.

'He didn't think we would get clearance so I said, "Well, it's on our way. The only way we can get back to Nairobi from Maputo is through Johannesburg. Why don't we just go from Johannesburg to Salisbury [now Harare] and then on to Nairobi."

'At Johannesburg the South Africans refused us entry and we had to stay overnight at Jan Smuts Airport in what they call a hotel. In fact, it's a cell. It has one door and no windows — and they charged us US$50 each for it. Next morning we flew to Salisbury.'

Amin and Saif separated from Dhollof as they passed through Immigration and Customs. He felt it better that Dhollof should not be identified with the camera crew. 'He was Danish, Scandinavian, and bad news in Rhodesia, as there was a lot of Nordic money behind the liberation fronts. We couldn't pretend we were anything else but a camera crew. The Rhodesians had good security and I thought it better we weren't linked together. There was no way we could hide our equipment so it was best to go in officially,' recollects Amin.

'Peter went straight through and got a two-week visitor's visa but Saif and I were held back because we were journalists. However, when Peter saw we had been asked to wait he came dashing back to ask if we had any problems. To which we said no. The immigration officer asked, "Is he something to do with you?"

'I said no but I felt the Rhodesians were very smart. Their security was   179 impeccable. We waited for thirty minutes or so and then were given a twenty-four-hour visa which was the normal practice for arriving journalists. You then had to report to the Ministry of Information. We checked in at Meikles Hotel and I went straight on to the information department.

'Bill Ferris was the information director and he sent us off to see a Colonel in charge of army public relations and also told us he'd get immigration to give us another week.

'The colonel, I forget his name, was full of charm and "No problem, old boy" shit. We told him we wanted to visit one of the protected villages [euphemism for concentration camps] and frontline operational areas.

'He replied, "No problem, old boy. Come back at four this afternoon and I'll have everything organized".'

The crew went to the Quill Club, Salisbury's version of a Press Club, to see the rest of the media pack. They asked Amin what he was doing. He told them: 'We're going to film protected villages and the front line. It's all arranged.'

Newsmen laughed. 'They told us the same — and we've been here for months.'

'I knew then we were being taken for a ride,' Amin recalls, 'and sure enough when we saw the colonel he said, "Sorry, old boy. Didn't have enough notice that you were coming, but never mind. Next time you're here we'll arrange everything."'

Ignoring the military bureaucracy, the crew drove to Mount Darwin, a front line area. 'We couldn't work there without someone knowing so we went to see the commissioner [military commander].'

The commissioner had served in Kenya and was charming and helpful. They spoke a few words in Swahili and he asked where they wanted to go. Mo told him.

'I assume you've got permission?'

'We've seen Bill Ferris in the Ministry of Information and a colonel and they've been extremely helpful.'

'Fine then. I'll organize everything. What do you want?'

'We'd like a Rhino or a Leopard.'

These were mine-proof trucks, designed to roll if they detonated a land mine. The crew were sitting in the commissioner's office but Dhollof was clearly nervous. 'After a while,' says Amin, 'the chief began to suspect something was wrong. He rang the Ministry of Information in Salisbury. You could see the expression on his face change rapidly. Then he asked us to wait outside, downstairs, where I filmed whatever was going on around. Then he came down and said, "I'm sorry. All the mine-protected vehicles are busy."'

He refused them permission to go in with their own car. It was too dangerous, he said, because of land mines. They filmed an interview with him and left, apparently to return to Salisbury.

Amin, however, took the first turning off the main road and came to a European farmer's house where they stopped and did another interview.

'He had everything – dogs, guns, electric fences. The whites were living under siege.' As the crew were leaving, he asked the farmer if there were any protected villages in the area. 'Sure, just down the road,' he told them.

They drove down a dirt track similar to many in the area which had been mined, and finally came to 'Keep Seven', the 'village' run by a twenty-year-old South African called Mr James who, he says, 'was as thick as a pole and very hairy'. The African guards let the crew enter the camp and James asked if they had permission.

'We told him we had, and he said he couldn't check anyway as his radio wasn't working.'

They filmed everywhere and everything, including African mothers and girls who were stripped to their panties and searched when entering the 'village'. 'They must have thought their knockers were booby traps,' he jokes, adding: 'It was really degrading.

'James told us that the night before the Ministry of Information had sent a film van to show movies. But he couldn't understand why they'd stoned the van. He was that thick.'

The crew stayed too long. 'We got greedy as usual. It was all great material but just as we were packing up our equipment a Leopard rolled in and out comes a guy very different from James — loaded with rows of medals and says, "Good morning gentlemen. How are you? Have you got all the pictures you want?"

'We nodded and he smiled as sweet as apple pie and said, "Have a good day — and a good journey back."

'I thought, "This is bloody simple." But it was too good to be true. Sure enough, down the track we found our way blocked by two Land Rovers and we were arrested. They said it wasn't arrest, but we didn't have any options. We were taken to Joint Operational Command headquarters at Bindura where I was asked to surrender my film.

'I refused on the grounds that we had done nothing illegal. Then one of the soldiers shouted for the "keys to the dungeon".'

Mo had never heard the word before and didn't know what it meant, but Dhollof turned white and started shaking.

'Now we're in trouble.'

'When I asked him why, he said that we would be locked up in the cell. But they didn't do that.'

The cameraman steadfastly refused to part with his films and finally the officer ordered the crew to report to the Ministry of Information in Salisbury and leave the films there. Amin agreed only that he'd go and talk to them.

They left unescorted and during the drive he unloaded the film he had shot and hid it away. Then he took two 400-foot rolls of unexposed film and marked the cans Roll 1 and Roll 2 in large letters and wrote down his 'dope' sheet on the outside.

In Salisbury he stormed into Bill Ferris's office and told him he was disgusted at the crew's treatment. He threw the two reels on the table. 'I don't think you have any right to it, but there's the film.'

Ferris, who didn't know what to say, mumbled an apology. 'Once we've seen the film and found nothing objectionable we'll give it to the Visnews man in Salisbury, and you'll get it in London.'

Seething outwardly, smiling inwardly, Amin charged back out of the office and the crew drove quickly to Meikles, settled their bill, and caught the next plane out. Ten days later Visnews were told by Salisbury that Peter Dhollof, Saif Awan and Mohamed Amin would never again enter Rhodesia.

The reason it took the Rhodesians so long to discover they had been duped was that the film had to go to Johannesburg for processing. This involved a ten-day delay, by which time the documentary had already been shown on Danish television.

By contrast, a deeply moving experience for Mohamed Amin this year was his assignment as producer-cameraman to film the first full television documentary of the Hajj, the pilgrimage that each Muslim is enjoined to make at least once. This astonishing and inspiring spectacle of faith, called *Journey of a Lifetime*, was made into 500 copies in twenty-seven languages.

'Since you have to be a Muslim to visit the holy places like Mecca and Medinah, it had to be an entirely Muslim crew. I was asked if I would like to be involved in it and since there isn't a Muslim who would not like to go to Mecca I said yes. I went with Saif Awan, who is also a Muslim, and a number of other Muslims including two Egyptians.

'My father and my mother are very devout in their religious convictions. My brothers, sisters and I were punished if we did not pray. There were no two ways about it. It was something to be taken seriously. The fact that I'm a Muslim is definitely family influence.

'I'm not a fanatic. I'm just a great believer. I pray, for example, whenever I take off in a plane, and when landing. It's not that I get on my knees and pray. You can pray sitting down. You don't recite anything but you just say it in your own heart.'

The Hajj was a significant moment in Amin's life. Over the years he would often return but could recapture neither that first feeling of euphoria nor his hard-nosed newsman's astonishment at seeing some three million people all gathered in one place, as the pilgrims did that year, on the plains of Arafat. He wrote of his feelings in a series in the *Nation*.

> The Muslim pilgrimage of the Hajj, which takes place every year, is the most staggering act of logistics the world has seen, an unparalleled movement of three million people by air, sea and land who live together for a night and a day in a massive tented city on the barren plains of Arafat, a few miles from the walls of Mecca . . . yet despite this incredible army of followers, despite the hustle and bustle of the hawkers and vendors, government officials and police who control the crowds, the over-riding atmosphere during the Hajj is of peace, a oneness with all these different disciples, of every race imaginable, from more than seventy nations.

Mohamed Amin in Mecca's Grand Mosque filming *Journey of a Lifetime* and photographing *Pilgrimage to Mecca* — a commitment on which he staked not only his reputation but all that he owned.

But neither that nor the film was enough. In his mind, he conceived a book, with perhaps 200 to 300 colour illustrations. It was the only way he felt it possible to convey the sense of the Hajj as both a physical and a spiritual experience.

'This was my first visit to Mecca and I was totally awed by what I saw. It was the finest experience of my life and it was during this trip that I felt that I should do a book on the Hajj.

'When I investigated the market there was very little available. Certainly nothing on the scale I envisaged, which was a large-format, high-quality illustrated book. So I decided I would go back and photograph the Hajj over the next two years.

'Getting permission to work on the Hajj was near impossible but because I had been involved on the film I had made the contacts. We had backing for the film from the King and the Crown Prince so it was much easier. I went back for the next two years to collect the material for the book.'

11 Lust to Kill: the Fall of Idi Amin

Despite his love of creative photography, Mohamed Amin hates any form of imposed discipline, either as studio work, or any kind of filming and photography not closely related to action. 'If it moves, shoot it,' might well be his credo.

His picture collection, which began with black and white prints of the 1958 Safari Rally, has grown to more than a million colour transparencies and black and white negatives. It is the single, most comprehensive picture library on Africa in existence. Many were taken in circumstances most people would find impossible. Bruised and battered by crowds or angry mobs, threatened and intimidated, or under fire on a battlefield, Amin's sure hands and eyes have an innate instinct for the picture that says it all.

Sometime in 1976 he made a journey to Juba, capital of southern Sudan, to film a story covering the integration of the two armies after the peace treaty between the south and the north. There he met British photographer Duncan Willetts. They talked. 'He indicated an interest in coming to work in Nairobi,' recalls Amin. 'A job was always a possiblity, but unless you get a work permit it's very difficult.

'I wasn't very interested in taking him on, but Duncan said, "If I get a permit, will it be possible to get a job?"

'I told him "fine".'

Months later, in 1977, Willetts walked into Mohamed Amin's office and said, 'Now I've got a permit. Can I have a job?'

It was at this stage that Amin began to take Duncan Willetts seriously. He hired him to run the Camerapix studio.

Amin's lack of enthusiasm for studio work is well known. On one rare occasion he agreed to do some brochure work at the private house of a friend who had a reputation for being a bad payer. When he had finished a hard morning's work, the friend asked what the bill was. Amin said, 'Call it a hundred Kenya shillings.'

'Is that right?' queried his astonished friend. 'I thought a thousand was your basic half-day rate.'

'It is. But I'd rather be owed a hundred than a thousand.'

Willetts soon established himself as the best commercial photographer in Nairobi depite the strong local competition. Amin encouraged him to do more and more outdoor work. Together they covered the private visit to

Kenya of the world's most touted eligible bachelor, Prince Charles, heir to the British throne. Fleet Street's tabloid newspapers, convinced there was a love affair between the Prince and some unknown girl, were desperate for a picture of the two together.

The script to Amin's film of the royal heir meeting Kenyatta at Nakuru State House said: 'Kenya is believed to be particularly popular with the Prince for its large wildlife reserves where he can escape pursuing newsmen.'

In fact, he went into hiding in an Aberdare mountain retreat. Willetts, on assignment for the Fleet Street tabloid the *Sun*, camped out at the Outspan Hotel in Nyeri with the rest of the pack. The royal heir read tabloid headlines about his 'blonde bird' and plotted a royal revenge.

Before leaving Jomo Kenyatta International Airport, the Prince handed a shoe-box to the *Daily Express* photographer and said: 'Don't open it until I've gone.'

As the Royal plane took off, the photographer unwrapped the shoe box. There, lying inside, was a stuffed pigeon — with a blond wig stuck on its head. Willetts' picture, under the headline **Charles gives press the bird!** made the *Sun's* front page.

By then, however, Amin was in Samburu country. Seers had been studying the stars. After fourteen years or more, all was propitious for the tribal circumcision ceremony: perhaps the last that would be held. Few outsiders are allowed to witness the ceremonies. However, Amin knew one of the senior elders, a civil servant in Maralal, capital of Samburuland, who arranged for him to take the first-ever photographs of this almost sacred Samburu ritual on the high Leroghi Plateau, 6,000 feet above sea level.

But when the photographer turned up on the day of the ceremony, Wilfrid Thesiger, the reclusive explorer and author acclaimed for his work among the nomadic Marsh Arabs, who had been cultivating the Samburu for weeks and was actually living with them, was resentful. In his usual fashion, Amin began organizing everybody, and Thesiger complained he was interfering with 'his' people.

Amin never did discover the reason for the fascination that the Samburu held for this philosopher, but he was astonished to find Thesiger almost begging to be allowed to perform the circumcision of the initiates. 'In the end,' he recalls, 'the Samburu were quietly laughing at this strange *mzungu* [white man]. They decided to charge him twenty bob for each initiate on whom he operated.' Since it's normal for the sponsors to pay the circumciser, Thesiger's deal must have pleased the thrifty Samburu elders.

But the big story which continued to dominate the headlines remained Idi Amin. Early in 1977 there had been another exodus of Ugandan refugees across the border. The refugees were nearly all members of the Christian Langi and Acholi tribes whose people had been systematically purged from their jobs, imprisoned, and were now being massacred in their tens of thousands.

Idi Amin never recovered from the humiliation of the Entebbe raid and I suggested to Mo that we should produce a book based on the dictator's rise and predictable fall written while he was in power and updated regularly so that it could be published within days of his demise. The proposed title was *Lust to Kill — The Rise and Fall of Idi Amin*. Based on drafts of the early chapters, the British paperback publishers Corgi paid a substantial advance.

Idi Amin was no friend to his neighbours. He made it impossible for the East African Community of Kenya, Tanzania and Uganda to function, and eventually financial and political differences resulted in the Community's collapse. One of the victims was East African Airways. On the back of a leased Boeing 707 Kenya swiftly launched Kenya Airways, and Tanzania, in a fit of pique, slammed shut its doors on Kenya.

On 17 February after a confrontation with the power-crazy dictator, the world learned of the murder of Ugandan Archbishop Janani Luwum provoking fears among the All-African Conference of Churches that he was about to unleash a reign of terror against all Christians. Then came news of an assassination bid against the Uganda Ogre himself.

Not long afterwards, Idi Amin, bedecked with medals he had awarded himself and sitting on a shooting stick in the corridors of the Libreville Conference Centre, Gabon, during the OAU summit, summoned Mohamed Amin with a movement of his podgy fingers.

'Where's Osman?' the dictator demanded. With Mo as cameraman, John Osman, the BBC correspondent in Nairobi, had interviewed Idi Amin at least twice.

'Tell him I am the Conqueror of the British Empire and I've awarded myself the CBE.'

It was Idi Amin's facetious response to the reaction he had roused in the British Press following his threat to grace the London Commonwealth summit which he was entitled to attend as head of a Commonwealth member state.

That same day he told the OAU delegates: 'On 30 June this year, in order to make it absolutely clear to you, I have been honoured by the highest order of the Conqueror of the British Imperialism in Uganda. The members of the Defence Council [his own] consider the official government of the British which made Ugandan slaves of a hundred years have run away, therefore they consider me the Conqueror of the British Empire.

'I captured some of the people who tried to assassinate me. Let me tell you I have got them but there will be debate on this particular point and that they told me the whole western Press knew exactly what was going to happen to me.

'But they said that their team was well planned, they were responsible. I wanted just to tell you because I'm sorry the President and the leader of Benin [formerly Dahomey] is not here. They told me officially their plan, their mission was to kill, move to Angola, to kill the President of Angola, 187 move to Uganda and then go to Guinea.'

To presidents or pressmen alike, none of this made sense. The megalomania and paranoia were unmistakeable. Just how chilling it was to work in this man's shadow emerged on 8 September 1977 in an interview the cameraman set up and filmed in his Nairobi office with former Uganda detainee John Sekabira, who first disclosed atrocities to Associated Press reporter John Edlin.

With worldwide conjecture about the fate of Dora Bloch who had been taken hostage during the Entebbe raid, it was a major scoop at the time. Sekabira claimed he had been conscripted into her burial party. He told of a big military truck, which came to the prison full of bodies.

The Visnews transcript continues:

How many?

Sekabira: There are 200 of them. After the raid at Entebbe International Airport, the Israeli raid, they used to bring in some bodies of airborne officers and some from the marine. Then, one day, it was very early in the morning, when they told us to prepare two graves. We prepared them. Then in the evening at five they brought in two bodies, one of a policeman who was in the uniform of a policeman and the other one, an old European lady.'

Do you think this was Mrs Dora Bloch?

Sekabira: That is what I think . . . after . . . when I told the people that's what they told me. And the prison officer who was the witness when the policeman was being shot, he told us that was the body of the Israeli woman. We asked him why the policeman was shot and the prison officer told us that when the secretary of police came to snatch away the radio from the hospital where she was being given treatment the policeman doubted that he was a police officer and ordered that he introduce himself to him. So instead they shot him, drag his body to the jeep, they brought them together, they were still breathing.

What kind of wounds did Mrs Bloch suffer?

Sekabira: They shoot in her head and the policeman had three shots, gunshots in his body.

Four days later the Visnews cameraman discovered Idi Amin's former cook, Moses Aloga. It was another of Mohamed Amin's world exclusives on Idi. The gruesome thread of this particular story still remains vivid:

You worked for Idi Amin in Kampala for how long?

Aloga: Four years.

You were doing what?

Aloga: I was working as a servant. For his, well office or residence. The Old Command Post, the New Command Post.

And this put you in charge of the room where he kept his drinks in a refrigerator?

Aloga: Yes, yes. I was in charge of that.

He kept something else in the fridge?

Aloga: Yes, he started it because he have got, you see, very big size fridge where he keeps human organs.

What kind of human organs?

Aloga: Just you'll find some head for the people who've been killed because if you're killed there, if he wants you he can get it. That I need your head for him. Then they bring the head he put it in the fridge and keep it for time.

Moses, when Sarah [Idi Amin's wife] opened the fridge she saw something very horrifying. What was her reaction to this?

Aloga: She pressed me to open that fridge. When I opened, in it she see the head of her [previous] husband, I know, which was very bad to her. She fell down. I tried to push her out, when I fell. . . .

How many heads did you see over the years you worked?

Aloga: No, I can't say because sometimes he kept five there, sometimes six. And stay there for any time he wants, you know. Because unfortunately his girl-friend found the head that was there. The girl was going with other men.

This same year Idi Amin's contemporary despot, President Bokassa, of the impoverished Central African Republic, announced his intention to crown himself Emperor of his arid, Sahara-edge bushland.

The event became Africa's greatest spectacle of the year. It was allocated a budget of £20 million, and written, produced and directed by former French army sergeant Jean-Bedel Bokassa. He was President-for-Life, President of the Government, Keeper of the Seals, Minister of Defence, the Civil Service, Social Security, the Interior, Telecommunications, Agriculture, Information, Health and Population, Grand Master of the Order of Operation Bokassa, Commander of the Order of Merit for Agriculture, Industry and the Postal Service, Holder of the Gold Medal for Work, and Knight of the International Society of Philatelists.

The opulence included:

Thirteen costumes worn at Napoleon's coronation (on which Bokassa based his), done up by the 200-year-old French firm of Guiselin;

The Emperor's thirty-two-pound robe, with its 785,000 pearls, and more than a million crystal beads at the bargain price of £75,000;

The Empress Catherine's gown from the House of Lanvin, dazzling with almost one million sequins and gold pieces, cost about £32,000;

The crown, topped with a diamond, sceptre and the Empress's diadem: cost £2.5 million;

Two hundred and forty tons of air-freighted champagne, wines, caviar, flowers, doves, and a seven-tier cake, sixty brand-new Mercedes limousines and thirty Peugeot 504s, together with 150 800cc BMW motor cycles, flown in at a total cost of more than £1 million.

Like the other newsmen covering the coronation of Bokassa as Emperor of one of the world's twenty-five poorest countries Mohamed Amin needed a morning suit.

'When I heard about the coronation,' Amin recollects, 'I was determined to cover this story. I offered it to Visnews who said there was no way 189 anyone was going to be allowed to cover the story because French television had bought the exclusive rights. They also told me that a French picture agency had bought exclusive stills rights — all being sold and marketed by a Frenchman who was the master-mind behind the organization of the coronation.

'I still wanted to go. Missing one of the biggest stories of the decade in Africa was just not on. The Associated Press assigned me to cover the event. Then I was told that you had to follow the protocol laid down by Bokassa himself. You had to be properly dressed — topper and tails, a morning suit.

'If you were not properly dressed, we were told, you would have an ear cut off. For fear of losing an ear,* I decided I had to be properly dressed. I was going to take no chances. I thought there would be no problem getting a morning suit since so many Englishmen wear one on wedding days.

'But when I called round friends who had recently got married, they all laughed. It was out of fashion, they told me. Eventually, I went to the Donovan Maule theatre in Nairobi and hired a morning suit. Newsweek's Nairobi bureau chief, James Pringle, who was on the flight with me, was so short he had to have his suit specially cut by the Donovan Maule to fit him.

'We went via Douala in Cameroon, the best way to get to Bangui. At Douala we were still worried that if we took a wrong step at the very least we might lose an ear. So we went to the British Embassy for advice.

'We saw the Number Two who spent the next half hour telling us that we shouldn't go there and that the British Government would have absolutely nothing to do with us if we got into any trouble.

'He was a typical British diplomat who was telling us in effect, "Look, you're a nuisance, so why don't you just go home and keep out of trouble instead of creating work for us".

'Next morning on the flight to Bangui I decided that there was no point in taking any chances, so I dressed up in my morning suit on the plane to arrive properly attired. The other three hacks on the flight decided to do the same.

'But when we stepped out of the plane it must have been around 100° Fahrenheit. As we came down the steps in our morning suits, cameras dangling round our necks, we looked absolute fools.

'The immigration officers were falling about laughing so we had no problem getting into the country. Then we went to the Ministry of Information for accreditation, but we were told it was impossible as the French had all the rights.

'Anyway, we decided we would cover it as best as we could. But all the hotels were full. Finally we spent the night inside a church. Next morning, when we arrived at the Coronation Palace, which had been built specially

*In 1972, Bokassa personally supervised the public amputation of the ears of thirteen convicted thieves.

for the occasion, we walked in without any problems.

'We were so well dressed that the security guards just assumed we were diplomats or state guests. My other colleagues went and sat down, but since I was photographing, I hung around the place where the Emperor was going to be crowned.

'The French television and stills guys came up and asked me who I was. I said I was just a guest from Kenya taking a few pictures. They left me alone until one of the French news guys recognized me and realised that I was not just taking pictures for fun, that I was a professional in fact.

'They tried to throw me out as the bugles heralding Bokassa's grand entrance sounded. In the scuffle, my leg hit the tripod of the French television camera and it came tumbling down.

'Desperate to get the camera back on its stand to film Bokassa, they stopped hustling me, but this particular camera missed his entrance.

'After that, everybody was too busy trying to get their own pictures to worry about throwing me out. I was only about six feet from the Emperor and it would have been noticed. That certainly would have caused problems.

'After the coronation, Bokassa drove in his horse-drawn carriage to the church, and the entire road from the palace to the church — about a mile or more — was covered with red carpet. Nobody realized that hundreds of cars would follow. At the end of the day the carpet was in shreds.

'We were kept some distance from the Emperor in the church. But near the end of the service I decided to make a dash to get some close-ups where Bokassa was sitting — and also his departure from the church.

'The security guys got very uptight. There was absolute silence in the church when they pounced on me. But when the Emperor spoke to them they left me alone. I had the best position for photography in church and for his departure. There were hundreds of security guys around, but I walked backwards right in front of the Emperor, working on a twenty-millimetre wide-angle lens. He loved being photographed and I got the best pictures of the day.

'That evening, we attended the banquet at the palace. Much later, when Bokassa was in sanctuary in France, it was alleged that human flesh had been served there. I don't know what I ate.

'That same night I left on the Paris flight and on to London to get my pictures out. I was determined to beat the French. My pictures were extensively used, not only by AP but by many magazines. But I remember it as the most bizarre story I've ever covered.'

The real news focus, though, remained on Idi Amin. When the BBC's David Lomax interviewed him in Kampala early in January 1978, he received such a grilling that Mo began to worry for their safety.

Despite Idi Amin's denials, Lomax kept insisting that Dora Bloch had been murdered by his men. The dictator grew angrier and angrier. The cameraman, who had studied him better than most for the last seven years, thought: 'He'll kill us all.' The confrontation only came to a halt 191

Another grotesque figure of Idi Amin's era in contemporary African history was Jean-Bedel Bokassa, dictator of the impoverished Central African Republic. In 1978, Bokassa staged a lavish £20 million coronation to invest himself as Emperor. Despite the exclusive rights being sold to French television and print media, Mohamed Amin was assigned to cover the event by the Associated Press and took an exclusive portfolio of pictures of the Emperor, his wife and sleeping son. But before he was admitted Amin was told that morning dress was mandatory. He solved the problem by hiring topper and tails from the Donovan Maule theatre in Nairobi.

when the reel ended and he had to change films.

'You could hear the silence. It was pin sharp. Then, as I was busy in the black bag, loading a new magazine, Idi Amin chuckled and wagged his finger at Lomax:

'"You know I'm only giving you this interview because of my friend Mohamed Amin."'

He arranged television interviews with Idi Amin on behalf of many world broadcasters. They came to him because of his reputation. No one else had his contacts.

Every Easter, Mohamed Amin's spectacular film reports of the East African Safari Rally demonstrated his sense of commitment. They have become something of a legend. Amin enjoyed nothing more than to follow this classic test of endurance and speed through five gruelling days and nights without rest, and still does.

During the 1978 event which was run over the Easter weekend of 25 March, Amin parked his Land Cruiser close to a flooded dirt track and set up his tripod and camera on the roof. The leaders came speeding through this section like power boats on a stormy sea, sending up a great wave of water on either side, drenching both Amin and Willetts who was savouring the 'delights' of the Safari for the first time. The *Nation* caption story tells what happened next:

Disaster in the making

Japanese ace Yoshio Iwashita struggles with the wheel of his Datsun as it begins to broadside at eighty miles an hour on a flooded stretch of bush road near Emali.

Seconds later the car leaves the road and rams into the Land Cruiser of Nairobi's international news cameraman Mohamed Amin. Amin and colleague Duncan Willetts are hurled through the air into a muddy ditch below.

And as Mo struggles out of the ditch, shaken, battered, with a suspected broken wrist, the camera is still whirring — bringing the reality of the Safari's ever-present dangers and excitement to millions of viewers worldwide.

The crash damaged Mo's cine camera and other expensive equipment. But he was back at work last night, out on the third and final leg of the route — still ready for the unexpected.

Said Mo: "I've covered nineteen safaris without a break [he filmed some of the 1971 Rally when he returned from Pakistan] so far. My wrist hurts but I wouldn't miss the finish for the world."

The film brought Iwashita a frantic telephone call from his wife in Tokyo. He had chosen not to tell her about the crash, but Amin's film, via Visnews, had shown it to the world.

In May, Amin was assigned to cover the Shaba war in Zaire. Shaba Province, formerly Katanga, is energy and mineral rich. Lying in the extreme south-east of Zaire, it provides much of that vast country's wealth, mainly from copper exports. Its people had long sought secession. Now, once again, they were fighting to forge their own secessionist nation.

In Kinshasa, Amin again met his friend and former Visnews colleague, Neil Davis, a unique and universally admired Australian cameraman-correspondent, who was working for NBC in Zaire. He was renowned for his incomparable front line action reports from the bloodiest battles of Vietnam and other Indo-Chinese wars. After many years of service, he had quit Visnews when the management wanted him to take a desk job in London. Like Amin, Neil craved action and loathed the very idea of desk work. He signed up with NBC and remained in the Far East, where he was killed in action, along with his soundman Bill Latch, filming an abortive coup in Bangkok on 9 September 1985.

Shaba was the last time that he and Amin worked together.

Before they could get near to any action, however, Amin encountered what to him was a much greater trauma than any war. It was the Kinshasa hotel's telephone system. Anxious to let Visnews in London know what was happening, he found he could not get through no matter how much he tried. Comparing notes with other reporters, he discovered the solution. He had to place calls 'on the system'. Back in his room he tried again. 'On the system, please.'

Thirty seconds later he was speaking to Visnews.

Then came the knock on the door. A waiter wanted 50 zaire (the national currency).

'What's this for?'

'Your telephone call, sir.'

'That's okay. Just put it on my bill.'

There was a discreet cough.

'But, sir, the call was "on the system". It doesn't go on the bill.'

'The system', however, did not apply to incoming calls. When London called him, the operator simply said he was out; and then told Amin so that he could call London to know what they wanted. 'On the system', of course.

Amin was in Zaire ten days, four of them at the front line. With other journalists, he and Davis flew down to Shaba where they hired a bus to take them to the action. Nearing the front, the driver would go no further. Parking the bus, he urinated by the roadside, insisting that it was the end of the road. Immediately Amin took his place at the wheel and, eager as Davis to get to the action, drove on.

'That war was the last time I saw Neil. It's like that with cameramen all around the world. Each of us has a beat and our paths don't cross as often as we would like. Certainly for someone like Neil. He was special. A fantastic man,' Amin says with a trace of sadness.

Asked once how he would want people to remember him, Amin said: 'If I die tomorrow, I'll be forgotten within a few months. It's as if you didn't exist — even to close friends. Possibly the family may remember a little bit

Splattered with mud, choking with dust, for more than twenty-five years Mohamed Amin has covered every stage of the gruelling five-day-long Safari Rally, frequently risking his life to film the action and sometimes coming to grief — as in the 1978 rally when, while he was filming from the roof, Japanese driver Iwashita rammed his Land Cruiser, throwing him and colleague Duncan Willetts into a ditch.

longer because they might have a bit of grief. But colleagues that you work with? Memories are very short.

'Neil Davis, for example, was one of the finest journalists I have ever come across and ever had the pleasure of working with. But very few people now mention his name. He's gone. His name may come up from time to time — as a good solid operator, in terms of a newsman. But, in terms of people sitting there, discussing him over a beer or cup of tea, no, there'll be very little.

'As the days and the weeks go by, he'll be forgotten. But I think that's how life goes. I mean, John F. Kennedy. How many people talk about him?'

That same month his organizational ability was recognized in Nairobi when he was unanimously elected chairman of the East Africa Foreign Correspondents Association, a position he filled with flair and success for five years. In that time, he achieved his personal ambition of housing the foreign Press corps under a single roof — creating, in effect, the Press Centre in Chester House, Koinange Street, in the heart of Nairobi.

This year, too, he was about to complete the production of his book *Pilgrimage to Mecca*. Passionately striving to produce his own testament to his Islamic faith, he had told Visnews earlier of his enthusiasm for a book, and indeed he and the company had signed an agreement to produce one.

Nothing came of it.

Since then, he had come close to abandoning the project, but he persevered. Nobody had ever done a pictorial book on the forbidden city and the rites of the Muslim Pilgrimage. Now he produced a dummy and, with this in his briefcase, he flew to London to pound the pavements, knocking on publishers' doors.

'I never had any ambition to become an international publisher. But publishing always was, and is, the fun part of the organization. I was driven into it by accident, purely by the fact that I was unable to persuade any publishers, and I saw most of the English publishers and several American publishers, to take *Pilgrimage to Mecca* when I walked up and down London and the gangways of the Frankfurt Book Fair,' Amin says sanguinely.

'Not having been able to place *Mecca* anywhere, I went round the printers to get prices for cost comparison. I got the addresses by going into a big book shop and looking at the printers of the best quality and writing to them. One of these was the Italian giant, Mondadori.

'When I got Mondadori's quotation, I spoke to Keith Lilley, who was then the managing director in London, and he asked if I could go and see him.

'I was on my way to the airport, as I was leaving that day, but he persuaded me to call in and spend some minutes discussing the book with him. He was obviously very interested in the subject.

'Keith soon discovered I knew little or nothing about printing or publishing, but I agreed prices with him for 30,000 copies and 120 days credit from delivery. To this day I have not been able to find out why he agreed. I was just a complete stranger from Africa asking for 30,000 books. He never even asked for a reference, never mind a guarantee.

'The separations cost £18,000. But because the deal was to pay 120 days from delivery I didn't actually have to pay at that time. Obviously, I was very concerned. I had incurred what for me was a massive debt. I didn't have £18,000.

'So I went around looking at the dark side of life. I had my house valued and I figured out, without telling her, how much Dolly's jewellery would bring in case the book was a disaster and I had to pay. To this day Dolly does not know that was the deal I was thinking about.

'The house and her jewellery would just have about paid for the books. What I would have done with the 30,000 copies, God alone knows. But it all worked out. Before we went to print, I was able to sell five different language editions to some of the top publishers in the business and in the event I paid Mondadori in thirty days. From then on, Mondadori and I, and particularly Keith Lilley, have been the best of friends.'

He wanted to launch the book in style with an exhibition of larger-than-life full-colour photomurals at the Hilton, Nairobi. Dr Munyua Waiyaki, Kenya's Minister for Foreign Affairs, agreed to be guest of honour.

In the middle of arranging it all, Amin flew to Khartoum to cover the annual OAU summit, when Brendan Farrow, then regional editor of Visnews, worked with him in the field for the first time. Farrow recalls:

'Our bus reached the hotel for us to find it surrounded by troops with fixed bayonets who wouldn't let us in. The government protocol man was unable to persuade the Sudanese troops to let us into the hotel. So, with no idea what we might do, we gathered in groups waiting for somebody to do something.'

At this point Farrow noticed that Mohamed Amin was already inside the hotel – sitting in an armchair.

'He turned, grinned and waved to us and went on with a telephone conversation he was having. How did he get in? I never found out. But the person he was talking to was the minister of information, and in no time at all the hotel doors were opened and we all checked in.'

Later, in the conference hall, he saw Amin in action. . . .

'We gained a perfect spot right up front, nicely angled across the stand from which President Nimeiri would make the opening address.

'Mo left me guarding the tripod while he went off with the camera to film the delegates in the hall seated behind their country identification plates, and finally the entry of the President and his progress to the rostrum.

'He then had to barge his way through masses of Press and TV cameramen to get his camera back onto the tripod for the start of the speech.

'Just as he was ready for the start of Nimeiri's address, an official placed two great pots of flowers — one on each side of the rostrum, totally blocking Mo's view of the speaker.

'"Get that fucking thing down!" yelled Mo. There was a solid mass of reporters and equipment between us and the stage and security all round. He barged back through the pack of cameramen, reporters, photographers, soundmen and lightmen, over all the cables and camera bags, and the backs of crouching sound recordists, snatched the pot down on his side and was back filming the opening speech before anybody quite realized what had happened.

'Nobody complained. And nobody tried to put the flowers back.'

Back in Nairobi, on Tuesday 22 August, Amin received a morning telephone call from Kinyanjui Kariuki, President Kenyatta's Press secretary. 'He was very vague, but he told me I should stand by for a big story. He told me to listen to VOK.

'I was intrigued. I knew Mzee was staying at State House, Mombasa, but Kinyanjui was ringing from State House, Nairobi. I telephoned State House, Mombasa. The switchboard operators were stunned. You could tell something was seriously wrong. I couldn't raise any of Mzee's aides. I rang Kinyanjui back but got no sense, sq I decided to drive to State House, Nairobi.

'I managed to get in, and when I found Kinyanjui he confessed: "Mzee's dead".

'They'd flown his body up from Mombasa and they still hadn't announced anything. Kinyanjui prepared the announcement, but when he rang the director of broadcasting at VOK, the man told him there was no way he would broadcast the news unless he was given a signed order.'

Amin filmed Daniel arap Moi as he was sworn in as Mzee's successor, in accordance with the constitution. 'Then I filmed the new President and the cabinet filing past Mzee's coffin.'

It was feared that Mzee's death would trigger a political crisis in Kenya. For five days Amin filmed the aftermath of the announcement, the lying-in-state at State House, and finally, after a statement to television by Jomo's old adversary, Oginga Odinga, who was only too keen to capitalize on the death of a political foe, the impressive State funeral, which Voice of Kenya televised live around the world. To everybody's relief, Kenya remained calm and stable.

On 31 October 1978, just seventy days after the new President took office, the Mecca exhibition opened at the Hilton. But as the crowds queued to see the pictures of Mecca, the Holy of Holies never before photographed comprehensively, Idi Amin ordered his troops on an inexplicable adventure into north-western Tanzania.

In retaliation, President Nyerere sent his troops into Uganda on the western side of Lake Victoria to start the bloody six-month-long struggle that removed the dictator. It was the first time in Africa's post-colonial history that one country had invaded another. Sensitive to criticism of his role, President Julius Nyerere likened Idi Amin to Hitler, and defended his
200 military intervention by pointing out that Amin had brought it on by his

own cross-border excursion into Tanzania territory. 'People accuse me of breaking international law. But should a thief be allowed to get away with his crimes?' Nyerere argued.

When Nyerere launched his counterattack, it seemed his objective was simply to teach Idi Amin a lesson. But as the Tanzanian army ground its way northward toward Kampala, it saw the chance to put an end to the regime once and for all. With the aid of 122-mm. artillery, the estimated 4,000-strong Tanzanian army and 3,000 Ugandan exiles pounded Amin's army until it broke and ran.

The world saw most of this action through Mohamed Amin's films and photographs as he flew in and out of the battle-torn Pearl of Africa with unflagging energy, while still finding time to hire freelance writer Angus Shaw to complete *Lust to Kill: The Rise and Fall of Idi Amin*.

The key towns of Masaka and Mbarara quickly fell to the invading forces even though Libyan leader Moamar al Gaddafi flew in a support force of 2,000 troops. But the Libyans had little stomach for a war that was not their concern. By early April it was clear that neither Idi Amin nor his capital, Kampala, could hold out much longer.

'The trouble was that nobody knew what was going on,' Mohamed Amin recalls. 'There were no communications with Kampala at all. The border was closed. I was fairly certain that Entebbe had been taken and the only way to go in was by air charter. Under that situation you could only go in on the winning side. If you went in on the losing side, there was a very definite possibility of losing yourself.

'Starting with Boskovic, my regular company, I went to all the charter companies in the hope that they would fly me in. There was no way we could get any permission. And nobody knew what was happening. Nobody was sure of the situation.

'The charter companies flatly refused. But we persevered, and finally on 13 April I met Dick Knight, a veteran pilot who runs one of Kenya's largest air charter companies, at the Dambusters Club at Wilson Airport. He was interested in taking us in. From my experience in the past, I told Dick that the problem was getting down. If he could get us down, we would have a reasonably good chance.

'He asked what I thought they would do. I said that they might shoot us down before we landed. We knew that there had been a pitched battle at the airport between the Libyans on Idi Amin's side and the Tanzanians.

'Dick said he wasn't worried about being shot down. "Tanzanians can't shoot straight, so we'll be all right."

'He was more worried about what would happen after we landed, and I said that once we had landed it would be all right, he should just leave everything to me.

'I came back to my office, put my equipment together, called my contact at State House in Dar es Salaam to tell him what we were doing and asked for some help.

'"Absolutely no. You'll be shot out of the sky. We have no contact with

Above: Mohamed Amin filming the first cabinet meeting of the second Republic with, from left to right, the late James Gicheru, defence minister; President Daniel arap Moi; the late Mbiyu Koinange, minister for state; Dr Gikonyo Kiano, minister for water development; and, in the foreground, back to camera, attorney general Charles Njonjo.

Right: Tearful Vice-President Daniel arap Moi mourns the death of Kenya's founding father, Mzee Jomo Kenyatta.

One of the big stories of 1978 was the death of President Mzee Jomo Kenyatta on 22 August at State House, Mombasa. The body of Kenya's founding father was flown to Nairobi where it lay in state at State House. Mourning, at extreme right, is his widow, Mama Ngina Kenyatta, and, second from right, his daughter by his first wife, Margaret Kenyatta.

Entebbe and the only way you can get in is if you come down here because we're arranging a special charter to take in the Press."

'That was the best they could offer. The fact that they were arranging a charter gave our mission a sense of urgency.

'I went in with BBC correspondent Brian Barron and Eric Thirer, the BBC cameraman-soundman in Nairobi. We flew in total silence. Not a word was said on the plane. I think deep down we were all completely shit-scared. It was one of the hairiest assignments I've ever gone on. It reminded me of the flights into Biafra at the height of the Nigerian civil war, but this felt much more dangerous. We had absolutely no control on the ground.'

They all knew the risks only too well. In the past few weeks, four European journalists had been killed by the Ugandan forces. 'There were two Germans and two Scandinavians, Swedish, young guys,' Amin recalls. 'The Germans were working for *Stern*, which is a heavyweight magazine. They came to me and *twice* — once in the office, once on the border — said, "We're going to go in by boat to Jinja and then walk our way to Kampala."

'I said I wouldn't. There's no way I'd go. Because a) you're going in on the losing side, b) you're going to see troops with no discipline whatsoever. The last thing they would want is to be filmed — or meet journalists — because when you're running away you don't want to be filmed, particularly in a place like Uganda. For so many years the evidence out of Uganda was such that you knew that at the best of times these people would chop you up. In a situation like this, you knew there was no question that they would leave you alone.

'It was very sad that these guys decided to go. They must have taken advice from other people as well, but their principals, I think mostly *Stern*, sitting in Germany, were putting a lot of pressure on them. And they were young, trying to make their names, which really isn't worth making if you're going to get killed. They did something that was very foolish. Sadly, within hours of getting off the boat, all four were dead.'

Mohamed's plan was different. It was a calculated risk. His team was going in on the victorious side, and if they weren't shot out of the sky, he felt pretty sure they'd be safe on the ground.

'We saw Entebbe quite early,' he remembers. 'It was very bright, early afternoon and Dick lost altitude quickly, coming in very low over Lake Victoria and touching down right on the lip of the runway. This runs uphill, so you can't see the airport buildings — or be seen — until you taxi in.

'But the first thing we saw — which I filmed as we touched down — was a blazing C-130 Hercules from Libya. It had been shot on take-off minutes before.

'When we reached the terminal we were stunned. It just wasn't a war situation. There were tribal dancers and a line-up of dignitaries — a real welcoming party — and I thought, "Shit. Now we're in trouble. They're expecting somebody important."

'I was first out and you could see the shock hit them. There was a big guy — a short, fat guy I knew — Rashidi Kawawa, the former prime minister of Tanzania, then minister of defence, and also the commander of the Tanzanian Army. He was not amused.'

Where were they from?

Kenya, Amin replied.

The welcoming party went into a huddle. In those days, Kenya was not exactly good news in either Tanzania or Uganda. They talked in Swahili, which Amin could follow clearly.

'It was not a good conversation. They were concerned with how we had got in to Entebbe and what they should do with us. And this was a discussion taking place at the top level.'

Before there was any outcome, however, another plane dipped low over the lake and came into land. It carried the expected dignitary, Yusuf Lule, flown from Dar es Salaam, to be sworn in as president that day.

'The trouble was that nobody knew what to do. It was obviously being done at very short notice. They didn't even have a decent Presidential car, just Land Rovers,' Amin remembers.

'We were virtually forgotten now and OK — part of the party — so we just followed Lule and his entourage into the VIP lounge where they discussed this and that and then decided to go to nearby State House to discuss the affair there.

'We tagged along after we found someone with a car which we hired. He had no fuel, but we'd taken along petrol. Actually it was Avgas [aviation gasoline]. Dick didn't want to carry regular fuel because it was unsafe. Avgas makes your car go like a bomb, but it buggers up the engine.

'State House was a shambles. Everything had been looted. The Tanzanian troops had been bringing in planes loaded with troops and flying them back to Tanzania loaded with Idi Amin's goodies — carpets, furniture, you name it.'

It was decided Lule should be sworn in on the steps of Kampala's Parliament Buildings. 'They even got together a reasonable crowd and we got some good film.'

Then they toured the ravaged city. Corpses lay in the streets. Mohamed Amin and his colleagues were the first media men to discover the horrific truth of the crazed dictator's regime. The State Research Bureau — SRB — had been transformed into a 20th-century torture chamber where none who entered, save the inquisitors, left. Later, some of these inquisitors were to return under different circumstances. As prisoners.

Tanzanian soldiers allowed him freedom to film. More important, at places like the SRB and State House he found files recording the terrible atrocities which had been committed. Before the day was out he accumulated two suitcases full of documents — damning and irrefutable indictment of what had gone on in Idi Amin's Uganda. He also discovered the last film taken of Idi Amin. He saw it through the window of a locked office — twenty or so reels piled on a desk and in cupboards.

'We'll have to break in.'

'I'll have nothing to do with that,' said Barron. 'And neither will Eric. I'll wait for you in the car.'

Yet once he had the film, Barron wanted to send it to BBC London.

Amin carried everything back with him to Nairobi and Angus Shaw, who had been complaining of a lack of 'statistical evidence'. Now the impatient writer had more than enough for two books.

The end, however, was not the dramatic one the authors envisaged. Idi Amin got away. The besiegers left one escape route from Kampala — a corridor running forty-five miles east to Jinja, Uganda's main industrial city. Idi Amin seems to have fled from Jinja aboard a helicopter around mid-April, leaving the hungry and desperate remnants of his once-powerful, 20,000-man army roaming Jinja. Some lay in the streets dying from open wounds. Only about 400 to 500 hard-core loyalists remained.

Many of his henchmen, among them Colonel Nassir Abdalla, governor of Kampala, crossed into Kenya seeking refuge, together with a fleet of twenty Mercedes and forty trucks full of plunder.

Kenyan officials said about eighty per cent of the refugees were Nubians, a tribe from northern Uganda, who were among Idi Amin's loyalist elite. The well-to-do and powerful thus began exile in Peugeots and Alfa Romeos. The poor carted wheelbarrows loaded with mattresses, chairs and tables. All brought tales of massacres.

In the final days before his flight, the crazed dictator raced about eastern Uganda in a red TR-7 sports car, moving from his Lake Victoria villa to Kampala and from there east to Jinja, sending his bodyguards to collect medicines from the local hospital while berating his troops for cowardice. As Kampala was falling, Ugandans heard his voice on an English-language broadcast from a mobile transmitter. 'I would like to denounce the announcement that my government has been overthrown. This is not true.' He called the Tanzanians 'barbaric murderers' and claimed he still controlled ninety per cent of the country. In those last hours, there was a Richard the Third madness about his frenzied oratory.

More and more gruesome evidence of his reign of terror was uncovered as Mohamed Amin kept up his reports on the crucial and bloody frontline war, which dragged on for several weeks after the fall of Kampala.

Once, remembers Duncan Willetts, they drove to Uganda in a Land Cruiser with Andy Torchia of The Associated Press and John Osman of the BBC. 'As we left Nairobi for Soroti, I remember Dolly telling *me* to take care of *Amin*. Incredible!'

The Ugandan town was in ruins. 'There used to be a United Nations flying school in the town, but all we could find were smashed up MiGs littering the runway. There were Tanzania soldiers everywhere with AK 47s. Very hairy. They were walking around all over the town and they were very trigger happy, drinking and enjoying the fruits of victory — the grateful Ugandan lasses. We booked in at the Uganda Tourist Corporation's Soroti Hotel. There wasn't any brochure, of course. No water either — and very little furniture.

'I remember John Osman felt he should introduce himself to the major in charge of the liberation, but afterwards Mo didn't think he had been all that wise. I mean, John went into the room and did his usual courtesy bit, you know, "Glad to meet you, Major. I'm Osman of the BBC."

'This bloke, surrounded by a bevy of good-looking and willing girls, and getting very high on a large and varied selection of miniatures, was totally pissed off by the interruption. If John had said he was from Tass or Radio Moscow he couldn't have cared less.'

On one of these frequent missions to cover the war the team took an Africair charter from Wilson Airport, Nairobi, to Busia, the Kenya-Uganda border town, and crossed into Uganda on foot. Inside the border, they found a Tanzanian soldier in command of a brand-new bus.

'He'd taken it straight out of the showroom,' says Mo. 'I went over to him and in Swahili asked him if he could give us a ride into Jinja.'

'Sure, but I've no petrol.' There was no petrol on the Uganda side at all.

'That's no problem. Why don't you give me the bus and I'll cross over into Kenya, fill it up and bring it back.'

'Not without me. You might not come back.'

'So he came with me. The Kenya border officials were quite helpful, but they insisted that he left his gun with them.

'We drove across, filled up and returned, and Duncan and the rest — Andy Torchia of The Associated Press, the Voice of America correspondent, and other hacks — got in and on we drove to Jinja with this Tanzanian soldier at the wheel.

'At Jinja, we filmed the Tanzanian troops taking over the airfield and then went over to look at State House where Idi Amin had been staying.'

There was a beautiful carving of a large wooden eagle and Mo said to his driver: 'This is very nice.'

'Would you like it?'

'Yes, but how do I take it with me?'

'Don't worry. I'll put it in the bus and hand it over to you at Busia.'

At Busia airstrip, the young European pilot took off and headed for Nairobi. He wanted to go to Kisumu to refuel. But because it was a public holiday the Kisumu control tower said there would be a service charge of twenty shillings and the pilot chose to go on to Nairobi. But the weather broke and he had to divert to refuel at Nakuru.

'I looked out,' recalls Amin. 'and there was the terminal building and he still hadn't touched down. I thought, "Christ. This thing's not going to stop because he's not going to be able to pull up in time." At the end of the runway was the main Mombasa-Kampala road with huge trucks passing along it all the time.

'He then decided to take off again, which was worse because there was no way he was going to clear the power lines at the end of the runway. I thought, "This is it".'

Grim truth of Idi Amin's reign of horror: his last victims, incarcerated in the State Research Bureau, Kampala, were tortured, maimed and hammered to death as the Tanzanian forces drew near to the Uganda capital.

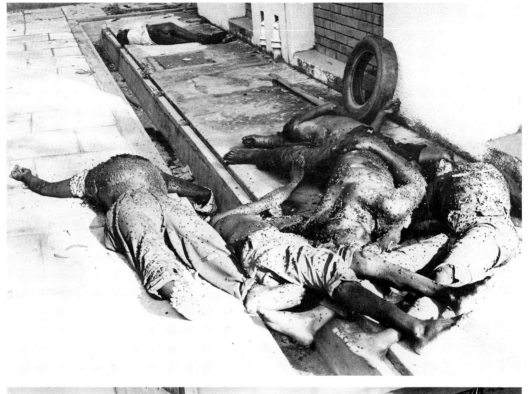

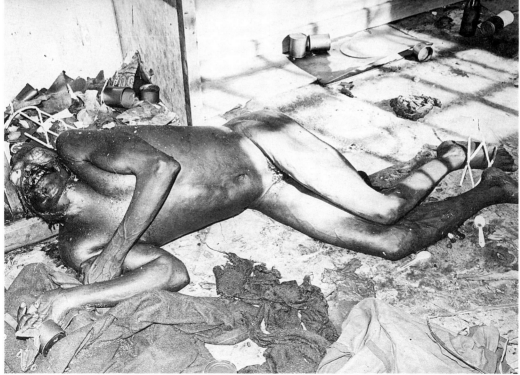

The plane powered into a stone dyke, spun around and collapsed.

'I opened the door and threw myself out and everybody followed,' Mohamed Amin recalls. The pilot was the last out and he just ripped off his epaullettes and threw them on the ground.

'I'm going to lose my job.'

'Damn right. I'm going to make sure you lose your job.'

Two weeks before the same pilot had landed at Maasai Mara with the plane's undercarriage up.

Idi Amin's fall was acclaimed by the whole world. The many filmed interviews and newspaper and magazine still pictures, broadcast and published everywhere, had portrayed him as the increasingly horrifying, deeply disturbing, if at times grotesquely comic, tyrant he really was. A significant amount of that exposure was from Mohamed Amin, either filmed and photographed by himself, or made possible by his efforts and his contacts.

Yet the British, thinking Idi Amin was a simple ex-colonial soldier, had been the first to recognize his government.

12 Expedition Where Man Began

Like most real camera aces, Mohamed Amin is a 'people person' and uses photography to express what he knows and feels about people. He tells thorough, intricate stories that touch people. They respond automatically. He is unpretentious and straightforward, and isn't afraid to move in close with his camera, somehow managing to penetrate almost to the soul of his subject.

It was the people who live around Lake Turkana who were the principal inspiration for his long-delayed expedition which he began organizing in earnest midway through 1979 to take place early in 1980.

As Kenya's fourth general elections, in November 1979, saw the first white Kenyan MP elected by an African majority, Mo was huddled over large-scale ordnance survey reference maps, planning the month-long journey round that rugged wilderness in Kenya's far north.

The concept of the book *People of the Lake* had changed. It had been planned as a book about the el-Molo, a small group living on Lake Turkana's south-eastern shores, illustrated with black and white pictures. The el-Molo, among the smallest communities in the world — fewer than 300 of them at that time — were not enough for the kind of book he now had in mind.

'The trip was for a purpose,' he says. 'For me it wasn't an adventure, although it was for some of the guys. There was a specific purpose to the trip. I didn't set it up just to have fun.

'I had been working on a book on the area for some time and I thought the best way to wrap it up was to go right round the lake, rather than working in sections. It also gives the feel of the whole place. It also added up to a bit more of an adventure in terms of a chapter in the book.'

He wanted the book to focus on all the communities around Turkana, the Merille, Rendille, Samburu, Turkana, and Gabbra as well as the el-Molo, and so be more colourful, as well as more challenging.

Aware of the tensions that can arise in a close-knit group isolated from society in hostile terrain he chose his team carefully. He included an Australian broadcaster, Stewart Sommerlad, and Andrew Johnson, Peter Moll, Saidi Suleiman, and myself.

Amin's planning for any event is impressively thorough. Sean Hawkins, who calls it 'a genius for logistics', says that 'behind his dramatic and beautiful photographs and films lie the realistic planning, the strategies and tactics, the precision timing — not to mention the courage — of a professional military commando. Without this, Mo the artist would never have captured what he did in so many situations.'

It explains partly why seasoned professionals are quite content to let Amin look after arrangements that will affect their safety — and sometimes their survival.

With everything organized to his satisfaction, only days before the expedition set off, he flew to Pakistan in the Ismaili leader's personal jet to cover the Aga Khan architectural awards in Lahore. It was his first visit since his arrest in 1971 and he was determined to ensure that his *persona grata* status in that country was restored under the new military regime of President Zia ul Haq. Knowing the new leader was a devout Muslim, he carried two large photomural prints of the holy places — Mecca and Medinah — to present to the Head of State.

During the awards ceremony in Shalimar Gardens, Lahore, he asked Siddiq Salik, one of the President's military aides, if it would be possible to present the pictures to Zia. He was told he could do it before the President left the ceremonies. 'But I hadn't got anything prepared. The pictures were still not framed, so I said "No", and thought I'd blown it. But next day I got a call to go to the Governor's House.'

The aide warned him that he had only one minute. In the event, the quietly-spoken President wanted to talk to him at length. 'He offered me tea and we had a long and interesting discussion. Then President Zia asked me, "Mr Amin, will you do something for my country? I would like you to produce a book about Pakistan."

'I told him that I would need time to think about the kind of book it should be and I would get in touch with him. Frankly, I thought he would forget all about it. He must meet hundreds of people like me every day.'

President Zia ul Haq, however, proved far from forgetful. But when he returned home early in January, Amin was swept up in the last-minute preparations for the expedition.

Amin left confident that nothing would go wrong. Nothing did. Until the eve of departure after we assembled in the morning for a Press 'photocall' in Total T-shirts and hats, atop the strengthened Land Cruiser with its piles of jerricans and volatile fuel. Departure was set for midnight from his house.

But at the last minute his two writers (Peter Moll and myself) were unable to make the start and the expedition was delayed about twenty-two hours. I had been beaten up a few hours before departure and taken to hospital. When Amin finally tracked me down I handed him my false teeth which had been broken into several pieces and promised to discharge myself from the hospital that night. But would he please get my teeth fixed.

Amin was driving the Land Cruiser and Stewart the Toyota Hilux. Both were heavily laden with water, fuel, food, and tents, even a trail bike. It was a complete survival kit for the four-week expedition. In addition,

Making a documentary on the Aga Khan architectural awards scheme,
Mohamed Amin wires the spiritual leader of the world's Ismailis for sound with
a neck mike.

Pakistani President Zia ul Haq talking to Mohamed Amin in the grounds of the Governor's House in Lahore, when he asked the cameraman if he would 'do something for my country'. The result of this meeting was the book *Journey through Pakistan*.

there was half-a-ton of camera equipment.

Heading off towards Rumuruti on a rather rugged murram road, Amin, who had not slept for two nights worrying about the delay, dozed off and the Land Cruiser hit a bank and rolled.

'Peter Moll was in the front with me and you and Saidi were in the back,' Amin recalls. 'You were all asleep but woke up very quickly. We all crawled out and fortunately nobody was hurt.'

He reminded me that I had just been released from hospital. 'You lost your pain-killers which you were holding in your hand but you were still clutching your bottle of beer.

'Soon after, out of the blue a police patrol car drove up. They were eager to prosecute somebody for dangerous driving. They talked to you while you sat there on the side of the road drinking your beer but you assured them that there was nothing dangerous about my driving. You had been advised to rest and avoid exertion.'

Shaking their heads, the police just drove away.

'We got the vehicle back on its wheels using the winch and the Hilux. All the windows were shattered and the top was totally bent. We drove back to Nyahururu and spent all day putting the vehicle back into some sort of shape so that we could drive on.

'We were unable to put any windows back as it was impossible to straighten anything.'

While this was going on I went to see the local doctor because some glass had gone into my eye causing intense pain but he could only give me some eye drops, so I cadged a lift in a Land Rover and went to hospital in Nairobi.

Mo remembers it best because I was back in the same bed in the same ward and no doctor or nurse believed me when I told them I had left. They all thought I had serious brain damage.

The actual story of the expedition and its drama, including the arrest of the entire team by Cuban-trained Marxists at a remote Ethiopian border post, is told by Mohamed Amin in the final chapter of *Cradle of Mankind*.

For more than half a century, largely during colonial times, the whole Turkana region was a closed zone kept isolated from the rest of the country and patrolled by British troops. Whatever the motives for this policy, it had the effect of insulating the peoples of the lake, and their traditions, from the changes going on around them. In the book, Amin writes:

> We took stock for twenty-four hours at Nyahururu, repaired what we could and hammered the worst protruberances back into the body-work. More equipment including a tent, beds and the refrigerator had to be jettisoned.
>
> But there were minor compensations. The lack of windscreen and windows, for instance, provided welcome ventilation when we eventually reached the Suguta Valley. A precipitous track, hand-made by an Italian missionary, leads down from Parkati for a few miles before petering out. And it was along these boulder-strewn 215

slopes, forty-eight hours later, that the much lighter station wagon crept into the valley, surely one of the hottest places on earth. From now on we became trail-blazers in the truest sense of the word.

Our two vehicles trailed a great cloud of dust as they raced across the floor of the Suguta Valley. The dried-up mud flats which we had to cross had turned into a giant shimmering saucepan.

We stayed in the Suguta for four days, braising slowly in our own sweat at noon temperatures of up to 137° Fahrenheit. While there, we climbed a perfect cone of ash called Andrew's Volcano, named after Lieutenant H. Andrew, a member of the Cavendish expedition to Turkana in 1897. Another climb, more rewarding, was across the Barrier, the coal-black crust of a vast lava flow which prevents just about any form of access to the southern tip of Turkana.

Our climbs proved what we already knew — that there was no way to drive over the Barrier to the Kerio Valley.

We decided to move on as directly as possible from the Suguta to Kalokol, halfway along the western shore of Lake Turkana. We estimated that the journey would take us two days. We could not afford to take much longer since our supply of water was already running low.

Two nights later, in fast-gathering darkness, we pitched camp as the sun sank behind a low hill. We had winched our way over screes and rocks and spent back-breaking hours clearing boulders from our path and, encouraged by our Turkana guides, had continued into a rugged wilderness. And now we were quite lost. What had begun as an adventure had turned into an ordeal of dehydration and energy sucking heat, fatigue and bewilderment. The guides we had hired finally admitted that they had no idea where we were.

Three more days passed before we finally reached Lokori, and then Kalokol near Ferguson's Gulf, the village where the Turkana Fishermen's Co-operative has brought the first signs of the industrial era to the region. A large filleting and freezing plant was nearing completion as we camped in the shade of some palms.

By now the station wagon needed a thorough repair job. Despite having taken off most of the weight, the rack was causing the roof to move around alarmingly: both front windscreen pillars had broken away and cracks were appearing around all the other pillars.

With the help of the Co-operative's mechanic, Stewart Sommerlad set to work. After almost three days the station wagon had a pipe frame that bolted to the floor in four places and also around the windscreen pillars. This kept the tottering superstructure more or less rigid and in place for the rest of the trip.

Once reassembled, the expedition set off for an exploration of Central Island, an hour away by power-boat from Ferguson's Gulf. A still active volcano, Central Island has three craters — one large, one small and side-vented, and the third submerged as a sand-fringed lagoon. It sounds attractive, but erosion has left the island looking hardly more scenic than a colliery tip.

Central Island could erupt at any moment and, amongst other damage, wipe out an important resting place for the migrant birds which come there attracted by the fruit of bright green *salvadora* bushes. There was no indication of an impending eruption when we were there, but the birds were clearly soon going to need another place to feed since the *salvadora* is being destroyed by the fishermen who camp on the island.

Back on the main track up the western shore of the lake from Ferguson's Gulf, there was nothing to relieve the monotony. We covered over a hundred miles of flattish, featureless scrub desert with nothing alive in it, or so it seemed.

It was not until after the Kenya border post at Todenyang that we were diverted by any incident of note.

The expedition had been cleared to enter Ethiopia by the highest authorities in Addis Ababa [the Ethiopian capital]. And, just to make sure, the day before taking the expedition across I paid a visit to the Ethiopian border post at Namuruputh. I was greeted warmly and told that the expedition would be welcome. When we arrived, however, we were arrested — the full drama, with rifles at our backs. The letters and visas meant nothing after all.

We persuaded the border guards to let us use our radio and eventually we got through to the Ethiopian Embassy in Nairobi who contacted Addis Ababa on our behalf. The response was an order, in Amharic morse, from the Ethiopian capital to let us into their country. The performance had taken forty-eight hours.

We then drove on a few miles to what I had always considered would be the biggest obstacle in any 'grand design' to drive round Lake Turkana — the meandering waters of the River Omo, more than a quarter of a mile wide at the village of Kalaam.

In the sixties, Kalaam had been a ferry-point for crossing the Omo, the sluggish fresh-water feed for the lake. The problem was that the American missionaries who built and operated the ferry had departed when Ethiopia became a Marxist state after the overthrow of Emperor Haile Selassie. Ethiopia's new revolutionary government failed to keep the Omo ferry in working order. Thus, although originally a well constructed unit consisting of a steel platform on top of twenty-five oil drums, it had fallen into decay. The drums had corroded into a mesh of holes and the pontoon lay half-submerged on the gentle slopes of the bank.

Hearts sinking, we drove fourteen miles upstream, directed by George Kistachir, the District Officer, to a place called Omo Rati where a second ferry was located. This turned out to be a series of planks on top of three large fibreglass dinghies. It looked solid enough, and it was floating, although a fourth dinghy was missing. 217

In 1980 Mohamed Amin's 'Round Turkana' expedition circumnavigated the 6,600-square-kilometre Jade Sea in Kenya's far north during a twenty-seven-day journey through some of the world's toughest terrain — filming and photographing the colourful and unspoilt cultures of the peoples who still live around the lake. Out of the expedition came the book *Cradle of Mankind*.

Opposite: The *Cradle of Mankind* exhibition drew large crowds in Nairobi and at the Commonwealth Institute, London, where it was opened by Princess Alexandra. Centrepiece of the larger-than-life photomurals was Mohamed Amin's favourite picture, shown above, of an el-Molo boy with a young crocodile he harpooned on the south-eastern shores of Lake Turkana.

The banks were steep and I worried that they might cause problems when loading and unloading. To overcome this obstacle we dug tons of earth out of the banks on both sides to make ramps.

One member of the team scrounged a broken-down outboard motor from George and managed to get it working. The rest of us set about strengthening and improving the ferry — a job that took a day and a night of hard labour, wiring oil drums and timber together. We christened the thing the 'Rati Queen' before we inched the station wagon aboard, very nearly losing it in the process. Then the unpredictable outboard seized in midstream.

The second crossing was less erratic and the pick-up was landed without mishap.

Originally we had intended to spend at least a week in Ethiopia but we were followed everywhere at gunpoint — 'for our own protection', I was assured — and repeatedly warned that photography was not allowed. So now that we had crossed the Omo I did not want to spend longer than necessary in Ethiopia. After an overnight camp on the eastern shores of the Omo I decided to head for Kenya.

It was not much later, after travelling for some thirty miles on the east bank, that our two-vehicle convoy drove over a small rise and we sighted a new Ethiopian border post. This was something we had not expected. As we approached it, two soldiers came out levelling their rifles at us as they ran down the hill. They seemed to have had a message about our expected arrival for they waved vigorously, presumably directing us into the border post. However, we picked up speed and ran straight past them, over the line to Kenya and did not stop until we reached the police station at Ileret.

The expedition returned to Nairobi on 13 February, after an absence of twenty-seven days. Amin's achievement in bringing his team successfully through such hostile territory received an accolade from Britain's Royal Geographical Society. That august body made him a Fellow of the Society, adding his name to a distinguished list which includes David Livingstone, Sir John Hunt and other famous explorers and pioneers.

Such fame attracts the most improbable characters in search of help. One was a zany character called Mihail Zimeonov, who had conceived the idea of moulding ten life-size bronzes, using dental alginate for the mould, from a living elephant. It was a perfect television story.

On 18 March 1980, Mo and Brian Barron drove up to Ol Pejeta ranch, then the private reserve of Saudi billionaire Adnan Kashoggi. It sprawled across more than 16,000 wilderness acres on the Laikipia Plains, north of Mount Kenya. It had its own herd of elephants as well as other wildlife. Peter de Mello, Ol Pejeta's game warden, had been instructed to find a suitable animal and Dr Ishtiaq Chawdri, from Kenya's Wildlife Conservation Department, was to drug the beast.

Kashoggi's pilot, a German hunter based in Kenya, took the ranch Cessna aloft and circled the area looking for a pachyderm to plaster. He found one just outside the chain mesh fence which isolates the homestead from the wilderness. Dr Chawdri fired a dart in the rear flank of the medium-size bull which, it was discovered too late, had a damaged right tusk.

The dart sent the beast charging madly through the tangled bush, a fleet of four-wheel drive vehicles in pursuit, stumbling crazily in and out of the thorn trees and lurching through the semi-jungle for almost two miles until it succumbed to the drug.

Amin, camera on shoulder, followed in the lead car as Mihail and his handlers moved in with their US$40,000 worth of plastic-like material — from which dentists normally mould dental impressions — which they slapped over the slumbering beast, white on its right side, before ponderously turning it over for pink on its left.

When Dr Chawdri gave the elephant the antidote to revive it Amin moved in close to film its awakening, despite warnings that it might get up suddenly and angrily. Being his soundman I should have stayed with him. But as the elephant trembled, and shook itself out of its deep sleep, I remembered his dash to safety with Peter Moll when filming Ahmed and I unscrewed the lead between the camera and recorder and took refuge on the lorry. He shot the end of the story without sound.

Though nothing was ever again heard of Mihail and his bronze elephants, that pink and white elephant put the finishing touch to one of the zaniest stories Amin ever filmed.

It was a year of high comedy and high drama for the Visnews ace. A few weeks after the Mihail sequence, Pope John Paul II paid his first visit to Kenya, arriving on 6 May. He was a charismatic figure and Amin was deluged with assignments including photography for *Newsweek* and *Time*.

'I heard that the Pope was a keep-fit enthusiast who went out jogging and also had a morning swim. I thought it would make great pictures,' Amin says.

'All we had to do was get him first thing in the morning. So with Duncan, I went to the papal nuncio's house in Lavington, Nairobi where the Pope was staying. It was just after six o' clock. The place was guarded by Kenya's paramilitary force, the GSU, who were reasonably friendly and let us in through the gates.

'We knocked on the door but there was no answer. I tried the door and it was open. We went from room to room looking for the Pope. But there was nobody around.

'About the seventh or eighth door, we ran into this big, tall man who looked like an American. In fact, I had seen him around the Pope before. He was Paul Marcinkus.'

It was clear that the two, who were carrying most of their gear, were news photographers. Marcinkus, all dressed up in a priest's clothes with the cassock and collar, was furious.

'What the hell are you doing here?'

Pope John Paul II blesses Kenya children during the Pontiff's visit in 1980 when Mohamed Amin had a confrontation with Archbishop Paul Marcinkus, known to many as 'God's Banker'.

'Father, this is a Holy house. Don't be so angry.'

'How did you get in?'

'Father, we came through the door.'

Mo said they wanted some pictures of the Pope jogging and swimming.

'He must have thought we were a bit around the bend but also pretty harmless. He told us that we had to leave and I said, "Look, we really need to get some pictures. If we can't film him swimming, can we take some pictures of him at breakfast?" — which he was probably having out on the patio. There was a firm negative.

'Although we had to leave the house, we were allowed to stay in the grounds to take some pictures of him as he left on his drive to the mass rally at Uhuru Park which was the highlight of his visit.

'While we hung around in the gardens I figured out that if we took pictures of him leaving the house we'd never make it to Uhuru Park in time, so I organised the convoy of cars outside. Since we were working from inside the grounds it was very easy for us to put our Land Cruiser in front of the Papal car, which in fact later produced some excellent material. We were the only ones directly in front photographing His Holiness and the thousands lining the route.

'If we had asked for this privilege I think it would have been refused, but the fact that we were working from inside the residence meant there were no problems.

'By this time a number of families of people who worked in the papal nunciate had gathered to be presented to His Holiness when he came out with the papal nuncio.

'He picked up little children and talked to the mothers, which gave me many first-class, human interest pictures, and the papal nuncio, whom I knew quite well, brought the Pope over to us and introduced Duncan and me, explaining that I had done a lot of work in Africa and also a book on the pilgrimage to Mecca.

'His Holiness gave us each a gold and ruby rosary. I treasure this.'

From the divine to the evil: mystery still surrounded Idi Amin's escape from Uganda. And, after all his years reporting the dictator's rule, Mohamed Amin was intrigued about the man's hideout. Nothing had been seen or heard of the fugitive dictator since mid-April 1979. Initially he had gone to ground in Libya in a big house just outside Tripoli where he had been told by Gaddafi to remain incognito. Idi Amin did not like this new kind of existence. Then the photographer heard that he had moved from Africa.

Using his network of contacts, following up one rumour after another, he discovered that his namesake had gone into hiding, together with his large family, somewhere in Jeddah, Saudi Arabia. The hideout was secret, but he was confident that, once in the city, he could track the tyrant down.

It was going to be expensive, however, and there was no guarantee that he would succeed. In April he discussed it with Brendan Farrow at 223

Visnews in guarded terms. The newsroom executive was enthusiastic, but the company's top management opposed it. Mohamed turned to BBC's Brian Barron, who thought Idi Amin was probably still in Libya. Barron was very keen to do the story and insistent that he and Mo go together. At no stage did the cameraman reveal Amin's whereabouts to Barron.

Slowly, however, the commercial possibilities of the story became apparent to the Visnews management and they agreed to underwrite the expedition. They were also strongly against any BBC involvement, fearing that BBC Enterprises, the corporation's powerful commercial wing, would gain the financial advantage at Visnews' expense.

Two lengthy messages to Brendan Farrow on 23 and 24 May tell the story. Referring to the BBC London approaches to Visnews London, Amin telexed:

> In case there are any misunderstandings, the circumstances surrounding this are:
> 1. I have been following this story for past two to three months when I was first tipped off by my contact about the change of the whereabouts of our elusive friend.
> 2. I maintained close contact but did not want to talk to anybody until I was reasonably sure the information was accurate and that I would have a reasonable chance to see the subject.
> 3. Barron and I discussed this story in very general terms about four weeks ago but he had no real information of the person's whereabouts.
> 4. As Uganda situation deteriorated further BB and I again discussed the possibilities as Uganda was now a hot item.
> 5. The fact that I discussed this with BB was in no way intended to mean that I was handing him the story. Over the past year I have suffered [a] great deal of frustration on several top stories due [to] your economy drive and there is no way I intend to hand over this story.
> 6. The joint operation idea was only discussed after Visnews said no to my proposition. At that point I had made it very clear to BB that the story was mine, the contact is mine, and if I agreed to do a deal with BBC (as VIS could not be persuaded to spend the money) it had to be in such a way that the BBC would pay all the costs, absolutely everything, which would have amounted to perhaps ten thousand sterling if the story worked — if it failed a lot less — and BBC would only have UK (repeat UK) rights and I would own the world rights.
> 7. That's the summary. As far as I am concerned the story is still mine and my loyalty is to Visnews. In other words since you now agree with me and are prepared to risk your money it's now yours too. You make a decision about the BBC. Personally I see no objection to BBC participation but doubt if Barron's presence is needed on the initial trip and if he insists on coming don't see why VIS should share his cost. Feel confident BB on his own would not even get near the hotel

as the authorities are none too happy about Limey accents at the moment.

Farrow phoned Amin to discuss the BBC joining the trip. Visnews realized that even he could not be sleuth, cameraman, soundman, lightman, grip and interviewer all at once, so they finally agreed to allow the BBC to join in. But explicit terms were agreed to protect Visnews sales rights.

In a letter of 28 May 1980 to Alan Protheroe, then editor, BBC TV news, Visnews editor-in-chief Robert Kearsley referred to 'the various discussions between BBC and Visnews people in Nairobi and London', and sought agreement for the Idi Amin Project. These included fifty-fifty shared costs for the three-man crew, Barron, Thirer and Mohamed Amin, exclusive UK broadcasting rights for BBC-TV news and exclusive international distribution rights outside the UK for Visnews. Another clause specified that 'Visnews and BBC Television News' would agree on the date and time of the first broadcast of the material.

The final clause read that 'the original negative would remain in Visnews hands', but 'that copies for BBC use . . . would be made free of any charge' — acknowledgement of Visnews copyright ownership. The letter, countersigned by Protheroe, was stamped with the BBC Television News seal. But Visnews staff remained unhappy.

On Thursday 28 May, the three flew from Nairobi to Jeddah. They entered the country professionally incognito for, unless cleared well beforehand by the highest authority, film crews were not allowed into Saudi Arabia.

Breaking his cine camera down into several pieces and adding theodolites and plumb lines and other bits of professional survey equipment Amin divided the camera and sound equipment among the three.

'All the bits and pieces were scattered through my baggage and Eric's. I was also carrying the sound equipment. We gave twenty rolls of Eastman colour negative to Brian who put it in his brown suitcase.

'We went through Customs separately so that we wouldn't look as if we were together. I was asked what I did. I said I was a surveyor and there was no hassle. He didn't connect the bits of camera and tripod with filming and I was through.

'Soon after, Eric was also out. Brian joined us about ten minutes later and we all looked at each other and said, "Everything OK?" And Brian said, "No. We've lost the stock." All twenty rolls of Eastman colour negative had been held. But he was given a receipt.

'But the Customs guys never connected the film with any of the equipment we were carrying. As there was not a lot we could do, we drove off to the Meridien Hotel. Immediately, I began to work on getting the stock. There was no point in finding Idi Amin if we had nothing to film him with.

'One of my Visnews colleagues, Maurice Thompson, was in Riyadh. He 225 was from the production division, which worked completely independent of the news division. But I was sure that he would help.

'He was surprised to hear that I was in Jeddah but didn't ask any questions. He gave me the name of a cameraman — who I realized later was actually working in the Ministry of Information — to call.

'The cameraman didn't have any Eastman colour film, but I still had to look for Idi Amin. Since it was a Friday, I thought the best place to look would be at the Friday prayers. But there are hundreds of mosques in Saudi Arabia and it was really a game of chance.'

Once again, 'Mo's Luck' came into play.

'I hired a car with a Pakistani driver and asked him if he'd seen the Ugandan leader as he was a friend of mine.

'He said Idi often went to Mecca, a forty minutes journey from Jeddah, which was a good place to look for him.

'The Holy Mosque in Mecca is the biggest mosque in the world and has several gates. I asked the driver to drop me at one of them. But when I got there the prayers had just finished and people were beginning to leave. Since it holds up to half a million people and because it was Friday prayers it was pretty full.

'I went inside anyway and looked around but I couldn't see him. While I was there, however, I decided to perform Umrah, which is the Lesser Pilgrimage, and I started my prayers. I performed Umrah, circling the Kab'ah seven times.

After praying Mo looked up and recognized, sitting close by, one of Idi Amin's bodyguards. He also recognized Mo.

'What are you doing here?'

'I've just come to pray. How's the big man?'

'Well, you just missed him. He was here a few minutes ago.'

Amin said he would like to pay his respects. Could he see him later that day?

'Give me your number. I will tell him you're here. I'm sure he would like to see you.'

'At least now I knew my information was correct. When I left the mosque and got into the car the driver told me, "Your friend Idi Amin came out two minutes after you went in".

'Brian and Eric were waiting at the Meridien. There was still nothing doing on the film side. I told Brian to leave it to me and not get involved.'

A little later an angry Thompson called Amin.

'Tell me, what are you doing in Saudi Arabia?'

'I'm just here doing a job for news division.'

'I've just been summoned by the minister for information to explain what a Visnews cameraman is doing in Jeddah.'

The government cameraman had reported Mo's call to his superiors.

'I told Maurice I was just checking on a story. In fact, I didn't even have any camera equipment in my room, which was true. It was all locked away in Eric's room.

Mohamed Amin pictured with deposed Ugandan leader Idi Amin after the cameraman tracked the Field Marshal down to his secret hideaway in Jeddah, Saudi Arabia, and persuaded him to give an exclusive interview.

Thompson insisted that the cameraman should tell him what he was doing. When Mo replied, he hit the roof.

'Here I am trying to sell a million dollar contract to the Saudi Government on behalf of Visnews and you're going to blow it and have us all arrested.'

'Sorry, Maurice. I know we work for the same company but I think you had better talk to head office. I am here to do a job and I'm going to do the best I can.'

'If you don't leave Saudi Arabia tonight I will have you arrested.'

'Maurice. You're not going to sell me down the drain are you?'

'Yes, I'm going to sell you down the drain.'

The telephone call gave Mohamed Amin an even greater sense of urgency. He went straight to the Kodak office in Jeddah to look for Eastman negative colour film. Now time was vital.

It was another instance of 'Mo's Luck'.

The manager said: 'We never stock this film. But somebody ordered twenty rolls which arrived here two weeks ago, after he left the country.' It was cheaper than the same stock in London.

Soon after he had a call from one of Idi Amin's sons who came over to the hotel.

'We drove back to Idi Amin's hideout and I was then taken in for a traditional reunion, an embrace and kiss on the cheek and we sat drinking tea.

'He was delighted to see me but when I asked him for an interview he said he could not do it. He was a guest of the King. I stayed on, however, and continued our conversation. It went on and on. I kept repeating my request. People in Uganda felt let down that Idi Amin had not spoken since leaving Uganda and the world was waiting to hear what he had to say.

'Finally, in the early hours of the morning, this got through and he said he would give me an interview "for one minute only".

'I immediately went to get Brian and Eric. Idi Amin had said he would not go outside the room but we had no lights. So we just drove through the market, which was open around the clock, and bought two "sun guns", which are readily available in Jeddah at throwaway prices.

'When we got back Idi Amin was dressed in a safari suit. I told Brian he could forget about a one-minute interview because "once he's got the lights on him and the camera is going you can ask as many questions as you want". In the end we had a one-hour interview, a world exclusive.

'When we came out I said we should go straight to the airport and take the first flight out no matter where it was going.

'I took the film and handed all the equipment to Eric and told him to catch another separate flight, wherever it might be going.

'We headed straight for the airport. Fortunately, the first flight was to London. I told Brian to take the receipt and collect the twenty rolls which had been confiscated. He did and so we had our unused film as well. The exposed film was in the suitcase. It was too risky to hand carry, especially with the security check. I thought we would have problems, and at that time there was no security on the checked baggage.' Thirer caught the next flight to Karachi — two hours later.

During the flight Brian Barron showed Mohamed Amin the draft of a press release announcing the discovery of Idi Amin's whereabouts by Brian Barron of the BBC and Mohamed Amin of Visnews. 'I didn't ask him to write it and it sounded OK and I told him, fine, and went back to sleep.'

They arrived at Heathrow around six in the morning. In the baggage hall, Barron phoned his editor. He came back asking for the film.

'No. The film goes to Visnews. It's not the BBC's film.'

'But we should have it.'

'The BBC can't process Eastman colour. Visnews can and we've got a twenty-four-hour laboratory.'

Amin kept his film, and they went their separate ways. Mo hired a car and drove straight to Visnews' Park Royal headquarters where the film was processed immediately. At that stage he didn't think that anybody in Visnews realized just how big the story was.

Checking in at a hotel, he cleaned up and drove back to Visnews as the BBC issued the following Press release:

935226 TVNEWS G
Amin talks exclusively to BBC TV news. Press Release
2nd June 1980

Idi Amin has reappeared and BBC television news will run in the nine o'clock news on BBC-1 Tomorrow (Tuesday June 3rd) an exclusive interview with the Ugandan Dictator.

For the first time since the overthrow of his regime fourteen months ago, Idi Amin talks to a journalist — Brian Barron, BBC TV news African correspondent, the Royal Television Society Television Reporter of the Year.

In a joint operation with Visnews, the London based international newsfilm agency, Barron tracked down and eventually met Idi Amin at his secret refuge in an Arab country.

Barron said: 'It was all very bizarre. Amin looked fitter and younger than when I last saw him — that was two years ago when he was in power.

He would not allow us to take pictures of the four sons he had with him — Maclaren, Mckenzie, Campbell and Moses — and before the cameras began to turn we conversed to the background music of Idi Amin's personal cassette — recording of the pipes and drums of the Black Watch.'

Barron added: 'Amin insisted that precise details of his whereabouts should remain secret.'

Amin told Barron: 'To tell you the truth, I enjoyed the war, the decisions, the command, though I'm very sorry about those who lost their lives.'

In a wide-ranging interview, Amin says he still sees himself as the saviour of Uganda, and dismisses reports of atrocities.

For further information: Peter Rosier,
News and Current Affairs Publicity,
BBC Television Centre, London W.12

Tel: 743 3000 ext. 7726/7

Not one mention of Mohamed Amin.

The London evening newspapers carried the story of Barron 'scooping the world'. Visnews staff were disgusted. Managing Editor Tom Hudson, now head of news, also badly upset, assured everyone that it would be sorted out and urged the news staff to leave it to the management.

But next day still, the morning papers told how that night's BBC Nine O'Clock news would feature 'Barron's' exclusive interview with Idi Amin. Driving to Visnews, Mohamed Amin tuned in the car radio to hear Barron 'coming out loud and clear on how he'd tracked down Idi Amin over six months. You'd have thought he'd been alone in the desert and across the poles. He came on like Lawrence of Arabia'. Seething, Amin stormed into Tom Hudson's office.

'What the hell's going on?'

Tom had heard Barron as well. Furious, Amin said:

'Just give me the film. I'll take it and we'll forget all about this.'

Just then Mo's editor-in-chief Bob Kearsley rang Hudson to ask if he knew where Amin was as the BBC wanted photographs of Barron with Idi Amin.

'Tell him to fuck off,' Mo told Tom.

Hudson handed the telephone to the Nairobi newsman.

'Tell him yourself.'

An ex-BBC man, Kearsley didn't understand Amin's anger.

'For God's sake, Bob, this is a Visnews story and we're letting the BBC walk all over us. It's an absolute lie that Barron got this story. It's totally untrue. We did it and it's ours.'

He remembers that when he left Hudson's office he said he was going to go to ITN and tell the whole story. 'But it's not something I would have done.'

Mo returned to his hotel pursued by telephone calls from Kearsley asking him to appear at a BBC Press conference at Television Centre that afternoon. He hung up. Kearsley rang back.

'Can we sort this out?'

'No, they're telling lies. If I go to the Press conference I'll tell them it's lies. It's not a BBC story.'

230   Finally, however, Amin reluctantly agreed. In the news room Barron

was too busy attending to requests for interviews from radio stations around the world to do much more than raise a hand in greeting.

Amin was introduced to the BBC editor who came round the desk and shook his hand.

'Congratulations Mo. It's a fantastic story.'

The cameraman stared at him.

'Don't congratulate me. I didn't do anything. It's all Brian Barron.'

'What's the problem?'

'Basically you're lying. Don't distort the facts. If I go to the Press conference I'll say so.'

The editor confessed a wrong had been done. That night, before the exclusive was shown on BBC, pictures of Barron and Mohamed appeared on the screen to introduce it.

There was a sequel. The London *Sunday Times* report of the Visnews discontent, in its 15 June edition, ended: 'The BBC, the major Visnews shareholder, is unrepentant and says: "If anyone suggests a cameraman should front a TV programme, sorry, that's not on. We employ journalists, and very good ones for that".'

Clearly the BBC at that time had no problem deciding who was more important to television news — the cameraman who got the story or the front man who tagged on to his coat-tail.

Amin was furious. But he had little time to fret. In Nairobi, he was immersed in the *Cradle of Mankind* book. He invited Richard Leakey, director of Kenya's National Museums whose own book on the origins of the human race, *The Making of Mankind*, was then in the final stages of production, to write the foreword, and sent him a copy of the manuscript. This had been revised to Mo's satisfaction, but he felt some pictures were missing. The book, he decided, needed aerial photographs.

Operation Drake, the adventure voyage run by Colonel John Blashford Snell which involved youths from all over the world in worthy assignments in far-flung places, including Kenya, supplied the answer. The team, which arrived in August 1980, was going to Sibiloi National Park, Lake Turkana. The expedition's transport included a thirty-three-year-old museum piece, a Beaver aircraft of the British Army's Air Corps based at Aldershot, England, which had been rehabilitated for Operation Drake. It was piloted by two veterans whom Mo christened 'Biggles I' and 'Biggles II'. Both were near their fifties.

He requisitioned the Beaver to report on the adventure safari, and to do his aerials of Lake Turkana. Though *Cradle of Mankind* was virtually finished, he wanted me to go with him to get the feel of the place.

The Beaver had a simple drop window which was pulled up and down by a leather strap. With no safety belt and perched on his upturned camera case, Amin sat by this, leaning out whenever he thought there might be a picture. Slowly, the burning waste of Suguta Valley receded and we were over the lake. Ahead, over the pilots' shoulders, I could make out the shape of South Island where two of Sir Vivien Fuchs 1934 exploration team 231 had vanished without trace. Not a place, I thought, to make a forced landing.

Suddenly, the single engine spluttered and died. Winking at me, Mo said, 'That's why they didn't let you carry your beer on this trip. It would have been wasted at the bottom of the lake.' Biggles I and Biggles II, who between them accounted for about sixty years of flying, were agitated, hands flying over buttons, switches, levers, eyes intent. The Beaver drifted on, only the rush of the slipstream through the open window could be heard. Unconcerned, Amin went on taking pictures.

As the Beaver drifted back over the land he suggested jokingly that they put it down on one of the beaches. Minutes later, after jiggling the wings, fuel flowed again into the engine and it restarted. But on the last leg to the landing strip at Alia Bay the engine spluttered out again and we came in wide and swift, the plane's shadow stampeding a herd of zebra grazing on the strip. That photograph made an impressive two-page spread in the book.

The day he returned he was off to the Rift Valley to photograph a Maasai village, manyatta, for another book, *The Last of the Maasai* (published in 1987). The following day, in Nairobi, he was discussing progress on the text of two other books: *Ivory Crisis*, by Ian Parker, and *Run Rhino Run*, by Esmond and Chryssee Bradley Martin, with his pictures. By now Camerapix had a regular stand at the main event in the publishing calendar, the Frankfurt Book Fair, where later in 1980 he showed colour proofs and the manuscript of *Cradle of Mankind* to potential buyers. The English edition was taken by Chatto & Windus, the American edition by the Overlook Press.

The sale concluded, he at once decided to start on another book. *Journey through Kenya* was conceived with the idea of publication in time for the OAU Heads of State summit in Nairobi in June 1981. Time was critical, so at the end of November Willetts and I began a five-week safari around Kenya.

It ended on New Year's Eve 1981 which Amin was spending with his family at a friend's house in Westlands, three miles out of town. As they celebrated the walls of the house shook with the force of a tremendous explosion.

'I immediately telephoned the police,' he recalls. 'They had heard this explosion, too, but didn't know where it was. I telephoned the fire station and they said they had heard it as well but didn't know where it was from. I phoned the *Nation* newspaper and they heard it, too, but didn't know where it was.

'I called the fire station again and they said they thought it was at the Norfolk Hotel, the capital's oldest and finest five-star hotel. Immediately I rang the Norfolk number. It was dead. I then looked in the directory and there was another number. For a call box.

'I called this and somebody lifted the receiver and just said: "Please help. Please help. We're dying here. I've just lost my leg. Please help."

Tragic aftermath of the Norfolk Hotel bomb blast in Nairobi on New Year's Eve 1980 which killed more than ten people and wounded many more.

'I rushed to my office, collected my cameras and went to the Norfolk. It was gruesome, shocking. A whole wing had been blown apart and there were bodies everywhere, wounded lying around. The restaurant above which the bomb had exploded was shattered and the place was ablaze.

'The police were there and the fire brigade and soon afterwards the fire engines from the airport arrived. But it took hours to bring the fire under control. I filmed the bodies being brought out of the restaurant and the wounded, some with hands and legs blown off, being taken to hospital.

'It was learned later that this bomb had been planted by a Palestinian organization apparently as revenge against the owners, the Jewish Block family, who helped the arrangements for the Israeli raid on Entebbe, but the truth will perhaps never be known.'

Amin took the finished manuscript and colour transparencies of *Journey through Kenya* to a Kenya Government ministry with the suggestion that they should buy presentation copies for delegates to the upcoming Organization of African Unity Conference in Nairobi. But nobody was prepared to back the enthusiasm they voiced and he soon abandoned the idea.

By then, he and Willetts were already working to complete photography on a parallel *Journey through Pakistan*. 'Duncan was never really involved in doing books or anything on the publishing side of the company until *Journey through Kenya* and *Journey through Pakistan*. I asked him if he would work on them. I thought it would be interesting to see how we worked together. Both books were a tremendous success. Since then Duncan and I have shared photography on virtually all our books.'

President Zia ul Haq was enthusiastic to see the book completed. Between them Amin, Willetts and writer Graham Hancock spent several months in that rugged country. Promised every facility and support, they discovered this was no empty pledge.

Later, in London, the secretary for the Pakistan ministry of information rang Amin to say that President Zia ul Haq, then in Paris, would like to see him — with the book proofs, if possible.

When Mo arrived, the Pakistani leader was addressing a press conference. While he fielded tough questions with intellectual agility, the photographer went into an ante-room and laid out the full-colour proofs on a large table. After the conference, Zia greeted Mo with warmth, then slowly and methodically studied each picture — of ancient Mughal forts, of camel nomads in the deserts, of K2, the world's second highest mountain at more than 28,000 feet, taken from the open doorway of a helicopter flying in freezing winter weather, rotor blades desperately clawing the thin air 3,000 feet above the chopper's ceiling with Mo's finger frozen on the shutter trigger. The President turned to the newsman. 'Mr Amin — I never knew my country was so beautiful.'

Mohamed wanted to publish the two *Journey through* books — *Pakistan* and *Kenya* — simultaneously. But *Kenya* still had no buyer. I suggested he write to film star William Holden — an old friend who knew Kenya well —

asking if he could publish the book as *William Holden's Journey through Kenya*.

Holden was enthusiastic. 'I congratulate you', wrote the star of *Stalag 11*, *Bridge on the River Kwai* and *The Wild Bunch*, 'for a truly remarkable job. I'm delighted to do the foreword.' He enclosed a 5,000-word manuscript, the first chapter. The first edition came out in 1983 and by 1987 *Journey through Kenya* had been reprinted in English five times. There are also German, Italian, French and Swedish language editions.

Then, in June 1981, while filming the OAU conference in his home town, Amin was asked to stage an exhibition of his work at the Commonwealth Institute in London. It was timely. He had just arranged for Kenya's Attorney-General Charles Njonjo to open his *Cradle of Mankind* exhibition in Nairobi in September and most of the work was already done.

Charles Njonjo, among the inner-cabinet in the Kenya Government, at that time was a close confidante and associate of President Daniel arap Moi. He opened the exhibition at the Nairobi Hilton on 23 September 1981. Mohamed Amin used the occasion to launch a trust fund to help educate the children of the communities around Lake Turkana. To do this, he produced a limited edition of *Cradle of Mankind* signed by Richard Leakey and himself. In an appeal to potential buyers, he pointed out: 'The cost of producing this special edition, printed on fine art paper, handbound in expensive simulated leather, with a gold blocked cover and elegant slipcase, is my own personal contribution to the Lake Turkana Education Fund.' It was a substantial contribution: running into several thousand pounds. The charity still functions.

The staging of the exhibition in Nairobi coincided with publication. Reviews were ecstatic. *Africana*, the most respected wildlife magazine in East Africa, described it as 'superbly illustrated . . . stunning pictures alone make turning the pages a pleasurable exercise'. And Britain's *Good Book Guide* said simply: 'The text . . . is informative and lively but the 164 full-colour photographs are brilliant.'

Richard Leakey's television series and book, *The Making of Mankind*, also stimulated interest.

Casting around for a notable personality to open the London exhibition, Amin wrote for help to his old friend Sir Anthony — 'Tony' — Duff, the former British High Commissioner in Kenya, who was then working in the Foreign Office, and who later became head of M15. As a result, the photographer was stunned to receive a letter from HRH Princess Alexandra agreeing to open the exhibition in London.

Ten days after it opened in Nairobi he took it down and packed it in special boxes to send to London. It took three days just to get the pictures into their large packing cases. Mo did most of the packing himself. Kenya Airways had agreed to deliver the exhibition to Heathrow and eventually to bring it back. He flew to London for the royal opening which attracted a great deal of attention. It included a brief speech of thanks by Mo and a longer and more detailed account of the things to be found around Lake Turkana by Richard Leakey. John Charlton of Chatto and Windus, Amin's London publisher, was clearly delighted.

During its run from 24 October to 31 December 1981 the exhibition drew an estimated 100,000 visitors. When it closed it was moved to the Royal Geographical Society's London headquarters where it ran, with like success, for another month.

Two days after the opening he received a warm letter of appreciation from Lady Mona Mitchell, the Princess's lady-in-waiting.

> The Princess, together with Mr Ogilvy and their son, James, greatly admired your wonderful photographs and they also enjoyed meeting many of the people who have been helping you. In saying how much they appreciated your kindness, Her Royal Highness and her husband would be glad if you would pass on their thanks to Mr Leakey, whom they were so pleased to see again and who made the tour round very interesting for Mr Ogilvy.

But by then Amin was in Frankfurt for the annual book fair — dummies, manuscripts and illustrations of *Journey through Kenya* and *Journey through Pakistan* in his hand. As *William Holden's Journey through Kenya*, the former was bought by The Bodley Head, news that delighted the Hollywood star. They also bought *Journey through Pakistan*.

Tragically, Holden, whose love of Kenya, its people, wildlife and landscapes was all-consuming, never lived to see the published book. Only weeks later he died in an accident in his Los Angeles apartment.

13   Uprising in Kenya, Bombs in Beirut

A demanding and often harsh taskmaster, Amin is an office virago. But aboard a long-haul jet or bouncing through the bush headed for adventure he's a different personality altogether. The prospect of yet another tough ordeal seems to remove the tension from his character: and the anticipation of another sixteen-to-eighteen hour day for several days on end seems to stimulate rather than tire him. Few can sustain his pace but in the end, however much they curse his incessant quest for perfection, most are thankful for his presence.

When he wants he can be ruthless and withering, but time and success have mellowed the sharp, aggressive edge of his character. But he has lost none of his steely nerve or sure touch.

Yet there are times he has had doubts. About himself. About his work.

New Year 1982 dawned with production of the two *Journey through* books in their final stages. With Esmond and Chryssee Bradley Martin's *Run Rhino Run* also in production, Amin immediately began work on two new publishing projects – *Portraits of Africa* and Ian Parker's *Ivory Crisis*.

The work was far removed from the demands of television news coverage of frontline battles but, in its own way, just as hectic and perhaps intellectually even more demanding.

Ever since Visnews closed its Africa Service, which used to be sent to broadcasters across the continent, Amin had had fewer television assignments. The service had been as close to a pan-African TV news network as anything could get at that time. He had wanted to develop and enlarge it, but Visnews found it uneconomical. Henceforth the agency's only interest in stories from Africa was if western broadcasters or some other media bloc would air them. Thus Mohamed Amin turned his energy to publishing.

He discovered he really enjoyed every stage of book production right up to the time the ozalids, blue-prints of the finished pages, arrived for checking, double-checking and final approval before delivery of the finished work. But he feared he might be over-reaching himself.

'I began thinking of retirement. With the amount of work I had taken on I felt I could easily ruin some of the projects because I felt it was not possible to cope.

'The answer is not to take on more people. I think you always perform better with a smaller team. As somebody said to me the other day; "If you are playing chess, the answer is not to have too many players on the board." That's when you get trouble. That's very true. The more people you've got, the more trouble. Because you're where the buck ends, and you're the one that has to do something about it.'

Other challenges occupied his mind, too. The idea of a *Journey down the Nile* — from its source in the Mufumbiro Mountains, high above the western shores of Lake Victoria, across the lake, through Uganda, Sudan and Egypt, to the Mediterranean — was gaining strength.

He had already identified the amphibious vehicles that he would use, and in May 1983 he asked John Turner of Sony to give him the company's latest ENG High Band camera gear for the journey. He even thought the expedition might carry its own mobile transmitting dish to beam live satellite reports to the world from the middle of the bush, and arranged a two-way space radio link with London and Nairobi from Marconi Space Communications.

Such an expedition offered everything Mohamed Amin enjoys in life — continuous travel among the toughest conditions man can endure, linked by mobile satellite equipment to the newsmaking business by which he lives and breathes.

In July, and in view of what was to happen the timing was providential, Dolly and Salim flew to Canada for a long summer holiday with relatives. But there was a problem. The Canadian High Commission refused to recognize Salim's British passport as a travel document since Salim had no right of entry into the country that issued it.

Mohamed Amin called the British High Commission and was told:

'Yes, we've made protests to the Canadians. They've been creating these problems for the last couple of months.'

'I don't think it's a Canadian problem. It's a British problem. You're issuing passports which have absolutely no value.'

'I'm terribly sorry, there's nothing I can do.'

'Look, there must be a way round. All my son wants to do is go and visit some relatives in Canada. Can't you issue him some kind of paper?'

'No, there's nothing that I can do.'

Amin pointed out that Salim originally had a proper British passport. But when it was renewed he had lost all his rights. Amin said the lad had been to Britain many times without any problems.

'Can you prove he was allowed into Britain unconditionally in the past?'

'He was allowed in many times when he had a proper passport which was not stamped. I don't see how I could prove that.'

'Can you find any old tickets or any other evidence?'

He couldn't. But when Amin was about to give up altogether he came across some old pictures of Salim feeding pigeons in London's Trafalgar Square and next to a statue of Robin Hood in Nottingham. He sent the official several prints of these. The official called back.

'This evidence is terrific. We'll issue him a proper passport.'

As his family flew to Canada, Amin took a Saudia flight to Jeddah to
interview Idi Amin on assignment for Britain's *Sunday Express* colour

magazine. 'They were doing a cover story, one of those "Where-Are-They-Now?" features on killers and dictators around the world. But Idi Amin had moved to another house.'

At Jeddah airport waiting for a bus to take him to the Meridien Hotel the driver of the Holiday Inn bus came along and asked if Mo remembered him. The photographer was nonplussed.

The driver said: 'You're Idi Amin's friend.' It was the Pakistani who had driven Amin on his last visit.

'I asked him if he knew where Idi Amin was living now. He said he did, so I checked in at the Holiday Inn instead, showered, dressed and came downstairs and drove with him to Idi Amin's new residence in the centre of Jeddah — a large house with perhaps ten or twelve bedrooms with walls all around.

'I talked to the guards, who allowed me in. I walked into the house where some of his children were watching a cartoon show on television. I asked them if I could see their dad. One went upstairs and soon after Idi came down and greeted me warmly. We sat in his living room and talked. He was very interested in what was going on in Uganda and we talked the whole day.

'I tried to persuade him to let me take some pictures but he refused. However, he agreed to the interview, which I recorded on his tape recorder. He asked me to come back the next day when we sat and talked again while his daughter cooked some beef sausages and made tea. I had taken along a Uganda map and when I showed it to him he got all excited. He wanted to know where Obote's troops were located.

'I'd no idea but I thought, "What the hell."

'So I said, "I think there's a battalion here, and a few companies here and possibly there's a brigade here."

'And I thought, "God, if he's planning to attack Uganda on my information then he's really got a surprise coming."

'With the map in his hands he then agreed I could photograph him. So I did several pictures of him with the map and then with his children.

'I returned to London and handed the interview and pictures to Pauline Peters on the *Sunday Express*. Next morning I had breakfast with Rita Perry at White's Hotel where I was staying and hired her to start my London office.'

Then, in what turned out to be another case of 'Mo's Luck', he left London that Saturday night, 31 July, to return to Nairobi aboard a leased KLM 747 operating under the Kenya Airways flag. As the Jumbo journeyed through the night, members of the Kenya Air Force attempted an abortive *coup d'état*. One of the key points they seized was Jomo Kenyatta International Airport.

As flight KQ103 neared Kenya, the rebels broke into the Voice of Kenya broadcasting station and announced that President Moi and his government had fallen. But as the pilot began the final descent to Jomo Kenyatta International Airport nobody aboard flight KQ103 was aware of this.

Flaps down, 'Seat Belt' and 'No Smoking' signs displayed, just before touchdown, the captain put on full power and began a steep, swift climb. Over the intercom he announced, 'I am sorry, ladies and gentlemen. We are diverting to Mombasa. We have lost radio contact with Nairobi control tower.'

Bitter fighting was taking place at the airport and it was closed. The rebels had already seized the city's other civilian airfield, Wilson Airport.

At Mombasa, Mo went to talk to the captain on the flight deck. He only knew that there had been an attempted coup. 'Nobody on the ground knew what was happening. I wandered over to the charter office and asked a young Asian pilot who was reading the *Sunday Nation* and clearly didn't know what was happening if he wanted to do a charter to Nairobi.

'We were about an hour out of Nairobi and he couldn't raise Eastair, the regional civil aviation control. Then some time later the Mombasa tower called him and told the pilot that there had been an emergency and that he should turn back to Mombasa.

'I told him, "No, we'll go on to Nairobi." After about five minutes I thought I had better tell him what had happened.

'If he could have thrown me out of the plane at that moment he would have.

'I believe quite strongly in destiny and fate. But only after you have put in everything that you have got. And then if something goes wrong then you can sometimes say, "Well I did my best and God just did not will it."

'Nature has given you a body and a mind with which to think, and if you've used all that *then* you'll get a helping hand to get in and get out. It was one of those situations.'

The pilot asked Amin:

'What do you expect is going to happen to us?'

'I've no idea. But if you're really scared, why don't you drop me at the polo grounds at Dagoretti Corner [on the outskirts of Nairobi]. Then you can take off and go to one of the lodges at Maasai Mara or Amboseli and I can walk home.'

'It's no problem landing there. But if you say there has been a coup and a plane is seen landing at the polo grounds that could cause us a lot of problems.'

'You're right. That's a bad idea. Let's just go into Wilson. I'm sure there'll be no problem. We might get arrested and pushed around a bit, but there'll no real problem.'

'So we came over Wilson and he waggled his wings as he passed the control tower which you normally do to indicate your radio isn't working or that you have another problem.

'That we learned later was the worst thing we could have done because the rebels could easily have taken a shot at us. We circled and landed and there was nobody around, but as we were taxiing off the runway about half a dozen soldiers armed with machine guns leapt out of nowhere and stopped us right in the middle of the runway.'

They were ordered out with their hands up and guns stuck in their backs. Asked where they were from, Mo calmly said Mombasa.

'What's the problem?'

'Don't you know?'

'No. We don't. We were told there was bad weather in Nairobi.'

'No, this is much worse than bad weather. Everything has changed. We've taken over the government.'

'Oh well. . . .'

The two were being walked towards the airport building while this conversation took place. Amin had no idea who was involved. It could have been either the army or the air force. In their camouflage uniforms the rebels looked just like any military.

'How long have you been here?'

'We've been here since midnight.'

The rebels complained that they were hungry but that nobody had been to check on them. They had no idea what was happening.

Said Amin: 'I'm sure you can get something to eat at the Aero Club.'

'We've been, but nobody's there.'

'The staff quarters are just next door.'

'Really?'

The photographer, the pilot and the rebels marched up to the Aero Club and Amin persuaded the manager and kitchen staff to make the rebels hamburgers and chips with sodas and tea. 'Actually,' Amin remembers, 'they didn't need much persuasion. Not with my escort.

'After this, Karim Bhaloo, the pilot, and I were left at the Aero Club. I then phoned a number of my friends hoping that somebody would give me a lift. I first got through to my doctor who I thought was my friend and asked him. But he said: "That's not possible. There's shooting all over the place."

'So that was the end of that. Other friends said much the same thing. I finally got through to Duncan Willetts, who gave me much the same story and told me he had been turned back twice when he had tried to go out. It was a dodgy situation, but I suggested that he should drive along a back road, via the mortuary, to Wilson Airport and after about half an hour he arrived at the Aero Club.

'I felt the first thing we should do was drop the pilot at his father's house, which was close to mine.

'We then drove to the office to get our cameras. At this point I realized that it was the air force that had rebelled and the army which was trying to put the place back into shape.

'At the roundabout on Uhuru Highway and Haile Selassie Avenue [in central Nairobi] we were taken out of our car at gunpoint. Luckily I recognized the colonel in charge and persuaded him to give us an armed escort of three soldiers.

'Two sat inside the Land Cruiser, one on the roof. We had this escort for the rest of the day while we covered the battle between rebels and army.

Aftermath of a failed *coup d'état* — Asian-owned shops in Nairobi's commercial suburb of Ngara after an army of looters swept down the streets following the 1 August 1982 insurrection by members of the Kenya Air Force.

Member of Kenya's crack GSU strides past passive civilians near the Kenya Air Force base, Eastleigh, in the turmoil that followed an abortive *coup d'état* in August 1982.

'Looting was taking place on such a scale that I think if they had been given another day they would have dismantled the entire twenty-nine storey Kenyatta International Conference Centre and taken the bricks home. In the few hours that the civilians and the rebels had the freedom to loot they pretty well cleaned out the entire shopping centres of the city.'

Amin and Willetts went on filming into the third day when flights resumed and Amin was able to ship his film to Visnews in London. The script noted:

The Kenyan capital Nairobi was slowly getting back to normal after the August 1 coup against President Daniel arap Moi failed. Almost the entire Kenyan Air Force, which was at the centre of the revolt, are in custody, said military sources on August 4.

A thousand civilians, also under arrest, have been described as looters by the authorities. Some are believed to be students, who came out openly in favour of the rebellion. The city centre has been under strict military surveillance since the coup.

Troops positioned at major junctions have been searching cars and passers-by, and police have mounted door-to-door operations to recover the contents of looted shops. Despite repeated government appeals for a return to work, many office-workers have been staying at home. But shopkeepers have started clearing away glass and other debris from their damaged premises.

On August 2, President Moi publicly thanked the armed forces for their support, and appealed for calm throughout the nation. At least 150 rebels and 100 civilians died, according to official estimates. No casualty toll has been given for government forces.

The rapes and the beatings inflicted on them during the first hours of the abortive coup were notice enough to many of Kenya's Asians that it was time to quit. Most, like Amin, however, shrugged it off.

In the end for him the would-be coup was just a brief diversion from the rapid development of his publishing interests. Almost on the back of the two *Journey through* books the first copies of *Run Rhino Run* arrived. Eloquently written, elegantly reproduced, it was to receive critical acclaim around the world, though its sales failed to match the enthusiasm of its reception.

Typical of the reviews was one by Ian Redmond in the influential *Wildlife* magazine: 'Large format "coffee table" books often have lavish colour photos that leave you gasping but poorly written, inaccurate captions that leave you cringing.

'Here the text is both well researched and readable, with an extensive bibliography, the photos, mainly by Mohamed Amin, are superb. Together, words and pictures put one message across loud and clear — we have very little time left.'

Most of the Press notices said much the same. But it was not the only success. In Islamabad, President Zia ul Haq honoured this Kenya-born son of the Punjab:

I am directed to inform you that the President of Pakistan has been graciously pleased to confer on you the award of Tamgha-i-Imtiaz on the occasion of Independence Day, 1982. This Honour has been published in the Gazette of Pakistan Extraordinary, dated 14 August 1982.

2. The conferment of this Honour entitles you to use the abbreviation 'T.I.' after your name.

3. The medallion of this award will be presented to you in due course.

Zahur Azar,
Cabinet Secretary

The award, Pakistan's second highest civilian honour, is equivalent to a British knighthood. But he didn't learn about this latest honour immediately. The letter came while he was in another frontline situation — stumping through the streets of shell-shattered Beirut in the wake of the 1982 Israeli invasion.

He arrived, via London, with boxes of chocolates and bottles of alcohol for what he imagined to be his deprived and beleaguered colleagues — to find there was almost every luxury available in the city's rubble-strewn streets from the 'stop-me-and-buy-one' vendors with their little push carts.

He checked in at the Bristol Hotel, down the street from the Commodore where the rest of the pack including NBC's large contingent were staying. 'They had about sixty guys in the field. They lived incredibly well. Every evening even when the shit was hitting the fan they laid on a full-scale banquet — complete with wines and all the trimmings.'

On one occasion this had disastrous consequences for the NBC team. As a Visnews subscriber, NBC had access to Amin's material and that of the Visnews Beirut bureau chief, Souheil Rached, and his team. In turn Visnews had access to NBC's material.

Nonetheless, the crews were competitive. While Amin and Souheil tried everything to get an interview with the PLO leader Yasser Arafat — who was finally quitting Lebanon — they heard that an NBC crew had beaten them to it at the Lebanese Prime Minister's house. Amin door-stopped at the Commodore to meet them on their return. But NBC's crew, waiting outside the Premier's house for Arafat to leave, were still feeling the effects of the evening's repast.

'The cameraman had drunk too much and needed a leak. The producer told him, "Don't be stupid. Arafat can come out any minute." But it got to the point where the guy just couldn't hold on any longer, so he shoved the camera into the producer's hands and galloped off to the john down the road.

'Just then, Arafat decides to leave so the producer switches on the ENG camera, focuses and starts filming as the cameraman comes galloping back in a panic and grabs the camera. The correspondent spoke to the PLO man who agreed to an interview. They all came back absolutely delighted.

"Wonderful. We've got a great interview. He talked for about twenty minutes."

'Straightaway I asked if I could get a "dub" for Visnews. "Sure," said the producer, "why don't you come on upstairs and dub it while we run it through the editing machine." You can imagine his face when they switched it on. The video cassette was blank. There wasn't any picture or sound.'

The cameraman had switched the camera off when he took it back from the producer thinking he was switching it on.

'Ah, well,' said the crestfallen producer. 'It wasn't such a great interview.'

'You can say that again,' commented Amin.

Next day he met Arafat and filmed an interview — which NBC gratefully dubbed.

His respect for Souheil, his Beirut-based colleague, is immense. 'He's a tremendous cameraman,' says Mo, 'and we really got some exciting sequences during those three weeks. His battle scenes were terrific. But he takes too many risks.'

One exciting sequence Amin did not film, however, was the bomb that blasted the hospital next door to the Bristol and that took off the hotel's top floor. 'I was asleep and I just grabbed my cameras and came out through the door into the corridor running for the stairs when I suddenly realized I was stark naked. I dashed back and threw on a pair of trousers and a shirt and went downstairs. There was a pretty large audience down there waiting for my entrance. I'm glad I realised in time.'

For three weeks he covered this bloody conflict and wrote a background piece for a Kenyan newspaper, *Coastweek*, entitled 'The Agony of Beirut'. It provoked a brief sensation with an allegation in the *Daily Nation* of 12 October that at the annual conference of the International Telecommunications Union at the Kenyatta International Conference Centre police had seized thousands of copies of the paper following protests by Israeli delegates. In a denial, *Coastweek* editor Adrian Grimwood concluded: 'The report and photographs were featured because they were an "exclusive" contribution from an award-winning correspondent well known to Kenyan readers for his often dramatic coverage of the world trouble spots.'

Amin went to Beirut, not his area, to enable Visnews staffers there to take a break from the constant pressure of work in Lebanon's war-torn capital.

Back on base in Nairobi he started planning to augment *Journey through Pakistan* with a large-scale photomural exhibition in Washington, attended by the President of Pakistan. The prints were produced in the ultra-modern Florida laboratory of his friend Masud Quraishy.

The two *Journey through* books were hailed as 'marvellous testimony to this lovely land' . . . 'travel books extraordinary' . . . 'perhaps unnecessary to add that they are superbly produced and printed like all Mohamed

Opposite and right: Children of war — young militants photographed by Mohamed Amin during his 1982 tour of duty in war-ravaged Beirut, the Lebanese capital; two honour the portrait of PLO leader Yasser Arafat.

Right: Bullet-riddled United Nations building in Beirut.

Opposite: Shattered ruins of Libya's embassy and fallen portrait of Moamar al Gaddafi in Beirut, Lebanon.

In Beirut in the early 1980s Amin relieved battle-tired colleagues at Visnews to maintain the agency's frontline coverage of the shattered Lebanese capital.

Amin's recent books' . . . 'heartwarming and delightful'.

They were solid evidence of Amin's skills as a publisher and invaluable to him at the Frankfurt Book Fair of October 1982. By now Camerapix had formed Camerapix Magazines Ltd to produce *Selamta*, the quarterly in-flight magazine of Ethiopian Airlines, and it was becoming a complex organization in its own right.

He also had to complete work on *Portraits of Africa*, for Collins-Harvill and set up his *Journey through Pakistan* exhibition. It was a formidable schedule to accomplish in the first three months of the year, but he was determined.

At this time he was also working to have his ban on entry into Tanzania lifted. It helped that Tanzania's Tourism Corporation had commissioned a *Journey through Tanzania* book. At the beginning of 1983 Willetts and writer Peter Marshall were in Tanzania working on the book, but Amin planned to do the photography for the final chapter, which involved climbing to the top of Africa's highest mountain, Kilimanjaro.

On Saturday 19 February he asked if I'd like to go with him.

'When are we leaving?'

'In about two hours.'

He had won his fight for re-admission to Tanzania. It was his first official visit since his 1966 eviction.

As he reached the lip of 18,700-foot-high Gillman's Point on the rim of Kibo Crater (highest point 19,340 feet) on 24 February 1983, his cousin Mohamed Shaffi took the picture which appears in *Journey through Tanzania*, although with goggles and parka it isn't easy to see that it's him. Nonetheless, it was a characteristically exuberant end to seventeen years exile.

Two days later he flew to Lahore to set up the *Journey through Pakistan* exhibition. Shipped from Washington, where it was first shown, the boxes were offloaded from the PIA 747 onto a camel cart, ironic contrast to the sophisticated processes that had been used to produce the exhibition material in Florida.

For once 'Mo's Luck' failed. A monsoon downpour laid several feet of water over Lahore's ancient streets. The official opening was cancelled. President Zia ul Haq, however, had resolved to put his personal seal of approval on the exhibition and Irish-born Begum Noon, head of the Pakistan Tourist Development Corporation, told Amin that the presidential opening would take place in the capital, Islamabad, soon. He returned to Nairobi on 22 March and the following night acquaintances, admirers and friends at Nairobi's Serena Hotel, celebrating Pakistan's National Day, saw him invested with the presidential award, the Tamgha-i-Imtiaz, by the Pakistan Ambassador to Kenya, Mr N. A. Ashraff.

Three days later, 26 March, he was filming on the island of Lamu off the Kenya coast when he received a message that the Pakistan President was opening the exhibition at the Islamabad Hotel on 29 March.

He immediately flew back to Nairobi, just in time to catch the only flight

Dolly admires the Tamgha-i-Imtiaz ribbon and medal, Pakistan's second highest civil award, conferred on Mohamed Amin by President Zia ul Haq.

Mohamed Amin presents a copy of the book *Journey through Kenya* to Britain's
Queen Elizabeth II at State House, Nairobi, watched by Duncan Willetts and
Brian Tetley.

that would get him to Islamabad for the event. Then he flew straight back to Nairobi on the return flight to cover the first leg of the Safari Rally.

He now planned a long swing with Dolly, Salim and myself through Pakistan and India, the latter to survey the possibility of a *Journey through India* book.

An interesting insight into his attitude to books and writers came about during this trip when I referred to *Journey through Kenya* as 'my book'. Salim, then thirteen, asked me:

'What do you mean by your book?'

'Well I wrote it, Salim.'

'Yes, but words have very little to do with books.'

He could only have heard that from his father.

Almost everywhere he went during this trip Mohamed Amin was treated as a hero. The *Journey through Pakistan* exhibition had just been used as the centrepiece presentation of a Presidential visit to Japan in the sixtieth floor Sky Lounge of the Tokyo Sheraton.

In Lahore, outside the museum founded by Rudyard Kipling's father, a taxi driver screeched to a halt opened his window and said: 'Mohamed Amin. May I have your autograph?'

In Bombay, a young photographer stopped him in the street, introduced himself, and invited us to his flat where he knelt at Mo's feet. 'You're my God,' he said. 'I'd do anything to work for you. Just tell me what you want.'

Coming out of the flat he turned to me and said puckishly: 'Why can't my staff treat me like that?'

He enjoys the company of those in power. Photographs of him with royalty, Heads of State, the rich and the famous, adorn his office walls. When Queen Elizabeth II of Britain was in Kenya in November 1983, Amin, Willetts and I attended the reception hosted by the monarch for the Press at State House. He had arranged through the Queen's Press Secretary, Michael Shea, to present a leather bound copy of *Journey through Kenya* to Her Majesty.

When the moment came to present the book, however, for once he fluffed his lines and forgot to mention its title (perhaps he remembered that royal admonition of twenty years before in Sudan). The Queen looked quizzically at Duncan who said quickly:

'It's called *Journey through Kenya*, Ma'am. By the three of us.'

'The three of you wrote it?'

'No, Ma'am,' I was able to say. 'They photographed it. I wrote it.'

Ironically, two months later Mohamed Amin received an unexpected letter from one of the Queen's aides. It said simply:

> I have the honour to inform you that The Queen has been graciously pleased to grant you unrestricted permission to wear the insignia of Tamgha-i-Imtiaz which has been conferred upon you by His Excellency the President of the Islamic Republic of Pakistan in recognition of your services.

14   There Are People Dying

Most TV viewers know BBC's Michael Buerk or CBS's Dan Rather or NBC's Tom Brokaw but few know the camera aces around whose material their careers have been built. The cameramen record the video and film images that provide television news with its living drama, moments of tragedy and triumph. It is their eyes and hands and brains that represent viewers at assassinations and coups, typhoons and air crashes, rescues and romances.

Why are they so anonymous? Visnews sells most of its syndicated services on the backs of its cameramen.

As Brendan Farrow once observed: 'Visnews surely relies on more field cameramen around the world than any other news organisation, and all our success stands through their skills, reliability and dedication. None of us can afford to forget that.'

But television news in the main, particularly solo networks and stations, have built their star systems first around the anchor person in the studios and, secondly, the front-of-camera reporters in the field.

Yet the stories cameramen tell about their work are in turn frightening, poignant, comic and almost always interesting. Some have long careers, others are cut down prematurely.

Michael Roe, another colleague at Visnews who used some of Mo's earliest work when he was deputy editor of the *Standard* in Nairobi during the 1960s, says: 'When there's a big story there's no better cameramen to have on your side than Mohamed. In addition to his superb eye for a picture and his ability to beat the bureaucrats who are so often a thorn in the cameramen's flesh, he has repeatedly shown himself fearless in his pursuit of the coverage that television news editors are clamouring for all over the world.'

All these skills came into play in 1984, the most significant year so far in Mohamed Amin's life. It began with a BBC special he filmed in Uganda in January. It continued with a three-week assignment in Nigeria for Danish television and diverted through two episodes of fun filming for a US television programme starring Brooke Shields, the Maharajah of Jaipur and film star Persis Khambatta, and an airlift of rare, wild game from Mombasa to a safari park in Florida before coming horrifyingly back to reality.

He produced more books: *Journey through Tanzania, The Beauty of Kenya,*   253 and *We Live In Pakistan*. For the latter he and I flew to Karachi early in March on a two-week cross-country trip. His energy was still phenomenal. He ranged across that large country, flying long distances and working relentlessly from 0500 until 2400 each day, before returning for his annual Easter assignment covering the exhausting Safari Rally, when he impressed me with his readiness to look at everyone's pictures. My own pictures and the work of his son Salim, for example, went round the world daily through The Associated Press. His only criteria was that the picture had to be good enough. He was also open to anybody's suggestions regarding things visual.

We had driven a long way ahead of the oncoming cars through a Nandi Hills tea plantation looking for a suitable location to film the rally action with his sixteen-millimetre Arriflex cine camera. At the bottom of one hill there was a sharp bend and a wooden bridge, favoured by a large number of film-makers and photographers. It was overcrowded, but as he came back down the track, he reckoned there was no alternative.

I insisted that there was a place well up the hill where he could film the fast climb up the dirt road, through a semi-hairpin bend, and catch the cars as they came into full frame before whipping through and on. He bet money there was no such spot. He drove back to the place I had in mind. Studying the situation, he framed it through his hands, shook my hand and said: 'Right. You win.' Jabbing a stick into the rocky soil to mark the spot, he set up his gear and sat contentedly beneath his Visnews parasol.

One week later, as part of a large Press party invited by the United Nations High Commissioner for Refugees to visit refugee repatriation schemes in Somalia, Ethiopia and Djibouti, he was in Ethiopia. Even as he flew north, beyond Lake Turkana, sparkling in the morning sun, there was the feel of drought and death beneath the speeding jet. That feeling was heightened during the fourteen days he spent in that tragic, hauntingly beautiful, but drought-ravaged region.

Relief and Rehabilitation Commissioner Dawit Wolde Georgis exploited the UNHCR Press visit to hold a conference at Bole Airport to warn of the risk of death by starvation for six to seven million people. Amin filmed a Michael Wooldridge interview with Dawit on the apron outside the VIP lounge while I listened, then the two newsmen flew out to another refugee area. Millions of Ethiopians were in the final stages of starvation.

The chief commissioner, who later defected to America, struck me as sincere. He was saddened and appalled at the enormity of Ethiopia's tragedy, shackled by his own frustration and the apparent insensibility of the western world to the mushrooming deaths from hunger. For months this unprecedented human tragedy remained cloaked in an almost universal blackout. Dawit's mood convinced Amin and Wooldridge who spent the next six months pressing for permission to film in normally restricted areas.

Ethiopia's Marxist regime issued few visas and fewer internal travel
permits.

One visit by Britain's Independent Television News may have confirmed Ethiopia's paranoia about western newsmen. The public relations director of the Save the Children Fund in Britain, Wendy Riches, explained to writer Brian Phelan in the *Listener* in February 1985.

'He [the reporter] was knowledgeable about the problems and sympathetic to our fears. He promised to do what he could and shortly visited Korem, where he filmed.

'But the reports he filmed focused on the political involvement of the USA and the guerilla war in the north, with only a passing reference to increasing food shortages.

'When he came back to England, he was genuinely disappointed he hadn't been able to do more about the impending famine but, as he explained, "There were no acute cases of starvation to film, so it wasn't *news*."'

This statement is incorrect. Months before that visit, by late 1983, many deaths had been recorded at Korem. Officials of Ethiopia's Relief and Rehabilitation Commission were angered by the report and alert to the danger of other reporters seeking to cover the rebel wars in Tigray Province and Eritrea under the pretext of getting visas and permits to report the famine. This was made clear to Amin by Ethiopian officials during his visit.

On 13 May 1984 Kenya's *Sunday Nation* carried a page one splash from Dire Dawa in southern Ethiopia, under Amin's byline, with the banner headline:

"Millions face death in Ethiopia"

The report warned: 'Between five and seven million people could die in the next two months — if the world does not act. The worst drought in Ethiopia's history has now spread into its once fertile highlands with more than a fifth of its 31 million people victims. During the last twelve days — by DC-3, helicopter and four-wheel drive — I have travelled thousands of kilometres across the Horn of Africa, in Ethiopia and Djibouti, to witness one of Africa's greatest tragedies in the making. Yet despite appeals at the highest level, the world has turned a blind eye to the starving nomads and refugees in Ethiopia, Djibouti, Somalia and Sudan.'

It ended prophetically: 'Wherever I travelled, the evidence of disaster on a massive scale was clearly visible. Compounded with confusion over figures, and the world's reluctance to step in and help, all the elements for tragedy on a big scale are in the making. The faces of the victims depict despair. The bloated corpses of their already dead cattle tell of even worse horrors to come.'

Some of his colleagues, foreign correspondents based in Nairobi, accused him of over-statement, but nonetheless the essence of the *Nation* exclusive was filed on the international wire services to major newspapers in the west.

Quite independently, around this time, British television director

Charles Stewart was in the Ethiopian highlands not far from Korem for several weeks filming an hour-long Central TV documentary, *Seeds of Despair*. It was scheduled for screening in Britain in mid-July. At the time that the Disasters Emergency Committee, DEC, made up of Britain's major fund-raising charities, decided to launch an eleven-nation appeal for starving Africa. The committee had had considerable trouble persuading Britain's Independent Broadcasting Authority that the crisis was large enough to justify a national appeal but Stewart's film *Seeds of Despair*, convinced them.

The programme, however, went out at 10.30 p.m. when many viewers were switching off and going to bed. The BBC had also agreed to air an appeal that same day, 'partly in competition, partly in co-operation'.

Mark Paterson, the appeal producer, asked the BBC foreign news desk for famine footage a week before it was to be screened, but there was none suitable. 'We wanted to do something,' said foreign news editor Courtenay Tordoff, 'so we got Michael Buerk to go from Johannesburg.'

Nothing so simple, of course. In fact, the BBC foreign desk rang Amin, as the Visnews Africa man, and asked him to go with Buerk. In the event, he passed on the job to Mohinder Dhillon. Amin was then already committed by Visnews to film a Brooke Shields episode of the US network show *Lifestyles of the Rich and Famous* for producer Robin Leach. Nevertheless, he spent time negotiating their visas and travel arrangements and also arranging transport to take them to a relief centre in the south.

The result was a first-class 'fireman's story' — a swift piece of film with an impressive summing up to camera, delivered with all Buerk's powerful charisma. Part of it was used as a news clip, between reports on the resignation of the French prime minister and a spectacular demonstration train crash. Another clip was used for the appeal, presented by Frank Bough. Linchpin of the appeal was a shot of Buerk holding a baby.

Over the next few weeks the two items inspired a startling response, amounting to almost £10 million. This surprised the BBC newsroom so much that foreign editor Chris Cramer belatedly telexed Dhillon via Amin: 'I am most grateful for the thought you put into this most harrowing assignment. Your pictures were superb and the overall coverage most professional. I feel very sure that this material will feature strongly in any television awards this year.'

Buerk, who had never met Amin before, recognized the crucial role the Visnews man had played and wrote to him on 20 July: 'A note to say thank you for all your help in the miracles that led to a very successful story. Without your contacts it wouldn't have been possible.'

Meanwhile, Amin was scoring a triumph of a kind far removed from the basics of news film coverage. The schedule for his *Lifestyles* assignment with Brooke Shields was a busy ten days that embraced large tracts of Kenya's beautiful wilderness. He set up a lion banquet on millionaire Kashoggi's Ol Pejeta ranch, and at Langata, Nairobi, there were many shots of Brooke with Betty Melville's Rothschild giraffes. The key

To Mohamed
It was
fun working
with you
Dangerous... but
fun!
Love,
Brooke
Shields
July 21 '84

Fun interlude before the tragedy — Mohamed Amin with Robin Leach's *Lifestyles* team and Brooke Shields on safari in Kenya.

sequences in the programme, however, were the star's meeting with Maasai warriors and her ride in a hot air balloon over the Maasai Mara's rolling grasslands at sun-up. The cameraman climbed inside the balloon as it lay on the ground and filmed a dramatic sequence of the gas burners blazing into flame, his camera, just feet from the roaring jets.

When Buerk saw it he asked for a dub.

Amin's enthusiasm for this kind of work was patent. The Visnews service report for 6 August commented: 'Visnews International Services notes Mo Amin's work near Nairobi which seems to be taking on epic *Ben Hur* proportions if the amount of tape and film arriving in London can be considered a valid indicator.' And an inter-office memo on 10 August noted sardonically: '. . . Mo Amin has concluded a "tough" special assignment for the U.S. [which] included trekking through the African bush accompanied by American actress Brooke Shields'.

The 7 September report concluded: 'To Nairobi bureau man Mo Amin has come a herogram — from *Lifestyles* (USA) who were very impressed by his work for them on his recent assignment with actress Brooke Shields. The result has been another *Lifestyles* assignment for Mo, though not in his own bureau area. Such was the success of Mo's coverage of actress Brooke Shields that the client has sought his camera work for another assignment in India.'

On 23 September, Amin flew to India for the second *Lifestyles* film with Persis Khambatta, directed by Hal Gessner and produced by Robin Leach. The junket involved lunch with the Maharajah of Jaipur, a prince named Bubbles because of all the champagne which flowed when he was born — the only son and heir of his father who, apparently, had been cursed and told he would have no male offspring. The Maharajah also took part in a polo match played on elephants. The game ended when one of the animals stepped on the ball. Amin also filmed a rich American couple's Indian-style wedding, for which they had flown out 100 guests; and then went on with the crew to film in Kashmir and at Tiger Tops in the Nepal jungle.

From the Nepal jungle Amin went to the Frankfurt Book Fair, and then returned to Nairobi after calling into Visnews London to check plans for his next trip to Ethiopia. The news desk wanted him to go immediately. He flew home on the night flight of 12 October.

Almost as soon as he stepped into his Nairobi office, on Saturday 13 October, Michael Buerk opened his Johannesburg telex machine with a message that became a keyboard conversation.

> Welcome back. TV News in London seem fairly desperate for me (and/or Mike Wooldridge, preferably and) to accompany you on your trip to Ethiopia on Monday.
> **Amin**. This Mo here. Go ahead with your message then we can talk over . . . while you sorting yourself out — I have just arrived straight from the airport. Mike Wooldridge is out of town till Sunday p.m. He left message saying so far that there was no firm go ahead from Addis

258

Sunday NATION

ABC — MEMBER OF THE AUDIT BUREAU OF CIRCULATIONS

No.1558., Nairobi, Sunday, May 13, 1984   Price 2/50

Millions face death in Ethiopia

Col Mengistu Haile Mariam: Government stepped in before. the drought gripped the country.

Branch threatens to sue Nassir

By SUNDAY NATION Reporters

The Mombasa North Kanu sub-branch has threatened to sue the district party chairman, Mr Shariff Nassir, for failure to endorse the recent decision to suspend Mr Said Hemed from the ruling party.

The sub-branch acting secretary, Mr Emmanuel Karisa Maitha, in a signed statement, said unless Mr Nassir convened a meeting to discuss the issue, his branch would not hesitate to take up the matter with the High Court.

Reacting to the statement, Mr Nassir told the *Sunday Nation* that nobody, except the President had the right to order him call such a meeting.

Mr Nassir, who is also an Assistant Minister for Lands and Settlement, told his critics to stop wasting time on the Hemed issue.

He said leaders in other districts were currently involved in raising funds for the new 8-4-4 education system, while his adversaries in Mombasa were

BACK PAGE — Col. 4

A famished grandmother and a child in Dire Dawa, Ethiopia, wonder when and where they will get a meal from.

Exclusive

By MOHAMED AMIN, DIRE DAWA, Saturday

Millions of people are starving to death in the drought-stricken Horn of Africa. In Ethiopia alone, between five to seven million people could die in the next two months — if the world does not act.

The worst drought in Ethiopia's history has now spread into its once fertile highlands with more than a fifth of its 31 million people victims.

During the last 12 days — by DC-3, helicopter and four-wheel drive —·I have travelled thousands of kilometres across the Horn of Africa, in Ethiopia and Djibouti, to witness one of Africa's greatest tragedies, in the making.

Yet, despite appeals at the highest level, the world has turned a blind eye to the starving nomads and refugees in Ethiopia, Djibouti, Somalia and Sudan.

"We need 250,000 tons of grain now," I was told by Ethiopia's Chief Commissioner of Relief and Rehabilitation, Mr Dawit Giorgis. "That will provide the minimum half of grain a day that the victims need to stay alive.

"Altogether, we need 900,000 tons of grain in the next few months if we are to save these poor people. It's a modest sum by international standards — about $40 million."

But so far only the United Nations High Commission for

PAGE 4 — Col. 4

Across the Kenya border in Ethiopia the question was not whether people would die of hunger — only how many would die.

so it is most unlikely we will go Monday. I will talk with Tafari Wossen, RRC's information chief, as soon as possible but unlikely he is able to do any more until Monday so it seems certain we will probably go Tuesday. The last I know from Nairobi — sorry, I'm jet-lagged — I mean from London was that permission was given for myself, soundman and Wooldridge. However, I still needed to get travel permits. Over. . .'

Buerk: Okay Mo. The thing is that Tafari wanted these [video] tapes and we sent them to him. One point. Will you go Monday if Mike Wooldridge or I have no permissions or will you await events regarding us and/or the travel permits for within Ethiopia?

Amin: I will wait until I have spoken with Tafari. There is no point me going if he does not have travel permits. Although I am 'friend' of Ethiopia I still need travel permits just like anyone else. Think it best for us to talk tomorrow p.m. when Mike back and also with some luck after I have talked with Tafari. Over.

Buerk: Okay Mo. You know best as always. The problem my end is that we have a story developing tomorrow down here and I don't know whether to go on it or not. London very keen on the Ethiopian trip but it's not to put Mike's nose out of joint at all. It's just that the film with Mohinder had such an impact that they wanted a piece on Ethiopia revisited from me. If you manage to speak to Tafari could you spell out the benefits of having a radio and a TV correspondent along as the different media require special individual attention etc. I would love to go so long as Mike doesn't get upset. Are you going to be in the office this afternoon? . . . Silly question, you always are, I know. I will call you there on the phone say in a couple of hours or so. Go ahead.

Amin: Don't think there is any problem with Mike. As you know he can never get upset. I will be in the office for another hour, then at home. I would say it's safe to decide now that it's most unlikely we will go Monday. I would think best bet is Tuesday's flight — so let's plan for that until I have Tafari in contact.

Buerk: Okay Mo. Will you be trying Tafari at home today (sorry I can't from down here for obvious reasons)?

Amin: Yes I will and will continue until I have him on the phone — even if it's late at night. As you may know, Tafari does not spend much time at home. But all we can do is keep trying and I will strongly urge him that it's important for millions of lives that you are with us.

Buerk: Great Mo. Will call you later and hope it all works out. Looking forward to seeing you again. Bye for now.

Afterwards, Amin called Tafari Wossen at his Addis Ababa home. 'When I asked him what the situation was, his immediate reaction was very negative. He said it had taken him a long time to get the permit for us and to add another name would be almost impossible.

'I put some pressure and explained the importance of a television reporter accompanying us. Being an old friend for more than twenty years, he said he would try but couldn't promise. There was no point in arriving on Monday morning because there was no way he could have the permit for Buerk so would I put the trip off for a day or two and ring him on Monday.

'On Monday I then pressed Tafari again and after several telephone calls he finally confirmed that we would have the permits. I also telexed Visnews.'

The telex read:

Travel permits still being sorted out. Now planning to go in Wednesday for one week with Mike Wooldridge and Mike Buerk. I am also offering an interesting find by Richard Leakey of a two-million-year-old man — probably the oldest ever found in almost perfect condition. Leakey will announce this find worldwide on Thursday but he has agreed, however, to let me film and also interview on Wednesday so that the material can be offered in London on Thursday. If I go to Addis Wednesday then I cannnot cover this as the flight is very early in the morning. If you are interested can arrange freelance cover.

Farrow: Thanks your message on Ethiopia etc. 1. Acknowledge you go Wednesday. Hope no further delay. Story already cooling in western minds. Is your permit also a problem or is it just Mike Buerk's? Prefer you go solo if this causes further delay. 2. Leakey old man. Yes, please assign a stringer if you go to Addis on Wednesday otherwise I assume you will cover.

Cheers.

Amin: Thanks your confirmation that I can go in to Addis Wednesday. The delay is due the BBC insisting on including TV correspondent which meant all the permits had to be re-arranged. Assigning Leakey.

15   All the World Wants to Give

If Buerk's presence only arose at the last moment, the consequences of his cajoling call from Johannesburg asking to join the party were, in many ways, providential. His ironic, restrained commentary perfectly underscored the graphic horror of Amin's film. But it could not overshadow the diligent planning and persistent persuasion carried out by Mohamed Amin during the previous six months.

Early on Wednesday 17 October 1984 Mohamed Amin and Michael Wooldridge met Buerk, who had flown up overnight from Johannesburg, in the Camerapix offices at the Press Centre, Chester House, in Nairobi's Koinange Street and drove to Jomo Kenyatta International Airport. There they boarded Ethiopian Airlines 0800 flight ET920 to Addis Ababa.

'I took one of our stills photographers, Zack Njuguna. He'd never done sound before in his life but I needed a soundman because in the past there had been complaints from the BBC. To satisfy the unions we had to have somebody.

'Michael Buerk, with whom I'd never worked before, was very concerned when he realised that Zack knew nothing about sound, not even the difference between a neck and a hand mike. But I kept telling him that the soundman was not important. As he'd been brought up by the BBC I don't think he really believed me.'

Three hours later the crew was in the headquarters of the Ethiopian Government's Relief and Rehabilitation Commission where they learned that their clearance to visit Ethiopia's 'politically sensitive' areas had been withdrawn.

'Someone, somewhere along the line, decided that we could not go to Mekele or Korem. Instead, they wanted to show us some of their settlement schemes. They accused us of only being interested in showing the horrors and not what the government was doing.

'I explained that was not the case, that you had to show the problems first and then the solutions.

'Tafari said: "That's a lot of nonsense. All you guys go away once you've got the story of the problems. You don't show the solutions."

'That is partly true. It's only the horror stories that make the screen. It's unfortunate that the positive side often doesn't. But I explained to him that in this particular case the problem was so big that whatever the solution it was a drop in the ocean. It was important that we get to the north where the problem was more critical.

'He wouldn't have it so I had a bit of a row and stormed out of his office, checked in at the Hilton Hotel and made more inquiries among my various contacts. It was absolutely clear that the places to go to were Mekele and Korem, which were at their worst.

'Generally, I will not scream at the bureaucracy. I just work around it, and let them feel that they're doing their job. Bureaucracies are set up to keep people in jobs. They're protecting their own jobs, and in actual fact by doing that they instigate more and more bureaucracy. For a guy in a responsible position to stay in that position he's going to get the bureaucracy below him so complicated that there's no way they can get rid of him. And the guy below him is going to do the same. I suck up to officials quite easily. You know, make them feel that they are doing their job; but at the same time letting *me* get away with something they shouldn't.

'I went back to see Tafari but he had gone away with the Canadian ambassador. I then stormed into the office of the commissioner who was out at a meeting so I went into the deputy commissioner's office and confronted him. He was surprised that we had got the permits and that they had been withdrawn. So he promised to reinstate them and give us permission to go to Mekele. I sat in his office while he called the head of security and various other people and we were finally told to pick them up in the afternoon.'

Peter Searle, director of British operations for World Vision, the Christian relief organization, says: 'There was a great deal of renegotiation to make it all happen, which Mo conducted and where he cashed in twenty years of favours and credits.'

There was one more problem. By road it was a tough, jolting journey through rebel-held territory which would take several days. 'We then had to find the means of getting to Mekele,' says Amin. 'Perhaps the deputy commissioner knew that it was not just the permit, that we were not going to get there anyway, that none of the civilian planes would take us there.

'We tried a charter from the only charter company in Addis Ababa, Admass Air. They refused to go. It was then that we went into the offices of World Vision, talked to the person in charge there and asked if it was possible to get their plane. He told me that they'd been trying to get permission to go to Mekele with relief supplies for three months. If I could get permission I could have the plane.

'So I went back to the deputy commissioner. He was horrified that we actually had access to a plane, but he was put in a position where he couldn't really refuse.

'We left Addis the following morning. Our flight plan was to go on to Lalibela, then Alamata and Mekele. However, once we were airborne I decided it would be better for us to go straight to Mekele in case something went wrong at Lalibela.'

Something did. At about the time their plane was flying over that 263 ancient city, Eritrean rebels occupied it.

'If we had landed we would have had an entirely different story – and it would probably have taken us two to three months to ship the film, since the normal procedure, if you get away, is to walk from the rebels' front line to the Sudanese border.'

The flight in the World Vision Twin Otter on Friday 19 October took two hours. They arrived in Mekele around midday. The whole day was set aside for filming.

'We were first brought face to face with the horror of the famine,' says Mike Wooldridge, 'in a corrugated iron shelter on the outskirts of Mekele. It was virtually cut off by rebel activity and had almost no food for the tens of thousands of famine victims who had trekked in from the parched countryside around.

'The shelter was full of people whose energy had been so sapped that they could only sit or lie on the earth floor surrounded by what few possessions they had brought with them from their homes.

'It wasn't just the small children and the elderly who bore the classic haunted appearance of the famine victim. Adults in their twenties and thirties looked the same. They barely reacted to us as we walked among them.

'They seemed utterly resigned to whatever fate had in store for them. From one corner of the shelter we heard sobbing. A man was dying, and a grief-stricken woman relative knelt beside him. Mo filmed his death as quietly and unobtrusively as possible.'

As they moved among the pitiful victims of this 20th-century 'biblical famine', a phrase that came to mind when the material was first screened in the Camerapix Nairobi editing room on 22 October, it was like moving through a living lithograph of the Valley of Lepers. Mohamed Amin felt crushed, demoralized.

Nothing, he was to say later, that he had witnessed in twenty-five years of covering wars, disasters, riots, and even the previous Ethiopian famine, prepared him for this. 'Everywhere I pointed my camera people were dying. Nurses were so short of milk they literally had to decide which of a hundred or so children out of 5,000 should live.'

Hundreds of millions were made present at these distressing deaths in a way which was bearable only because Mohamed Amin, their eyes at the scene, never intruded on the privacy of the victims. The dignity of the suffering and the dying passed through his camera to viewers every-where. The anguish and the compassion became transmutable in a rare moment of *cinéma vérité* reporting.

'Ethiopia has changed me. Definitely it's changed me. Before the 1984 story in Ethiopia, anything that I filmed was to me always just a story. I couldn't have cared less. There's not much you can do in most situations. I was just doing a job and that was it.

'I've got to protect my own ass and make sure that I don't get shot up while I'm doing a job. So I have never, that I can actually think of, become

Sheltered from the heat of the sun
and the chill of night by only a
flimsy piece of hessian, a weary
mother nurses her starving baby
as Mohamed Amin kneels to film a
tragedy that aroused the
conscience of mankind.

In the dying fields of northern
Ethiopia, the team that broke the
news that stunned the world —
Mohamed Amin of Visnews,
Michael Wooldridge and Michael
Buerk, both of the BBC.

Overleaf: Like a living lithograph
of a Biblical famine, hundreds of
starving huddle in the open in the
chill mist and smoke of early
morning at Korem.

Following pages: Images of
despair from Ethiopia.

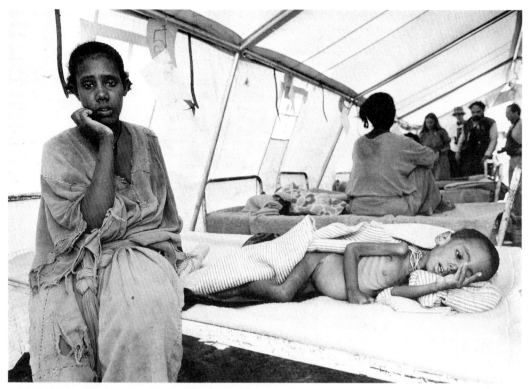

emotionally involved in an incident. And I've seen worse situations than Ethiopia. Where people have just been killed by other people. Just being shot by other people; mob justice and situations like that.

'But here in Ethiopia it was different because what we were looking at, simply in terms of numbers, were hundreds of thousands of people who were victims of a situation. First of all, they were dying simply because there was no food. And every time I think of this particular situation I get tears in my eyes because it's not imaginable that there are people, particularly in the case of the very proud Ethiopian people, who just took it for granted that they were going to die. They were not going to get the food. They were dying for months and months, probably for some years. The government couldn't care less. The world couldn't care less. They were totally helpless themselves. They couldn't do anything for them-selves. . . .'

Says Wooldridge: 'We saw and filmed other tragic scenes during the times we walked among the five thousand or so people who were gathered in and around the shelter. I remember being called to see the body of a four-year-old boy who had died minutes earlier. His parents had died a day or two before. He left three orphaned sisters and brothers. Whether they are still alive now is anybody's guess.

'Some might think filming such scenes is an intrusion, but the hope of church and relief workers on the spot was that it would jolt the world, which of course is precisely what happened. Mo and I were to be similarly horrified two days later when, at dawn, we watched bodies being lined up for burial on the edge of Korem camp.

'They were the men, women and children who had died during the night. It was bitterly cold, and many people had to sleep out in the open for lack of tents or room in the shelters. Some children had no clothes. Mo filmed the corpses of infants and mothers together, relatives wailing uncontrollably, a camp official fastidiously recording every death.

'I remember thinking it was like watching bodies being laid out after an air crash. Within an hour we saw forty, and the average daily toll at that time was around 100. But it seemed even more tragic because these deaths could have been avoided so much more than those in an air crash.'

Mohamed Amin filmed his nightmare images between 19 and 21 October 1984 at three places now as firmly inscribed in the history book of human horror as Belsen and Auschwitz; Mekele, Alamata and Korem. It was impossible to be a cool, detached observer. Amin tried a trick he often uses. He closed his left eye so that all he could see was what his camera let him see. Like watching a movie, the element of reality diminishes because the lens intervenes between the action and the observer. It had worked in the past. It had no effect in Ethiopia.

All that mattered now was to let the world know.

By persuading World Vision to fly them direct from Alamata to Addis on 21 October they were able to leave Addis aboard the 0930 Kenya Airways flight KQ403 of 22 October. It gave time to edit the nine cassettes in the 269

Camerapix office on the Monday evening.

In the editing suite, the images were replayed and once again the starving lay dying before the editor and crew as they would, too, in living rooms around the world. Nobody would escape this anguish.

Amin's telex to Brendan Farrow served notice: 'Fyi just returned exAddis drought footage stop Situation is worse than ever with thousands of people dying daily stop Will ship material on U-matic tonight stop Will telex detailed dope later in the day. Rgds.'

Shortly after, at 00.30 hours on 23 October, Michael Buerk flew out of Kenya, on a British Airways flight with the edited story. It was shown on the BBC's lunchtime news bulletin the same day. And the astonishing response began.

Even as Buerk was London bound, Amin continued work through that fateful night and all day Tuesday, printing up black and white still pictures of the famine victims and writing a 1,250-word news report which went out that day on The Associated Press wires together with five of his most dramatic still pictures.

The story made page leads in almost every newspaper in the western world and billions of readers shared the same sense of shock as television viewers. This is how the story was filed from Nairobi to New York and then around the world:

Ethiopia Famine 1
With Wirephotos NAI-1 thru NAI-5
Eight people waging battle against starvation of 100,000
[by Mohamed Amin]

Alamata, Ethiopia (AP) — Dr George Ngatiri and seven other medical personnel fight a daily battle to keep 100,000 people alive at this famine relief centre in northern Ethiopia. Every day they lose 90 to 100, mostly children. The people who come here are victims of perhaps the greatest famine in this East African nation's modern history, caused by a decade long drought and complicated by two secessionist wars in the north.

Ethiopia's Marxist government estimates the drought has affected life for 7.7 million in this country of 33 million, forcing 2.2 million from their homes and threatening 5.5 million with starvation.

Every day hundreds more arrive at this recently established camp along the border of Tigray and Welo provinces. Last week, 36 miles north-east of Alamata, Tigrain rebels claimed the capture of the town of Lalibela.

Reporters who visited the Alamata camp, 700 kilometres north of the capital of Addis Ababa, found Dr Ngatiri, one other doctor, three nurses and three nutritionists working with 100,000 starving people.

Twelve miles to the north, thousands more huddled at another emergency relief camp at Korem.

Ngatiri, a Kenyan, said at least half the victims are children. This day the doctor had turned away a group of mothers and their frail, emaciated babies — victims of pneumonia, scabies, relapsing fever and marasmus, the Latin medical term for starvation.

'I'm sorry,' he told them, speaking through an interpreter. He had no food or medicine for the new arrivals. With more than 90,000 waiting outside the camp, he had supplies for only 3,000.

'There is nothing I can do. I know your children need treatment,' the Kenyan physician told the mothers. 'I have to treat them. But I have nothing to treat them with. Come back in five days'.

As the interpreter translated into Amharic, Dr Ngatiri held up the extended fingers of one hand to indicate five.

Those turned away would have to wait out in the open. During the day, the tropical sun pushes temperatures to 100° Fahrenheit. At night, at this elevation of 12,000 feet, temperatures fall to below 50° Fahrenheit.

Most of the displaced people have no more than thin, worn sheets and ragged clothing to keep themselves warm.

Those accepted inside the camp run by World Vision International must leave at night — even the 100 or so patients on intravenous drips.

Ethiopian officials said they risk attack by the rebels if they remain inside the camp.

World Vision International, a US-based interdenominational relief group, is the only agency at work at Alamata. At the Korem camp, Catholic Relief Services, Ethiopia's Relief and Rehabilitation Commission and other groups have had more time to organize relief efforts.

But even at Korem there wasn't nearly enough food to go around. A reporter who visited Korem in March found 10,000 people going hungry. In late October there were up to 100,000.

About 80,000 people are camped outside Mekele, 90 miles north of Korem.

British nurse Claire Bertschinger said this camp feeds about 500 children a day on a special, high-energy diet of powdered milk and biscuits prepared in Britain. But every day, she said, 300 more arrive and there's not enough powdered milk and biscuits to go around.

Reporters visiting Mekele saw an old man die before their eyes as he took a drink of water.

At Korem, relief agencies are feeding nearly 17,000 children daily, said medical co-ordinator Brigitte Vessot of France. She said there are at least another 200,000 famine victims within a 60-mile radius of the camp, though all estimates are really guesses.

An Ethiopian man wearing a cowboy hat walked through the huddled masses at Korem and marked people on the head with a felt pen, apparently at random, to determine who received clothing and food.

And yet both Eurovision, Europe's prestige TV-news exchange net- 271

Above: Bereaved families at Korem lay out the bodies of the elderly and young as the Ethiopian famine reaches its height.

Below: Grieving families mourn the deaths of their relatives during the 1984 Ethiopian famine when Mohamed Amin's pictures sent a landslide of compassion sweeping across the world.

work, and NBC America, initially turned down Amin's film material. NBC's London staff saw the film as soon as it was run by BBC. Donna Ryan, duty producer in the London office, was so moved that she rang Cheryl Gould, *Nightly News* foreign producer in New York, and made a pitch to get the piece on the air that night before Gould had even seen it. She met resistance.

Paul Greenberg, executive producer of *Nightly News* remembers: 'You say, "yeah — terrible and horrible", and then you get back to your business, the election, and worrying about who did what to whom in Nicaragua.'

But NBC's general manager of news in Europe, Joseph Angotti, picked up the telephone and called Greenberg personally. 'We heard from New York that it was a really busy news day and there were all kinds of things going on and that they might wait until the next day to put it on. I called Paul and said that I just wanted to be sure that he understood how very, very exceptional this material was.'

As a result, Greenberg asked the London bureau to transmit the BBC version of Amin's report with Buerk's moving elegy, which arrived at five p.m., New York time, just as the newsroom was busily assembling the night's broadcast. 'There are very few times that a newsroom can be brought to complete silence,' Greenberg says, 'but this was one of those occasions. All the side talk and worried preparations for the evening broadcast, all the gossip and talk of the political campaign and concern for the night's stories just stopped.

'Tears came to your eyes and you felt as if you'd just been hit in the stomach.'

The 'problem' with the famine story, the perception — as NBC's anchorman Tom Brokaw put it that night, that it was just words from far-off places — was resolved. Now there were pictures, devastating, compelling pictures. 'I remember Brokaw saying, "We've got to put this on",' recalls Greenberg. The decision was made.

All around the world, the impact was immediate and overwhelming — first within the profession, a small tight circle of normally hard-faced and seemingly hard-hearted cynics and then among the general public. Amin's film had broken all barriers.

His colleagues in the BBC and Visnews were the first to react. From BBC TV News came an urgent message sent at 1428 GMT:

'Please accept the warmest congratulations from all at BBC TV news for your most impressive and moving coverage from Ethiopia. You clearly overcame the problem of covering a subject that has become all too familiar yet still telling the story in a highly graphic and compassionate manner. We ran 5.19 in news afternoon with 7.30 planned for Six O'Clock News and about five minutes plus for the Nine O'Clock. . . .'

From Brendan Farrow at Visnews: 'Allow me to congratulate your outstanding and superb coverage Ethiopia. Buerk voicer undoubtedly excellent but your pictures caused nothing less than shock wave of horror 273 throughout western broadcaster world. To eventual benefit those affected by famine. Newsbiz so often seems to end with recording disaster it must be immensely gratifying to you personally to know the positive side of your work from this grim story. Marvellously well done...'

From Kevin Hamilton, managing editor, Visnews, at 1545 GMT: 'Along with everybody else at Visnews, I watched your Ethiopian pictures on the BBC lunchtime news today with a feeling of pride and admiration as well as horror. To the BBC's credit they were put together extremely well and Mike's commentary was superb. But equal credit must go to you, not only for your camerawork but for the logistical efforts which obviously went into the entire exercise. I'm sure you'll be proud to know that we are breaking with all existing precedent and running all five minutes of your first piece on all our satellite feeds tonight. I have no doubt they will provoke the international reaction which the situation in Ethiopia warrants.'

From Brian Quinn, managing director Visnews, at 1650 GMT on 25 October: '. . . Apart from the profound reaction it has produced in the UK, the level of camera journalism was very high. The departure of the villagers with their dead was outstanding work and your discipline on wide angle during the rush for the "imagined" food arrival was technique of the highest order. You will know of the flood of support it caused in Britain but it was fed to Japan with a vignette of the British reaction and produced in turn a flood in Japan. Well done.'

In the daily report issued by Visnews on 24 October: 'Mohamed Amin's first report on the appalling state of the drought victims of Ethiopia has already brought an overwhelming response of horror and concern as well as offers of aid. Mohamed Amin's exclusive cover from Tigray Province being aired today is having similar impact. Eurovision who had turned down the coverage yesterday took both the first and the second report today once word of the state of the disaster in Ethiopia had spread.'

What this achieved was the greatest act of giving in history, unleashing a chain reaction which grew ever bigger and bigger throughout more than eighteen astonishing months, highlighted by the British Band Aid recording session and the USA for Africa album.

An unlikely Irish pop star, Bob Geldof, remembers watching Amin's film that evening in October. It changed his attitude to life. In Chapter Thirteen of his autobiography *Is That It?*, entitled 'Driven to Tears', Geldof recalls his anguish:

'From the first seconds it was clear that this was horror on a monumental scale. The pictures were of people who were so shrunken by starvation that they looked like beings from another planet. . . . The camera wandered amidst them like a mesmerized observer, occasionally dwelling on one person so that he looked directly at me, sitting in my comfortable living room. . . . Their eyes looked into mine. . . . Paula [Paula Yates, television presenter, pop star and Geldof's wife] burst into tears, and then rushed upstairs to check on our baby who was sleeping peacefully in her cot. . . .

'The images played and replayed in my mind. What could I do? . . . All I could do was make records that no one bought. But I would do that, I would give all the profits of the next Rats [Boomtown Rats is the name of Geldof's group] record to Oxfam. What good would that do? It would be a pitiful amount. But it would be more than I could raise by simply dipping into my shrunken bank account. . . . Yet that was still not enough.'

Next morning in the Phonogram press office, where he had a desk, Geldof suggested the Band Aid record that inspired Europe. In turn, his example prompted American singer and actor Harry Belafonte to initiate a similar effort in America. Together with Ken Kragen he organised the production of *We Are the World*, written and composed by Michael Jackson and Lionel Richie.

Their efforts in turn inspired ordinary people everywhere to give what they could. 'The depth of feeling behind these donations has awed me,' Oxfam director Guy Stringer said early in 1985.

Typical was the West family in a remote Scottish village. Mrs Alick West had burst into tears watching Amin's film. Afterwards she, her husband Alex and their sixteen-year-old son Patrick drew up a list of all the things they no longer needed. Put together, the china and glass, old furniture, a treasured thirty-six-year-old tractor and a caravan, raised almost £2,500 for Ethiopia's starving when auctioned.

Six-year-old Janet Joss in southern England put all her toys into a pram and went through the village selling them door to door. She raised £40.

Within seventy-two hours of the first report the ordinary people of Britain had already pledged a total of more than £5 million for an appeal which, officially, had closed the week before.

An unemployed man sent his own unemployment benefit cheque of £54 — 'all I have' — for the Ethiopian famine victims. A farmer's wife, in tears, rang relief offices and said: 'I've just looked in my larder. And I've come away feeling guilty'. She sent a ton of wheat.

In the words of reporter John Edwards who has often covered crises in Africa for the London *Daily Mail*: 'A tide of help had turned and it was starting to flow towards Ethiopia. Millions of people were involved now.'

Almost as soon as the phones started ringing John Eke, chief accountant of the Save the Children Fund emergency office in London, totted up the contributions – pennies and pounds mainly from the poor, but also much from the well-to-do and wealthy — and recorded a total of more than £10,000 from 160 donors. At week's end the fund stood at more than £14 million. 'That's a huge figure,' he said. 'We haven't had anything like this before.'

In Washington, President Reagan saw the NBC telecast of Amin's film and rang through immediately to pledge US$45 million. When Australian Prime Minister Bob Hawke saw a cassette replay before an interview he wept. Australia launched a nationwide famine appeal.

The London *Sun* passed on £100,000 from its readers' fund for children, 275 and within ten days over £400,000 had been sent to the *Daily Mirror's* special fund. A plane with thirty tons of food, medical supplies, tents and blankets organised by the *Mirror* and with proprietor Robert Maxwell on board flew out to Addis Ababa.

A remarkable effort by the small *Evening Argus*, Brighton, in Southern England, raised over £46,000 from readers and the money was used to fly out an Anglo Cargo Boeing 707 from Gatwick Airport loaded with blankets.

The appeal was launched with a front page splash written by editor David Williams, who flew out with the aircraft: 'The money was raised within six days and I reckon we will top £50,000. It is the most fantastic response to any appeal I have known.'

Some amusing ways were devised to raise money in Britain; a Miss Lovely Legs competition; a Miss Beautiful Eyes contest; a sponsored silence; and a sponsored slim-in where weight-conscious young British women shed pounds to raise pounds for famine victims.

In one South Wales village, a young woman organized a musical concert in aid of the Ethiopian famine relief. Sharon Harvey, who lives in the mining village of Arbertillery, pooled voluntary resources and talent to entertain local residents and raise money.

Ten-year-old Londoner Julius Harper raised £96 by busking with his recorder at Camden Lock open-air market. Six unemployed youths from Nottingham played a forty-eight-hour pool marathon that brought in sponsored takings of £673.

In Gillingham, Kent, hairdresser Jerry Harley set up his shaving stand in the High Street and brought in sponsored takings of £150 by shaving — blindfold — ten people in four minutes.

At St. Peter's Church, in Caversham, Berkshire, the Reverend Richard Kingsbury preached a nine-hour sermon to extract £2,000 from his flock. North Devon hotelier Leslie Oakland drove an old Land Rover through the towns and villages around Barnstaple, inviting people to throw in money towards a new Land Rover to send to the famine zone. Within three weeks, he collected £10,000.

Celebrities gave generously for a series of auctions that netted almost £8,000. Princess Alice, Duchess of Gloucester, donated a silver fruit bowl presented to her by the late Emperor Haile Selassie of Ethiopia.

Actress Joan Collins contributed a black silk evening gown; jazz musician Kenny Ball, a trumpet; Steve Davis, a snooker cue; Henry Cooper, a pair of boxing gloves. And the entire England football team gave their jerseys after their spectacular 8-0 win over Turkey.

Many people volunteered their labour. In Batley, West Yorkshire, two separate factory shifts toiled without pay through a Friday night and a Saturday morning to prepare ten tons of high-energy biscuits in time for an emergency flight to Ethiopia. At Birmingham Airport, members of the Aston Villa football team, who also helped to raise £86,000 for a West Midlands fund, loaded a Boeing 707 with food and medical supplies.

In Southampton, dockers ignored traditional union demarcation rules to work alongside farmers over Christmas, loading 10,000 tonnes of wheat. They waived overtime payments, thereby saving thousands of pounds in labour charges.

For some Britons, fund-raising brought a total change of life. After Cambridgeshire farmer Oliver Walston, forty-four, set up a famine-relief scheme inviting wheat farmers to contribute the £100-proceeds from sale of one ton of their grain, he found himself transformed into a full-time charity organizer. Turning the running of his 3,000-acre farm over to his foreman, Walston and his wife Anne struggled to deal with sackfuls of mail bringing donations for *Send a Ton to Africa*, not only from wheat growers but from farmers who sold lambs, calves and market-garden produce.

His telephone bill soared as he negotiated with bank officials, corn merchants, millers, transport firms and port authorities for his fund's cash to be turned into wheat for shipment to Ethiopia. But Wilson considers that the effort and his £9,000 expenses were more than repaid by the satisfaction of knowing that his scheme raised £1.9 million and shipped 12,000 tons of wheat to Ethiopia and Sudan.

Nigel Humphries, thirty-four-year-old managing director and chief pilot of the charter company Air South-West, simply dropped everything to go out to help. When he and his colleague Liz Amos decided that he should fly their one plane — a twin-engine Beechcraft Queen Air — to Ethiopia, they immediately appealed for funds through local press and radio. Within three days, they received pledges of £10,000. Humphries took off at once with a ton and half of plastic sheeting, tarpaulin and rope urgently needed by the Save the Children Fund for a feeding station.

For the next three weeks, Humphries provided an aerial taxi service inside Ethiopia, flying doctors, nurses and relief workers to feeding camps. The airstrips he used, perilously deep in valleys, were often little more than rough tracks.

By the time he returned to Exeter, Liz Amos had boosted the total of funds to £70,000, enabling him to go to Sudan for a further two months in February and March 1985.

From their own pockets Americans gave more than US$70 million to feed the starving. It had come from the hearts as well as the pockets of corporations and churches, parents and veterans, teachers and children — like six-year-old Sandra Nathan of Brooksville, Florida, who donated her US$5 life savings. And an Illinois company — Lauhoff Grain — put together a nine-company group to deliver a million meals to Ethiopia's famine-stricken children. Arna Aranki, a Michigan schoolgirl, raised money from her classmates.

It was not just Americans or Britons who rallied to help. From Europeans, Japanese, Latin Americans, Australians and Asians came gifts of the heart.

All heeded Mohamed Amin's call and the whole world came together as 277 one.

16 Together We Can Build a Better World

Television news lives by the size of the audience it attracts. Whatever Mohamed Amin's thoughts about stills photography there is no doubt in his mind that it was the *moving* images of television which served as the catalyst to arouse mankind's conscience.

'I don't think still pictures would have carried the same impact at all. It is certainly television because it's moving pictures, it's sound, that really pierced the hearts of the people who saw it.

'I shot still pictures as well and it is the most syndicated story I have come across. I have cuttings two feet deep.

'But it wasn't these photographs or the article that moved anybody. It was the television news clips that made the impact.

'Television certainly has more power than any writing you can do. Mike Wooldridge filed his story well before us because with radio you can pick up the phone and deliver your story. With television it's more complicated. Mike had better descriptions than we did of what was happening. He was twenty-four hours ahead.

'But I haven't heard many people talk about the radio piece. It was the television pictures.'

With Mohamed Amin's film, according to figures supplied by the broadcasters it serves, Visnews achieved saturation, reaching an estimated one billion viewers.

To any communicator the idea of reaching the minds and touching the hearts of one billion people at virtually one and the same time is awesome.

Yet, incredibly, once again, at first Amin's role in the achievement was virtually ignored. Rather like a replay of the publicity they put out about the Idi Amin exclusive — which had been entirely his work — the BBC built all their publicity around their reporter, Michael Buerk, and 'his' film.

Nobody denied the power of Buerk's superb commentary. But for a television company to behave as if pictures are secondary reveals something very strange at the least about its view of what television is all about, quite apart from the fact that Buerk — as he admitted — would never have got near the story himself. He was only there because Amin took him.

Later, BBC News did give Mo credit. But not before another injustice had been done. Around the world the report that galvanised the world into an unprecedented frenzy of giving was already known — as it still is, to many — as 'the BBC' or 'Buerk's' report.

Just how interested the BBC was in putting the record straight was to be made clear during the submission for the British Royal Television Society's Television-News award entries. It was agreed that the joint entry of Amin's film and Buerk's commentary would be submitted as a 'Visnews-BBC' entry. It went in as 'BBC-Visnews'; and the award was made to 'BBC Television News/Visnews.'

The cameraman was singularly unconcerned. Hours after the initial telecast he had telexed Buerk:

> Well done with all your pieces — the world is proud of you and eight million Ethiopians grateful. Please telex when you coming back through here. If you stay the night, I promise an Indian banquet. If you don't I will meet you at airport to collect tapes. . . . World Vision Tony Atkins and Jacob [Akol, World Vision's information officer in Nairobi] anxious to see all the footage. They have agreed to provide plane just about anytime we ask. For your information have told the Ethiopians we want to make a return visit in a couple of weeks. Assume you would want to join us. Bestest Mo Amin.

Later, at the award ceremony, Buerk stressed the more important part played by Amin. In fact, two weeks after the first report, Buerk telexed Mo: 'See from current edition of *Newsweek* the balance of credit for the Ethiopian masterpiece is adjusting itself. Quite right, too! I keep mentioning — and spelling out, however incorrectly — your name when interviewed by all and sundry. I will make you famous, Mo, given half a chance.' There was never any dispute between the two professionals.

But, as Visnews duty editor Tim Arlott says: 'The two stories the BBC claimed most credit for in the past ten years in fact were both Visnews stories, and both from Mohamed Amin — tracking down Idi Amin, and getting to the heart of the Ethiopian famine and bringing back the pictures that showed the world what it meant.'

It brought some droll repercussions for Visnews. Apparently unaware that the pictures were Visnews copyright, BBC Enterprises sold them to Visnews's opposition in America, ABC and CBS. And that wasn't the end. The Australian Nine Network — the only one in Australia without access to Visnews material — then got it off ABC America. UPITN (Visnews's greatest competitor) then got it from the Nine Network, who *sold* it to USIA (the American information agency). The final touch was given when USIA sent it to Visnews complete with American information which explained that this was BBC material shot by a BBC crew on a routine journey bringing equipment back to London for servicing. That particular error started with a London *Sunday Times* report.

The Visnews internal report which noted all this concluded, however: 'The obvious consolation is that the massive relief effort now under way, tens of thousands of famished people now receiving food, can be directly attributed to Mohamed Amin's Visnews pictures'.

The next report is also worth quoting: 'UPITN has made a donation to help the agency World Vision. The contribution was the UPITN profit from mistakenly selling the Visnews coverage to the USIA!'

In fact, as Peter Searle recalls, UPITN had legitimately used some of Amin's films. 'Imagine my shock' he says, 'when sitting quietly at home in October, I watched the amazing footage and heard Michael Buerk say "only the Red Cross can fly food this far north".

'There was the plane which I knew and loved delivering a bit of the Red Cross food, but on a World Vision trip. Michael Buerk and the BBC have not been allowed to forget that! There's no doubt at all, however, that the prime impetus for that visit, the genius of the camerawork and the contacts to make it all happen belong almost entirely to Mo.

'Both Buerk and Wooldridge were in the right place at the right time and nothing should detract from their professionalism — but it was Mo's footage.

'There was an interesting sequel to it which got lost in the subsequent excitement. Because of our involvement Visnews agreed that any un-shown footage could be used by World Vision. On the night of the first transmission I discovered that this was actually still with Visnews in London, though technically belonging to World Vision.

'After twenty-four hours of hectic negotiation I was able to go live on ITN News on, I think, the Friday with an agreed sixty-second clip from the spare footage and talk about World Vision International involvement and our plans.

'I think this is probably the only time that BBC and ITN have used part of the same Visnews trip by agreement, again a little bit of World Vision input.'

Mohamed Amin was unconcerned about the glory, only with sustaining the response. Six days after his return from Addis he telexed London: 'I am departing now for Addis with soundman and Mike Buerk. BBC clearly desperate to get anything, as last night they were talking about the possibilities of chartering a Lear jet from Nairobi for a satellite feed. BBC have now based their engineer and editor in Nairobi with massive equipment which at the moment has been impounded by Customs. I have told them what they should do to clear but they seem to think British High Commission will help, which I am afraid is wishful thinking.

'We are all going in without visas but I don't foresee much trouble except several hours delay at Addis airport while the authorities get the paperwork sorted. I am pulling out next Friday, however, and will be prepared to go back following Friday after Pakistan trip.'

On this second visit he made a firm commitment to himself to produce his own personal documentary about not only the Ethiopian, but the African famine, even though as a result of his coverage some forty television crews were now working in Ethiopia.

'I felt that it was absolutely crucial to keep this story on television as long as possible as the usual tendency in the media is that you have an
immediate impact when a story is shown. People respond and give what

they can when the story is on the screen and then the story is forgotten. Everbody's goes on to something else,' Amin says. 'I felt that it was my duty to do what I could to continue working on the story. Not only did I do dozens of news pieces after the initial story to keep it alive, but I decided that, at my own cost, I would do a documentary.'

His report would be called *African Calvary*, picking up a phrase used by the charismatic Mother Teresa of Calcutta who told Amin that the famine in Ethiopia was 'an open Calvary'. Perhaps it reinforced the sense of destiny that runs through his life when she put her saintly Christian hand on his Islamic shoulder and said: 'My son, God has sent you for this hour.'

And again when he approached the Vatican with a request for Pope John Paul II to deliver a special appeal: he flew with his film crew to Rome to record the message. This time there was no confrontation with Bishop Marcinkus — only a warm papal welcome.

Indeed Amin had inspired a great deal of activity as the Visnews log noted: 'The demand for camera crew days continues, not least for services in Ethiopia following Mohamed Amin's splendid pioneering efforts on the famine story. Recent requests have come from UNICEF and the UN's Rome-based Food and Agricultural Organization. World Vision, the American church charity which assisted Mo with his first coverage, have returned for additional coverage.

'Mo's efforts, incidentally, have formed the basis for two country-wide satellite broadcasts in the USA: World Vision linked stations to a question and answer session two weeks ago, and UNICEF produced a similar programme this week. Ed Helfer reports from Viscom that both were successful productions and well received.'

And Bob Geldof had by now turned himself into the world's greatest long distance fund raiser. Within days, he was organising the cream of Britain's pop stars to make a chorus record, *Do They Know It's Christmas,* which was to inspire the formation of USA for Africa, stimulate an even greater financial response from the American public for *We Are the World* and finally generate the ultimate, that incredible space shot, the sixteen-hour *Live Aid* concert marathon — the greatest single charity event in mankind's history.

As *African Calvary* neared completion, Amin also began to organize contributions of time, services and material from many people so that all the revenues from its sale could go to the charity fund he was establishing.

'To make a documentary on this scale is a very expensive business. I was prepared to do everything I could within my own resources but I obviously needed help and backup.'

One of the first persons he discussed this with was Peter Searle, the British director of World Vision, who remembers: 'I found myself in Nairobi in November 1984 having difficulties getting into Addis because all accommodation was taken for some Economic Commission for Africa junket. With a day or two to spare I decided to drop into the Nairobi Press Centre, not then appreciating that it was another wholly owned subsidi-

Left: Mohamed Amin talking to Mother Teresa after the filming of his documentary *African Calvary* — 'my son, God sent you for this hour', she whispered.

Left: Flanked by Michael Buerk, with whom he jointly received the British Academy for Film and Television Arts award for the Best Actuality Coverage of 1984, Mohamed Amin is presented to Princess Anne.

Left: Watched by former British Prime Minister Harold Wilson, Mohamed Amin and Michael Buerk share the Royal Television Society's 1984 award for International News at the presentations held in 1985.

Right: Mohamed Amin presents British Prime Minister Margaret Thatcher with copies of *Journey through Kenya* and *Journey through Tanzania* after recording her interview for *African Calvary* at 10 Downing Street.

Right: During the fourth Kenny Rogers World Hunger Media Awards at the United Nations Building in New York, Mohamed Amin was pictured with the country and western star and his wife, Marianne, and NBC anchorman Tom Brokaw. At far left of picture is veteran US broadcaster Walter Cronkite, who was master of ceremonies.

Right: Salim, Dolly and Mohamed Amin joined American Vice-President George Bush at the White House ceremony when the US leader signed a bill appropriating an additional one billion dollars in aid for Africa, attributing it all to the cameraman's courage in 'arousing the conscience of the world'.

ary of Amin Enterprises.

'I visited one or two people on spec and finally decided to go down the end and see whether the legendary Mo Amin was around. He welcomed me when we met for the first time. An hour later we shook hands on the outline deal which produced *African Calvary*.

'It was a unique and, I believe, divinely ordained meeting. Mo had produced the initial footage that exposed the drought to the world but knew well that the picture was bigger than Ethiopia and there was much more to tell.

'I represented the admittedly quite small British office of the world's largest private voluntary agency and was conscious of the fact that we were working in many countries that had not received the publicity which Ethiopia then had. It seemed natural that we should get together and, there and then, I committed my own office to make this film without consultation or authorization.'

Others rallied round, too. Sony Broadcast provided the equipment needed for filming. Mohinder Dhillon filmed the documentary with Amin. Bert Demmers of UNICEF also helped, as well as Diverse Productions in London who gave the editing and post-production facilities as a donation.

'Frank Dynes telexed me that the only cost would be the overtime of the engineers, the editor and the graphics personnel,' remembers Amin. 'A few hours later Frank telephoned to tell me that the staff would donate all the time that was needed to produce this film.

'The dedication of the people, particularly during the editing, was incredible. Mike Ray, who worked as the editor — and later in fact joined us — Frank Dynes, Philip Clark, spent night after night with us trying to put it together. Everywhere I went, all along the line, people were so generous it was incredible. The dedication was total and absolute.'

Visnews and the BBC made library material available and Visnews later provided the facilities to market the documentary at the MIP television fair in Cannes, France. About 7,500 video cassettes were sent free to libraries, schools, churches and hospitals: all done at cost by Twentieth Century productions.

'We provided many facilities and support for Mo when he shot the film and it was seen at Easter 1985 in Britain and subsequently around the world,' recalls Peter Searle. 'The proceeds from the actual sale of it to the television stations went to another charity but World Vision benefited very substantially — far above our initial investment — from spontaneous donations from the public who saw it. Thus, our involvement and investment were returned to us. We also had a hand in one of the most effective pieces of television documentary ever seen in this area on this theme.

'The effect of Mo's camerawork and his involvement continued both before and after the showing of *African Calvary*. I visited Ethiopia with him on a number of occasions and watched his own unique blend of dealing with officialdom.

'Arriving with half a ton of excess baggage he would seize the senior Customs official from his office, inform him that he was "a guest of the government again" and have the chalk cross placed on everything, including my own humble suitcase, so we received VIP treatment through Customs.

'While treating with appropriate deference those senior government officials who were helpful, he had a uniquely brusque way of handling petty, obstructive officials and the inevitable minders.

'The motivation was always the same. Mo was in a hurry to get the story and get it out: those who sought to get in the way of those he sought to help with his uniquely probing lens simply had to get out of the way or suffer the consequences.

'I watched him take risks with his safety, with his reputation, and with his contacts. Happily none of them seem to have suffered. I watched this normally smartly dressed and comfort-loving Kenyan sink to his knees amidst the excretion and vomit of desperately sick children to catch the images which would bring their plight to the attention of an increasingly jaded world. All considerations of personal comfort and health were secondary to what he was filming.

'Mo is an African and I am British. Mo is a devout Muslim and I am a committed Christian. Mo is a professional photographer, cameraman and entrepreneur. I serve with a relief agency.

'In many ways we have little in common: in others we have much. I remember bouncing along with him and the crew in the back of a World Vision Land Cruiser from a camp in northern Ethiopia. I said, "Mo, I know we believe different things about Who is up there, but I think we could both agree that someone up there has decided that we deserve one another."'

Slowly the balance of credit for Amin's work began to be restored. In both Europe and America he won, or shared, some of the greatest honours his profession could bestow. They included the Royal Television Society award and a British Academy of Film and Television Arts trophy, which was presented to him at about the same time that Michael Jackson, Bruce Springsteen, Diana Ross, Lionel Ritchie and almost fifty top stars, organized by Harry Belafonte and Ken Kragen, gathered in Los Angeles for the lengthy recording of 'We Are the World'. Five days before the Royal Television Society's event, the premier European television festival awarded Buerk and Amin the Monte Carlo Golden Nymph Award for International News. A snowball began.

Soon, in the company of such distinguished names from the entertainment world as Albert Finney, Jim Henson, Charlton Heston, Burt Lancaster, Dame Peggy Ashcroft, and Kirk Douglas, Amin was sitting with Michael Buerk, this time at the British Film and Television Academy Award ceremony — the British Oscar — to pick up the trophy for Best Actuality coverage of 1984.

The BBC-2 premier of *African Calvary* on 2 April received glowing critical tributes from the cream of Britain's television pundits; acknowledgement not just of his superlative skills with the camera, but also of his remarkable talents as a producer.

'Unbearable in its unwinking, almost poetic portrayal of Africa's famine . . . Margaret Thatcher, Julius Nyerere, Kenneth Kaunda, the Pope and many others voice their concern. Otherwise there is very little commentary . . . none is needed.' — *Daily Mail* (3 April 1985).

Hugh Herbert of the *Guardian* also noted the producer's definition of the film as 'not a news story, nor an orthodox documentary; more a requiem for the dead in Ethiopia and elsewhere on the continent.'

Similarly, his name was already being acknowledged in the United States. The day after the première he was in New York to receive the Long Island University's coveted George Polk Award for Best Foreign Television Reporting at the Hotel Roosevelt, and later the Overseas Press Club of America award.

During this visit, after addressing members and representatives of the United Nations and affiliated non-governmental organizations at a showing of *African Calvary* in New York and the School of Journalism of Columbia University, he was feted and honoured at the White House by US Vice-President George Bush.

Hundreds of important guests in government, defence, business and private voluntary organizations were invited to witness the Vice-President put his signature to a unique American Congress Bill. It gave an appropriation of an additional one billion American dollars as emergency aid to Africa. Bush ascribed it all to the power and persuasiveness of Mohamed Amin's visual reporting.

Introducing him as the man who 'mobilized the conscience of mankind', Vice-President Bush told the guests, including the US Assistant Secretary for African Affairs, Chester Crocker, that by the end of February 1985, Americans privately had donated US$70 million through the mail alone while the US Government had already allocated US$700 million, none of which would have happened 'if the world had not first seen the misery for itself' as a result of Mohamed Amin's persistence and courage 'in risking his life time and again' to bring the world the first television report. Many millions were alive because of his photography, the Vice-President said.

Thanking the government and people of America for their generosity, in reply Amin presumed to tell them what else they needed to do to avert a major crisis in Africa. The continent, he told the Vice-President and Chester Crocker, desperately needed long-term help to recover and rebuild.

And, recalling that the United States had shown the way after World War II, under the Marshall Plan by rebuilding Europe and its economy, he expressed the hope that Africa, too, in its hour of need, might now look to American compassion.

286   Subsequently, the two US awards and his other wholly individual

awards became the pennants not only of cameramen colleagues in Visnews but of photographers and cameramen throughout the world. 'Could not have been better deserved,' cabled an exultant Souheil Rached, his Visnews contemporary in shattered, war-torn Beirut.

In Kenya, however, Amin gave himself no time to reflect on the honours which were being showered on him. Instead he threw himself into an endless round of assignments and planning. Indefatigable in his efforts to help the starving, his 1985 air travel record equalled perhaps his accumulated mileage of the previous decade. He flew across Africa, Europe, and America regularly. One immigration officer at London's Heathrow Airport leafing through his passports asked him disbelievingly: 'Are you resident in a plane?'

Yet in mid-year he found time to dedicate two weeks to an air-ground safari across East and Central Africa with Harry Belafonte, Marlon Jackson and Ken Kragen, USA for Africa's top management, and other executives and stars. Treasurer Len Freedman, the same age as the cameraman, dropped out in the middle from exhaustion, and looking at him asked: 'How the hell do you do it?'

Amin also organized pool coverage of the tour for the American television networks, as well as a meeting for the USA for Africa group with Julius Nyerere, then President of Tanzania, Abdul Rahman Sowar el Dahab of Sudan, and Chairman Haile Mariam Mengistu of Ethiopia.

The group flew to the gravest-hit areas to decide how the funds raised could be used most effectively and humanely. 'It will be a momentous occasion for USA for Africa,' executive director Marty Rogol had said before he set off. It was more. It left this extraordinary mixture of show-biz stars, business executives and marketing experts who whistle-stopped through Ethiopia, Tanzania, Kenya and Sudan, somewhat sadder, wiser and profoundly moved, all inspired by what *We Are the World* was to achieve.

Amin's energy remained unflagging. He was contacted by an American entrepreneur, Lou Falcigno, who was in the satellite television promotion business. With World Vision, Falcigno had dreamed up one of the most bizarre spectaculars ever conceived, to mark the first anniversary of Amin's historic Ethiopian famine film.

It involved lifting into Ethiopia and hopefully cutting through their top-heavy bureaucracy, something like 100 tons of heavy transport and the latest and most sophisticated transmitting equipment. Amin had agreed to be chief regional consultant and liaison specialist.

In the end, as the outline became more and more stupendous, the detail more and more vague, the Ethiopians more and more incredulous, and Amin more and more cynical about the project's viability, he withdrew. He had considerable concern for the loss of funds for the famine victims and he was convinced this programme could only end in trauma for all involved.

Within days, World Vision abandoned the project in favour of a much more realistic project — a twelve-hour live telethon fund-raiser to the USA out of Nairobi. A team of expensive US television executives arrived to set this up and Mo sat on the sidelines until, panic-stricken, Lou rang and asked for help.

Swiftly he moved into action. Together he and Brendan Farrow organized meetings with Voice of Kenya. It seemed as if it would be okay. They could use the VOK studios. Then came a snag. He told Farrow to see the principal at the KIMC, a large, government-run, mass communications training complex in one of Nairobi's inner suburbs. It was agreed the transmission would originate there.

The visiting television *hoi polloi* moved in to start rewiring and rehearsing. They were delighted. Hours later came a call from Lou.

'My bums have been thrown out, Mo. There's only twenty-four hours to go before we start transmitting. You gotta studio in the game park or something?'

As he left the office that night, Mo told me to wear a suit. 'We're going to see the permanent secretary in the morning.' He had no appointment, but when we got there the permanent secretary agreed to see him. An hour later he had permission to use the KIMC facility until the Monday morning. The Americans moved back in.

What remained for Mohamed Amin was to travel to Europe and America to receive three more awards, perhaps the most distinguished awards of his career; the A.H. Boerma Award from the Food and Agricultural Organization of the United Nations in Rome on 11 November, the Distinguished Achievement Award of the University of Southern California on 19 November and the Kenny Rogers World Hunger Media Award at the United Nations Headquarters New York on 26 November.

'I believe', observes Michael Wooldridge, 'it meant a great deal to him that a cameraman from Africa — from outside the European and North American mainstream of television journalism — had won such prestigious awards. And he always used the platform that these award ceremonies gave him to plead for help for the famine victims, that the world might not forget, once the memory and the horror of his own pictures had faded.'

Says Amin: 'Since the story I have changed in a number of ways and one is that every time I look at a situation it comes to me very strongly that I am very fortunate, that my colleagues, my friends, my family, are very fortunate.

'Ethiopia has left a scar on me which will last the rest of my life. It has made me constantly aware of how desperate the situation is for a very large part of the world.'

The list of journalism award winners at the University of Southern California glitters with the names of all the greatest American communicators of the last half of the century; people like Henry R. Luce and Walter Cronkite, Art Buchwald and John Chancellor, Alastair Cooke and Dan

Rather, Drew Pearson and many more. On the night of 19 November 1985, at the alumni's annual awards dinner in the Sheraton Premiere, Universal City, Los Angeles, Mohamed Amin's name was added to this impressive roll of honour.

Despite the misspelling of his name on his award (Mohammed), it was vindication for many injustices delivered professionally, as well as compensation for a life sometimes spent in the shadows and slurs of racial prejudice.

In selecting him as the first non-American in its twenty-six-year history to receive its Theodore E. Kruglak Special Award the USC Journalist Alumni Association was not breaking with tradition and precedent simply in the fact that he was a non-American. The award signified a major and radical shift in the thinking of those who decide why — as well as who — a person should be honoured for their work in journalism. The letter inviting him to accept the award noted the importance of the cameraman:

'If one of the basic goals of journalists is to present the public with the information it needs to make decisions and take action, then your work is a true model of noteworthy achievement. . . . Your acceptance of the award and presence at the banquet would be something of which both you and our university could be very proud.'

For the guests, as for the recipients, it was an evening charged, like all such evenings, with expectancy. The atmosphere at the Sheraton Première, a hotel built up in the backlot of one of the oldest of filmland's production companies, was drenched in glamour. Universal Studios was just about to finish post-production work on their Oscar-winning classic *Out of Africa*, filmed in Kenya, so it was fitting, perhaps, that it should have been chosen as the setting.

Six hundred of the film capital's leading citizens had donned formal attire to feast on the double boneless breast of chicken laced in champagne sauce, followed by hazelnut ice cream with praline sauce, and to listen to Norman Corwin, for many the 'father' of American broadcasting, conduct the ceremonies staged with all the fanfare and glamour for which Hollywood is renowned.

Introducing Amin, Norman Corwin said: 'In the twenty-six years of these occasions, the proceeds of which are directed always to scholarships for deserving journalism students, awards have gone to reporters, editors, publishers, broadcasters, columnists, networks, newspapers, magazines, film-makers, foreign correspondents, educators and government officials.

'Tonight for the first time, a photojournalist will be added to the roll. . . . It's a little late . . . to be sure, but then, we're only in our second quarter-century.'

As he spoke, Amin's thoughts drifted back to the night thirteen months before when, soaked to the skin by a mountain mist, his soul had been chilled to its depths. The satisfying sense of acknowledgement, which he had travelled 12,000 miles to savour, faded.

Now Norman Corwin launched into his eulogy.

'It takes minimal scholarship to know that journalism has no season; no day or night; that it's an estate both local and global; that it probably was started by the first talking head, a spear-thrower just back from the hunt; and that it progressed through the classic agencies of pen and pencil, through generations of printing presses and typewriters and daisywheels, to a point where even the magnificent Linotype is now a museum piece, displayed for its quaintness in the lobby of a great newspaper — something out of an early dynasty. And now the tools are electronic and the sky is not the limit, as we witness a communication satellite which at this very moment is riding in stationary orbit 23,000 miles above the Galapagos Islands — an instrument owned and operated by one of tonight's awardees. . . .

'And journalism is a photographer working for months in Nairobi, day after day, week after week, seeking permission to cover a famine, trying to persuade assorted political and military people who distrusted journalists of all stripes, that he was not interested in spying on army installations in the region . . . that what he wanted was to document the ravages of hunger . . . to make it *known*. And finally he got what he was after — and what he was after turned out to be so grave and tremendous that it stirred the conscience of the world. All this in reference to Mohamed Amin of Nairobi, Kenya — known to his friends as Mo. . . .

'Mohamed Amin, when he sought entry to the afflicted regions, knew that the dimensions of the famine were little understood. After all, hunger is not uncommon in the world. Not even here at home. Right now the US mails carry a stamp showing emaciated faces, brown, black and white; beneath is printed the stark appeal, HELP END HUNGER.

'It was to do just that, to help end hunger, that Mr Amin packed his cameras and went across the border into Ethiopia.

'The pictures that he took there are not the kind you put up on your wall; but then neither is a good deal of pictorial news in this cruellest of all centuries. The pictures were first shown, not without hestitation let it be said, in Britain; then, in this country, by *NBC Nightly News with Tom Brokaw*. The rest is journalistic and humanistic history.

'It would be inappropriate for me to tell you much more about Mr Amin's work in the sub-Saharan dying fields, and about its effect, because he and his pictures tell the story so much better than anyone else.'

Now the lights dimmed and for Amin the glitter of the evening again palled. On a large screen, above the guests, stunning life-size images of skeletal babies and human beings in their last moments of life seemed to fill the banqueting hall.

Even seen for perhaps the third or fourth time the video footage still shocked. It was like being swept overboard into an icy sea, the body left breathless, numb and sick. The festive mood of the evening had changed, too. There was a solemnity about it that had been lacking before, as Norman Corwin wound up: 'Mohamed Amin, I invite you on behalf of the

Journalist Alumni Association of USC, to add a few more steps to your

1985's MOST-HONORED JOURNALIST, Mohamed Amin, African bureau chief for Visnews, is shown with USA for Africa founder Ken Kragen and "Live Aid" organizer Bob Geldof at ceremonies for 1985 World Hunger Media Awards in New York. Mr. Amin was co-recipient of the "Best Television Coverage" award with the BBC's Michael Buerk for their reports on the Ethiopian famine. Left to right: Mr. and Mrs. (Dolly) Amin, Mr. Kragen, and Mr. Geldof.

long journey, to accept the first award given to a photographer in the twenty-six-year-old history of these celebrations.'

He took those last few steps on the journey begun so long ago in Dar es Salaam when he first discovered the magic and the power of photography.

To Tom Hudson, head of news of the world's largest television agency, he is 'the greatest pictorial journalist I have ever known, and I have known some . . . courteous and kind, with a highly developed intelligence, the ability to "talk a bird out of a tree", which has enabled him to talk himself into the most secret enclaves, and out of some of the most dangerous situations.

'. . . the world will always remember that he once trod this earth, with dignity and stature.'

The way for this son of a poor railway worker had been gruelling, paved with frequent injustice and studded with ordeals. But he persevered. In doing so he had inspired compassion and generosity in millions of people all round the world.

Now, with sincerity and characteristically uncompromising directness, he used the platform and the mood of the evening to make his own personal statement about the politics of hunger, a mood reflected in his opening words:

'For me this is a sad occasion. The reports which win this award were of half a million deaths which need never have happened.

'There are in my mind two serious questions. And, in thanking you for the honour you do me, I ask you briefly to consider them with me. The first question is: How long are we to allow the political divisions of the world to obstruct the supply of basics like food and medicine to the needy? And the second: Does television act responsibly regarding Third World problems or simply exploit them for their emotional impact?'

Saying that the political question raised itself he charged that governments and international organizations knew of the situation in Ethiopia 'long before my reports, yet did little or nothing'.

He spoke of UN warnings in 1980 and again in 1983. 'Yet no government heeded the cries for help to any significant extent.'

Was it, he asked, the politics of Ethiopia which were behind the West's failure to respond?

'Ethiopia received nothing matching its needs, despite all the warnings. Whatever the reason for it, combined with drought and other factors, it produced the most appalling tragedy we know of only too well.

'That surely is a scandal for which no right-minded government anywhere can duck the responsibility. There can be little doubt that had the matter been left in the hands of the world's governments an even more ghastly tragedy would have developed and might yet be going.'

Nor did he spare the very television organizations which aired his pictures. 'I believe this Ethiopia tragedy has proven beyond doubt that they do underestimate the amount of public interest there is in the Third World. Why do I say this?

'You may find it hard to believe now, but when my first report about the famine in Mekele was offered to Europe's broadcasters they turned it down. . . . I understand the story was pretty much the same here . . . but when they [the viewers] saw, they proved beyond all question they were not as small-minded as some of the people who run the media . . . the power of television news could not be demonstrated more clearly. . . .

'But there is a responsibility that goes with that power. We fail in that responsibility if we do not report the often horrendous problems of development facing the peoples of the Third World. We must report them courageously, without favour to East or to West.

'If we do that, we can then trust the people of the world to see that their governments will take their responsibilities to the Third World seriously.

'If we do that, I believe . . . that the day will quickly come when no child, or man and woman, anywhere, need ever again go hungry to bed or starved to the grave.'

Postscript

Nairobi, Kenya
January 1986

Not for nothing is Mohamed Amin known as the Man Who Always Gets His Picture. Now forty-three, he has been scoring world scoops ever since he was the first television and press cameraman into Zanzibar after the 1964 coup.

The secret of his success is incredibly hard work, painstaking and thorough planning, a meticulously updated list of contacts, an uncanny knack of anticipating the big story — and an enviable measure of luck.

Combined with incredible timing it all came together last weekend when, on Friday 24 January, all radio and telephone links with Uganda and its capital, Kampala, went down.

Early in the week, Yoweri Museveni's National Resistance Army closed in on the city for an expected showdown with the troops of the discredited President Tito Okello.

Amin decided that the fall of Kampala was imminent, that it was time to move. Too soon, of course for such a highly volatile situation and he could have found himself stopping a bullet; too late, and somebody else would get the all-important *first* story.

But travel to Uganda out of Kenya was banned; and in eastern Uganda bordering western Kenya all the border gates were locked and barred.

So on Friday, when he went to cover the arrival of Tanzanian President Ali Hassan Mwinyi on a brief official visit to Kenya, he also saw Habib Halahala, the new President's press secretary, at the Inter-Continental Hotel.

With his exact knowledge of East Africa, his canny mind planned an adventure across Lake Victoria to Tanzania and by road from there into Uganda through long-held NRA territory.

But there was a seven-day moratorium on all departures to Tanzania too which was the reason for his early morning visit to the senior Tanzanian Government man on the Saturday.

Later that day Boskovic's Africair — who've been flying Amin around Africa for the best part of twenty-five years — telexed the Tanzanian aviation authorities to obtain landing clearance for an early morning Sunday flight from Nairobi via Mwanza to Bukoba.

'If you ever want to beat the opposition,' notes writer Angus Shaw, 'study that location on a map — Mwanza is so far from the action only a fool would go in that direction.'

294

Meanwhile, Mohamed Amin's TV rivals CNN and WTN went the obvious way, travelling overland to the Kenya-Uganda border, where they filmed activity at the gate and what could be seen of Uganda from the Kenya side of the fence.

But Africair's Cessna 404 5Y-HCN was cleared to depart from Nairobi's Jomo Kenyatta International Airport before sunup, bound for Mwanza and Bukoba.

Arriving in Mwanza for Customs and Immigration clearance at 7.30 a.m., Amin and Duncan Willetts had to make a ten-minute walk to the Customs officer's house. The cheerful but reluctant Tanzanian official, a woman, agreed to get up and come down to the airport to clear them. But she insisted on having her bath first, which created a one-hour delay.

'There was no sign of Immigration,' Amin recalls, 'so we decided to check in the other side of the lake in Bukoba.' There was another snag. Because it was Sunday the Customs lady did not have a rubber stamp. She gave them a clearance letter instead.

With that the Cessna, carrying Amin, Reuter's Michael Rank, the BBC's Michael Wooldridge, and Duncan and Mohamed Shaffi, both of Camerapix, flew the second leg across Victoria to Bukoba.

When the plane landed in Bukoba both luck and planning began to play their parts. First, Amin found the driver of a pick-up truck waiting for a coffin at the airport and persuaded him to give them a lift into town. On the way the driver stopped to introduce him to the region's Number Two civil servant.

Impressed, this man said he would contact his superior, the regional director – the Number One man in Tanzania's West Lake Province — and arrange for him to meet Amin at the Lake Hotel. The kindly motorist then shipped all the cameras and other equipment to the hotel as the party walked down from the airport.

When the director arrived, a photograph showing Amin and Duncan with the recently retired President Julius Nyerere, together with a presentation copy of *Journey through Tanzania*, opened all doors.

'We've transport,' said the regional director, 'You can use it to get you to the border. But we've no petrol.'

Amin had foreseen this probability and carried his own — 200 litres in ten jerricans. He says: 'Always remember, in a war situation there are plenty of vehicles but never any fuel.'

So by noon the party was walking across the Uganda border at Mutukula — still without formal Tanzanian immigration clearance. The man in Bukoba had no stamp either so he too had given them a letter.

The border officer reading through this sniffed huffily but gave them a 'transit' pass. On the other side they were welcomed by a twenty-two-year-old Museveni army chief called Commander Fred who said he had been instructed to meet them.

'I'm not sure if he really had been,' says Amin. 'But we certainly weren't going to argue.'

Commander Fred — elderly by comparison with the rank and file of what the party began to call the Schoolboy Brigade — had an ordained minister, the Reverend Samuel Kiwanuka, as his driver.

Stopping for refreshments on the rough road journey, they met a driver with a pick-up who had just driven down from Kampala. Questioned for news, he was so overcome by the party of world pressmen he got out of his pick-up and offered it to them:

'You've got to get there quickly — and you'll never do it in that truck. Take this. Please.' He even topped it up with petrol.

They arrived at Masaka well after sundown and were given rooms at the Laston Hotel. 'You wouldn't have thought there was a war,' says Amin. 'It was spotless. And although they had no water and no power they filled large drums in the rooms so we could all have baths.'

Though they were dubious about the NRA promises that their driver would show up for them on time the next morning, the Reverend Kiwanuka brought the pick-up to the front of the hotel on the dot of five.

Mist shrouded the road to Kampala and the cold was piercing, but the party made it to Kampala in time to film, photograph and report — exclusively — the entry of Yoweri Museveni into the city. There the drama ended except for one other extraordinary element of 'Mo's Luck'.

Entebbe Airport was closed. The only way out was back to Bukoba or through Kassese into Rwanda. On an off-chance, Amin asked Museveni if Entebbe was clear and if there were any planes they could commandeer.

The new President summoned a top military commander and assigned him to Amin with orders to do everything possible to get them back to Nairobi that day.

Fighting was still taking place on the road from Kampala to Entebbe and hundreds of prisoners were still being seized. The party arrived just minutes after Entebbe Airport was grabbed by Museveni's National Resistance Army. In fact the officer in charge was on the intercom refusing permission for a Bellair plane piloted by Colin Stewart — carrying vital drugs for the United Nations — to land. The NRA's Number One man for Kampala countermanded these instructions and gave Stewart clearance to land.

And when the drugs were offloaded, he told Stewart: 'Now take these gentlemen back to Nairobi.'

That night Mo Amin's Visnews film went by satellite from the VOK broadcasting station, via the Longonot ground station to the Eurovision network and, via Visnews, to almost 500 million homes around the world.

From Nairobi take-off to satellite transmission, the entire operation had taken less than forty hours. Another Mohamed Amin success. Another world first.

Epilogue

This is by no means the end of Mohamed Amin's story.

In the year after the awards ceremonies in Rome, Los Angeles — an event which the *Los Angeles Times* said clearly belonged to Mohamed Amin despite the other prestigious winners — and New York, he was as busy as ever. Not only filming events like the overthrow of Milton Obote's second regime, but also in filming for a third time Pope John Paul II on his second visit to Kenya.

The Pontiff made history by visiting an African wildlife sanctuary, the Maasai Mara National Reserve. As the highlight of this visit he blessed an orphan rhino calf flown more than 300 miles by light plane from its haven in northern Kenya specially for the event. Amin filmed the flight two weeks before the papal visit.

Then he was told that the visit to Maasai Mara was strictly off-limits to the media. Indeed, if the Press attempted to cover it His Holiness, he was warned, would cancel that section of his itinerary. It was another challenge to be overcome.

Amin flew to the Mara with his cameras at the personal request of Kenya's then Minister for Tourism, Mr Andrew Omanga. As usual, Visnews got its expected exclusive.

This third meeting also gave Amin the opportunity to present the Pontiff with copies of three of his books which he thought appropriate on such an occasion: *Run Rhino Run, Journey through Kenya*, and, in reciprocation for the papal rosary he treasures, his testament to his own faith, *Pilgrimage to Mecca*.

In December 1986 he flew to London to receive the Order of Christian Unity's Valiant for Truth award, perhaps to him the most cherished recognition of his work for the world's starving and for the homeless.

For by then he was completing *Give Me Shelter*, a major 27-minute documentary marking 1987 as the International Year of Shelter for the Homeless. He had been among a list of nominations that included Lord Denning, Mary Kenny, Sir John Junor, Bernard Levin, Bishop Desmond Tutu, Peregrine Worsthorne, Winnie Mandela, and Dr Wendy Savage.

He was chosen from a short-list of three. The others were the late Charles Douglas-Home, editor of *The Times* of London, and Mo's contemporary, the late UPITN cameraman George De'ath.

Both, I am sure, would have agreed he was a worthy winner. Lady 297

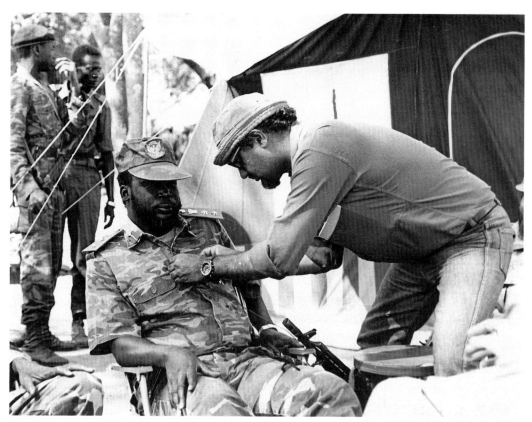

Above: Interviewing Sudan's rebel leader, the SPLA's Colonel John Garang, deep in the heart of southern Sudan. A British television producer in the same area was tragically killed when his vehicle detonated a land mine.

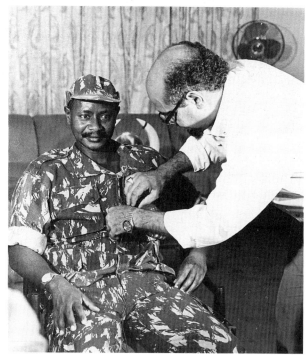

Right: Mohamed Amin prepares Uganda's newest President, Yoweri Museveni, for an interview after his troops marched into Kampala in January 1986.

Mohamed Amin has continued to bring important news of Africa and the
Middle East to world viewers since the 1984 Ethiopian famine story. With
producer John Penycate he filmed for BBC *Panorama* the tragic story of Yoweri
Museveni's young soldiers, orphans of war and terror.

Lothian, the chairperson of the Advisory Council, told guests at the award ceremony in London's Arts Club in December 1986, that the aim of the award which carries no financial reward was 'to annually pay tribute to the individual or group working for Press, television, radio or literature who has best used modern means of communication courageously to convey the truth in the public interest'.

Presenting the award, the head of the international Salvation Army, General Eva Burrows, described it as the antithesis of 'chequebook journalism' that highlighted two strong human qualities, courage and honesty, 'qualities seen in Mohamed Amin who is honoured this evening. But I would add a third quality, which is a key to the powerful visual presentation which so stirred the world – the quality of compassion.' She described the outcome as a 'landmark in human history'.

Expressing gratitude to him for 'this heightened awareness', General Burrows said the media had the power and the responsibility to feed the young with those things which the Bible listed as 'whatsoever things are true, whatsoever things are honest, whatsoever things are just, whatsoever things are pure, whatsoever things are lovely, whatsoever things are of good report'.

Receiving the award, Mohamed Amin said that he was proud to join the list of 'brave and distinguished people' who had won the twelve previous awards. It gave him special pleasure, he said, that he, a Muslim, had been chosen by a Christian organization.

'In a world where religious difference is so often the pretext for violence, I find this heart-warming.'

Of his Ethiopian film reports he said the dignity and patience of the victims had reminded him of some of his favourite words from the Holy Qur'an.

Surely God is with the patient.
And say not of those slain in God's way,
'They are dead'; rather they are living
But you are not aware.

Two things had become evident to him as a result of the world's reaction to his reports. 'One — ordinary people do respond when they know the truth. 'Second — not enough is done, or the wrong solutions are applied, when people do know the truth.'

He concluded: 'As a commuter between the underprivileged and privileged worlds I want to say that the western media have to face the fact that they too live in a global village.

'John Donne said four centuries ago:

No man is an island entire of itself
Every man is a piece of the continent . . .
Any man's death diminishes me, because I am involved in mankind;
and therefore never send to know for whom the bell tolls;
it tolls for thee.

'It does indeed.'

Mohamed Amin returns frequently to the arid mountain fields of northern
Ethiopia to keep alight the flames of compassion which blazed across the world
as a result of his work.

A former editor of the *Observer* and vice chairman of the Award's Advisory Council, Iain Lindsay-Smith, in his reflection, said the responsibility for deciding what was of good report was quite awesome. In *Midsummer Night's Dream* Puck had said he would 'put a girdle round the earth in forty minutes'.

'And now, of course, we do. The communications girdle round the earth, laced laser-tight by satellite and land station, is an instantaneous conductor.'

Yet just as the victim of war was truth, so the first victim of instant, high-tech communication was meaningful perception.

'What makes people become players in the way that the films of Mohamed Amin made the world play a role in the fund-raising for famine?

'For what we see here is one of the great hopeful movements of the twentieth century. Perhaps even an historic turning point.'

He closed with the thought: 'As to the valour of Mohamed Amin's telling as Milton wrote:

'"I cannot praise a fugitive and cloistered virtue, unexercised and unbreathed, that never sallies out and sees her adversary, but slinks out of the race where the immortal garland is to be run for, not without dust and heat."

'The dust and heat, in this case, about famine in Africa.'

Three months after this ceremony, in March 1987, when this biography was completed, I went with Mohamed Amin once more to Pakistan: this time he was gathering film on the limited war being fought between India and Pakistan in the highest frontline in the history of warfare, along the snow-clad peaks, ice cliffs and cornices of the Pamir Knot where the four greatest mountain ranges in the world merge in a tangle of lofty spires and plunging ravines.

He whirled around these filming from the open doors of Pakistan Army helicopters. Stunned by the sheer savagery of the scenery, I tumbled out of the Puma helicopter at the army base at Gore, around 16,000 feet along the Baltoro Glacier, and refused to go higher.

But Mo swept into a high-altitude Alouette, doors removed, and was about to take off to circle the lower flanks of 28,250-foot-high K2, the world's second highest mountain, when he was ordered back to the Puma. It could not wait and had to return to Skardu.

His frustration as he climbed into the helicopter was enormous, almost surly. He looked just like a cat who had taken its first lick of stolen cream before being caught in the act.

He found some compensation in the days that followed, making supersonic bombing runs in the Pakistan Air Force's F-16 jets when he pulled the full nine Gs these aircraft impose. After two such runs the group captain told one questioning subordinate pilot: 'Don't worry about him. He's a fighter pilot.'

And finally he did get to 25,000 feet on the slopes of K2 — in June 1987.

But all this must surely be for the second half of a remarkable life.

Salvation Army leader Dame Eva Burrows presents Mohamed Amin with
Britain's most coveted media award, The Valiant for Truth Trophy, at a ceremony
at the London Arts Club in December 1986 for his continuing work in bringing the
plight of the hungry and the homeless to the attention of the world.

Index